D0947065

Financing Techology's
Frontier

SECOND EDITION

Financing Technology's
Frontier

Decision-Making Models
for Investors and Advisors

SECOND EDITION

Richard P. Shanley, CPA, MBA

WILEY

John Wiley & Sons, Inc.

Library of Congress Cataloging-in-Publication Data:

ISBN 0-471-44432-4

Printed in the United States of America

10   9   8   7   6   5   4   3   2   1

contents

foreword

Nobody can really guarantee the future. The best we can do is size up the chances, calculate the risks involved, estimate our ability to deal with them and then make our plans with confidence.

—Henry Ford II

This is not a book about raising money. This is a book about creating the future.

It is a book for entrepreneurs, entrepreneurial hopefuls, and managers of emerging companies that want to know how to size up the risks involved in their venture and, knowing them, improve their chances for success. Consider it a road map to help you get where you want to go.

In *Ten Lessons from the Future*, author Wolfgang Grulke wrote that in order to be successful in business, you cannot simply look at today and ask, "What do I need to do to get to tomorrow?" He suggests that what you need to do ask is "Where do I want this company to be in ten years? Where do I want this technology to be in ten years?" Then project yourself to that place, ten years in the future, and look backward to see how you got there.

Easier said than done? Maybe. But what Richard Shanley has achieved in this edition of *Financing Technology's Frontier* goes a long way toward providing the tools necessary to build a successful technology company and to providing the perspective that company builders must have in order to compete in today's global and challenging business environment.

The world needs entrepreneurs—people with vision who are willing to take risks for the future. Over the last 20 years, we have witnessed an interesting phenomenon, both in this country and around the world: emerging companies in the "hottest" technologies becoming, for a time, the darlings of Wall Street and riding an unrealistic wave of publicity to a public offering. Perhaps those days are gone for good, but the need for technological innovation is not. And technological innovation is not permanently slowed by even an extended downturn in the economy. Tech trends ride exponential waves and, once moving, have extraordinary momentum.

Looking back over the tech wave of the last 20 years, biotech companies were the first technology pioneers to catch the public imagination in the 1980s. In the 1990s Internet-related technologies excited investors and analysts with transformational promises of e-commerce, communications, and access to information via the World Wide Web. At the beginning of the 21st century, it is clear that these two fields—biotechnology and Internet technology—are working hand in glove to create the breakthroughs of the future.

And the world needs these breakthroughs. We need the developments that are coming out of the efforts of technology pioneers: developments that will not only identify, control, and cure diseases, but also will have a far-reaching impact on manufacturing, agriculture, and the environment. Industries at the frontiers of technology—biotechnology and web-based technology companies—are still considered high risk by financing sources, and the number of investors and advisors knowledgeable in these areas is still relatively small.

The knowledge shared in this book comprises a tool kit for companies that are embarking on the path to growth, success, and, perhaps, a public offering. One of the biggest dangers for a company in its early stages is in not knowing what it does not know. Within these pages, chapter by chapter, managers will learn what they do not know and can reinforce what they have already accomplished. Whether it is raising capital, forming strategic alliances, creating compensation plans, tax planning to maximize cash flow, or preparing your board for an initial public offering in a post-Enron, Sarbanes-Oxley world, *Financing Technology's Frontier* answers questions you might not even have known to ask. Shanley has created a compendium of invaluable information written in lay terms and supported by case studies from the real worlds of business and finance.

These are not easy times in which to grow a company. But the right company in the right market, well conceived and well executed, will always garner positive attention. In this time of uneven and unstable economies, global conflicts that threaten to do us all harm, sharp population growth in areas that can handle it least, and unexpected change on a day-to-day basis, we still need our scientists and business people to persevere.

As citizens of the world, we need all the energy and the outcomes that these new ventures can bring. If this book can help even one entrepreneur with one breakthrough that can improve the lives of others, it will have been a success. We want to help that one entrepreneur succeed. And this is a good place to start.

John Bigalke
National Industry Leader Healthcare & Life Sciences
Deloitte & Touche LLP
September 2003

The investment community alternately embraces and shuns high-risk technology and biotech companies. One month, Internet technology is fueling a stock market wave, the next month it is undertow. One year, biotech is stunning market makers with innovative alliances, sophisticated deals, and successful clinical trials. The next, promised new cures evaporate and disillusioned investors move into a "wait and see" position. These love-hate cycles can be painful for the founders and management of the technology companies who rely on these investors for the capital to develop their new cutting-edge products and services.

The most important question asked by every start-up and rapidly-growing technology company with whom I have worked over the last two decades is: "How do I find the money to keep going before commercializing our product?" Of course, the solutions for raising the money to fund research and development are as various as the companies themselves.

Company founders begin at the earliest stage with personal funds, seed money from private individuals, credit cards, and bank loans. The goodwill (and bank accounts) of family and friends does not last long, and technology companies typically need millions of dollars and many years before their products are marketable. Accredited (angel) investors and government-sponsored programs are attuned to the needs of early-stage companies. An entrepreneur's financing options, when successful, progress through venture capital financing, corporate partnerships, and then, ultimately, to the public market through an initial public offering, or to the sale of the company. Along the way, one of the best sources of money is through the conservation of available cash—in other words, by controlling the burn rate of cash on hand.

Many primers have been written for entrepreneurs by knowledgeable advisors offering instructions on how to write a business plan, how to approach the venture capital community, or plan the timing of an initial public offering. Very little is available that discusses the investment process from the point of view of the venture capitalists and investment bankers themselves. What criteria do they use when considering an investment in a company? What are their investment objectives?

To help entrepreneurs find answers to these questions and other issues they face in growing their companies, a two-day conference, "Financing Technology's Frontier: Investment Strategies for High-Tech and Biotech

Companies" was held in September 1996. A group of directors and partners from well-known venture capital partnerships and investment banking firms, along with several CEOs of technology companies, spoke about the decision-making processes their organizations employ, and discussed some of their personal experiences in helping found and develop companies on technology's frontier.

The second edition of this book is an extension and updating of the first edition, which originated with the discussions that took place over the two days of the original conference.

I am privileged to be able to work with some of the pioneers on technology's frontier. This book is dedicated to those people—both investors and entrepreneurs—who are even now shaping changes in the way we will live as the 21st century unfolds.

acknowledgments

I have truly been twice blessed. The first edition of this book began as a promising idea and a two-day seminar, was subsequently developed into a manuscript, and eventually became the original edition.

There were many contributors to that effort, including the numerous business leaders and venture capitalists quoted in the book, as well as two editors, Susan Wylie Lanfray and Michael Ramos, without whose contributions there would not have been a first edition upon which the second edition was built.

That was then, and this is now. Now I am happily ensconced as a partner in my current firm, Deloitte & Touche. And here we created the second edition manuscript, containing much new material and several new chapters, and by itself a tremendous project. My second blessing is to have such tremendous help in completing this latest project.

I want to send out a wide ranging thanks to the firm of Deloitte & Touche for supporting me in this endeavor. In addition, I want to send out specific thanks to my partners and colleagues who gave of their individual time, talents, and energy in commenting on the book or contributing material. Included in this list are: Dr. Pierre Anhoury, John Bigalke, David Black, Nathalie Duchesnay, Tom Feuerstein, Stuart Henderson, Larry Kraemer, Nigel Mercer, Peter Micca, Don O'Callaghan, John Rhodes, Akihiro Sano, Marty Somelofske, Hans Verloop, and Ken Weixel. Colleagues, each of your contributions added a measure of your individual and cumulative special knowledge to several of the technical chapters herein.

Three special people come in for pointed, special thanks. Lynda Bauer, a marketing strategist with our Tri-State Business Development Center, was the creative brains and dynamo behind this project. She believed in the project and in me. We have a terrific working rapport, and her contributions were invaluable. Renee Souleles was able to cobble together gobs of research from the ideas we all developed, helped me pull it all together, kept the master of the manuscript, and, despite pressures, always seemed unflappable.

Lastly, but not thirdly, in writing the first edition, I noted that I was fortunate to have a terrific contributing editor. I was, if anything, even more fortunate the second time around. Linda Jenkins not only contributed her finely-honed writing skills, she also brought a second set of skills, in that she has a deep understanding of the technology space that she brings to the task.

Linda gets it. No explaining technical terms here. Linda's combined skills made my tasks flow so much more smoothly.

In completing the second edition, we called on many in the business community to contribute their points of view through interviews they agreed to. I want to thank the following interviewees who are quoted in this book: Dr. Anthony Atti from SciVentures, Tom D'Ambra from Albany Molecular Research, Michael J. Donovan from Biosquare, Dina Elliott from Elliott Consulting, Dr. Howard Fillit from the Institute for the Study of Aging, Buck French from JPMorgan Partners, Margaret Horn from Genencor, Maria Gotsch from the NYC Investment Fund, Hugh Jones from Data-Monitor PLC, Ray Land from Genencor, and Dr. William Polf from New York Presbyterian Hospital.

In addition, I want to again thank the following people who contributed their knowledge to the first edition. We carried much of that wisdom on into this second edition: Jeffrey W. Casdin, James H. Cavanaugh, Ph.D., Patricia M. Cloherty, Peter J. Crowley, Stephen J. Epstein, CPA, Dean C. Gordanier, Jr., J.D., Charles M. Hartman, William A. Haseltine, Ph.D., Jeffrey R. Jay, M.D., Andrew D. Klein, Jeremy M. Levin, D. Phil, MB.BChir., Jay Moorin, Jack Nelson, Daniel J. O'Brien, Fredric D. Price, and Philippe L. Sommer.

Thanks to all.

about the author

Richard P. Shanley, CPA, MBA, is a partner in the Tri-state cluster of Deloitte & Touche's national Healthcare & Life Sciences practice. He has over 27 years of diversified professional services experience encompassing audit and public stock offerings for biotech, pharmaceutical, and high-tech companies. His experience in pharmaceuticals and biotech has been continuous and spans more than 20 years. Rich founded and led industry practices in both Life Sciences and New Media.

Rich also speaks regularly on various topics in the technology field. He recently moderated a panel at the IBF biotech conference in San Francisco; spoke on the topic "From Concept to Company" at New York Biotech Association's meeting at the NY Academy of Sciences; spoke about "Borderless Biotechnology" at BioSante in Montreal; spoke at the NanoBusiness Alliance latest two annual meetings in New York; moderated a panel at BIO 2002 in Toronto on the importance of project management in reducing the time from discovery to market; spoke at Connecticut and Pittsburgh Venture Groups' biotech events; spoke at the Nanotech Investing Forum in Palm Springs CA; was on the faculty of the Deloitte Healthcare College in Orlando, Florida; and moderated a panel in at BIO 2003 in Washington, D.C. on financing biotech.

Rich is an active member of the New York State Society of Certified Public Accountants and the American Institute of Certified Public Accountants. He also has been actively involved in the New Jersey Biotechnology Council, the New York Biotechnology Association, the Connecticut Venture Group, the New Jersey Technology Council, the NanoBusiness Alliance and the Biotechnology Industry Organization.

CHAPTER 1

Sharing the Excitement of Discovery

The pace of change is accelerating and has been since the inception of invention [and] this acceleration is an inherent feature of technology. The result will be far greater transformations in the first two decades of the twenty-first century than we saw in the entire twentieth century.

—Ray Kurzweil, author and inventor[1]

PACE OF CHANGE

As humankind stands on the edge of a new millennium, it is interesting and informative to take a look backward, and measure how far technology has advanced in the last 1,000 years and understand why the pace of change has accelerated so rapidly in just the last 100 years, and why it will continue to accelerate at an even faster pace over the next 100 years.

A millennium ago, the most advanced practitioners of the art of healing lived in the Ottoman Empire. The skills of these medical practitioners were essentially derivative, in that their primary goal was to interpret and revive the medical knowledge developed by Hippocrates, Galen, and other physicians of the Greco-Roman era. Indeed, in the year 1000, western civilization knew less about medical science than its ancestors did 2,000 years ago.

Throughout the Ottoman Empire, the most famous physician was Avicenna, a Persian, who wrote the million-word textbook, *Canon of Medicine*, which was considered to be the defining treatise on medicine until well into the seventeenth century.

A millennium ago, written language was reserved for society's elite. The Guttenberg printing press had not yet been invented, so the dissemination of information was a slow, painful process. For the average person, storytelling

1

(either oral or through the visual arts) was the most common means to communicate ideas between villages or across generations. To communicate across distances required the physical travel of a human being, which greatly limited the dissemination of information.

By the turn of the 20th century, the level of knowledge had increased tremendously. In medicine, vaccines were developed. Knowledge of germs as the source of infection was proven by Louis Pasteur in France, and this led to the first attempts at preventive medicine and the development of theories of immunization. Also at this time, the specific microbes responsible for tuberculosis and cholera were discovered by Robert Koch in Germany.

In communication, voice transmission over phone lines had become available, which made possible verbal communications between people who were miles apart. King Kalakaua, sovereign of the small and far-off kingdom of Hawaii, was one of the first monarchs to install a phone line in his palace, allowing him remote communication with his staff. By 1878 the first commercial phone exchange was put into service in New Haven, Connecticut, and AT&T was born.

The other communication breakthrough that occurred at the end of the 19th century was the teletype or teleprinter. This technology was in widespread use for over 50 years and only recently was rendered obsolete by computer printers and visual displays.

Within the last 20 to 40 years, the knowledge boundary has been pushed even further, and the pace of change has picked up considerably. The genetic code has been cracked; monoclonal antibodies have been produced; the human growth hormone has been synthesized; human insulin has been produced in genetically modified bacteria, becoming, in 1982 the first biotech drug approved by the Food and Drug Administration. Technology for "golden rice" recently has been made available to developing countries in hopes of improving the health of undernourished people and preventing some forms of blindness; the DNA fingerprinting technique was developed in 1984, and one year later, genetic fingerprinting was entered as evidence in a courtroom; the Human Genome Project, an international effort to map and sequence all the genes in the human body as well as the genomes of key experimental organisms such as yeasts and nematode worms, delivered an initial analysis of the sequence fully two years ahead of schedule. The implications of these and countless other breakthroughs on disease treatment and food production are enormous. Biotech and genomics have revolutionized the industry, approaching disease from its source and not its symptoms. Real cures are emerging as science comes to understand causation at the genetic level.

In communications, we now send and receive a wide variety of data instantly and globally. These transmissions include text, images, and sound, and enable users to access vast sources of information stored in databases from remote locations. In 1990, when researcher Tim Berners-Lee developed the HyperText Markup Language (HTML), the concept of a global communications network was understood by very few. Just four years later the World Wide Web emerged and has arguably become one of the most important technological breakthroughs in the history of humankind.

Today's computers are performing tasks that were considered unthinkable just a decade or two ago: real-time voice recognition, responding to natural language, recognizing patterns in medical procedures, and so on. It is estimated that computers doubled in speed every three years at the beginning of the 20th century, every two years in the 1950s and 1960s, and are now doubling in speed every 12 months.[2]

But the high-tech and biotech industries are not solely functions of advances in science. These industries are actually defined by *two* spheres, of which science is only the first. The second sphere is business—the ability to introduce new products valued by customers into the marketplace.

> *Venture capitalists invest for the long term. I think, and most of my colleagues would agree, there is a great future in this area and a wealth of opportunity. The thing to remember is that the science moves on extremely fast, and the key question is how you harness the science into a viable business model.*
>
> —Nicholas Galakatos, Ph.D., Former Partner, Venrock Associates (now Vice President, Millennium Pharmaceuticals, Inc.)[3]

Like the underlying technology, the nature of business has changed dramatically over the last millennium. A thousand years ago, society was largely based on agriculture, and great wealth accrued to large landholders. Commerce was conducted predominately at the individual level; for example, a cobbler or a draftsman plied his trade to others in the same town. Conducting business usually required the physical presence of all parties, such as a farmer's market in the town square, which brought together all the farmers, their products, and their customers.

In the 19th century, the Industrial Revolution changed the scale of business dramatically. Manufacturing and production were performed by large factories and, in order to build these, access to capital was critical. For the first time, large numbers of investors outside of the company itself were needed to build factories and realize economies of scale. And so the corporation as we know it today began to emerge. Since the Middle Ages, business had been conducted at the whim of a sole proprietor or a small partnership. The emergence of a corporation—with multiple divisions and responsibilities and managements—changed the world of business forever.

Once again, the size and nature of business is changing. To compete successfully, companies must be lean and nimble, able to respond quickly to changing market conditions. Sheer size alone does not guarantee a sustainable competitive advantage, and neither do traditional economies of scale. Instead, *knowledge* and *information* are seen as the key resources for companies that allow them to provide value to their customers. Finally, it is no longer necessary to establish physical locations for the conduct of commerce. With Internet technology, companies establish virtual marketplaces from which they sell their goods on a worldwide basis.

These changes—in the world of business as well as the world of science—are the driving force behind opportunities in the high-tech and biotech industries.

CHARACTERISTICS OF HIGH-TECH AND BIOTECH COMPANIES

Think about the nature of innovation in the drug industry. What exactly does it take to have the kind of scientific breakthrough necessary to create a new drug, one with significant therapeutic value?

In short, it takes entrepreneurial spirit and scientific insight.

You can array data that is common knowledge across the industry and ask ten scientists, "Is there a drug in there or not?" Nine will tell you no, and one person will say yes. Maybe that one person is wrong, and maybe that one person just found a breakthrough, it happens all the time. That intangible element of insight makes all the difference in our industry.

—Judy Lewent, Chief Financial Officer, Merck & Co. [4]

High-tech and biotech companies operate in separate industries with vastly different products, yet they share important similarities. These similarities stem from a common goal, namely to capitalize on scientific insight and create products valued by customers. The following characteristics are common to both high-tech and biotech companies.

- Success in the medical, communications, or any other technology-driven field requires a steady flow of innovative products. To create these new products, high-tech and biotech companies are extremely research intensive. The Biotechnology Industry Organization (BIO) reported that the biotechnology industry is one of the most research-intensive industries in the world and that, in 2001, the United States alone spent $15.6 billion on research and development (R&D). Similarly, the BIO reported that the top five biotech companies spent an average of $89,400 per employee on R&D in 2000, while the average for all U.S. industries is about $8,000 per employee.
- The structure of the company must be compatible with this research-driven nature of the business. According to Gabriel Schmergel, president

and chief executive officer (CEO) of Genetics Institute, Inc., "Innovation thrives better when decentralized. The truly innovative people tend to migrate away from the large organizations, whether academic or industry, and move to smaller ones. That is where true innovation is taking place."[5]

- High-tech and biotech companies tend to be smaller with fewer employees, and disparate functions exist side by side rather than in the different departments found at larger corporations. The aim is to be able to translate ideas quickly into action. Technological change is rapid, and the company must be able to keep pace.

- The working environment of high-tech and biotech companies tends to attract people who are motivated by an intellectual curiosity and drive. It is common for high-tech and biotech companies to offer their employees stock options and other forms of equity-based compensation, such as restricted stock and restricted stock units. Microsoft recently announced the suspension of stock option grants. The company will replace its option granting program with a program focused on restricted stock units. The goal of all these forms of equity-based compensation is to provide a strong incentive for performance and create for the employees an intense, personal stake in the company. Stock options are also valuable because they help the company conserve its cash.

NEED FOR FINANCING

Perhaps the most important characteristic shared by high-tech and biotech companies is the long lead time required before products are sold and revenues are realized from research projects. Financing this research and product development can take hundreds of millions of dollars, and there is no guarantee of ultimate success. For example, in the biotech industry it takes, on average, in excess of $500 million and 10 years to bring a drug to market. Once there, 7 out of 10 products fail to return the cost of the company's capital.

CEOs of high-tech and biotech companies are under tremendous pressure to continually raise financing from a variety of sources. Unfortunately, as the high-tech and biotech industries have matured, investors have become more pragmatic and cautious about the companies they back financially.

Merck invests approximately $1 billion per year in research, which has given us extraordinary insights into the risky nature and high cost of pharmaceutical research. We know that scientists will probe an idea they feel has merit for as long as they possibly can, which is great. You get advocates, you get champions, and you never say die. The challenge from the point of view of the finance department is

EXHIBIT 1.1   Financing Decision Tree

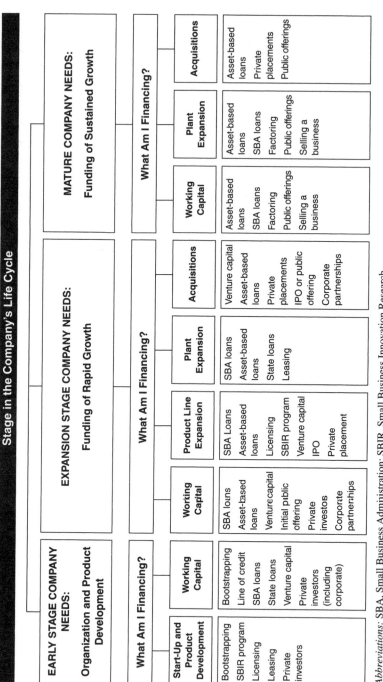

| Stage in the Company's Life Cycle | | | | | | | | | | | | | |

EARLY STAGE COMPANY NEEDS:

Organization and Product Development

EXPANSION STAGE COMPANY NEEDS:

Funding of Rapid Growth

MATURE COMPANY NEEDS:

Funding of Sustained Growth

What Am I Financing?

Start-Up and Product Development	Working Capital
Bootstrapping	Bootstrapping
SBIR program	Line of credit
Licensing	SBA loans
Leasing	State loans
Private investors	Venture capital
	Private investors (including corporate)

What Am I Financing?

Working Capital	Product Line Expansion	Plant Expansion	Acquisitions
SBA loans	SBA Loans	SBA loans	Venture capital
Asset-based loans	Asset-based loans	Asset-based loans	Asset-based loans
Venture capital	Licensing	State loans	Private placements
Initial public offering	SBIR program	Leasing	IPO or public offering
Private investos	Venture capital		Corporate partnerships
Corporate partnerhips	IPO		
	Private placement		

What Am I Financing?

Working Capital	Plant Expansion	Acquisitions
Asset-based loans	Asset-based loans	Asset-based loans
SBA loans	SBA loans	Private placements
Factoring	Factoring	Public offerings
Public offerings	Public offerings	
Selling a business	Selling a business	

Abbreviations: SBA, Small Business Administration; SBIR, Small Business Innovation Research.

Source: The Financing Decision Tree was developed by Meryle J. Melnicoff, Ph.D. and is being used with permission.

to put parameters around that curiosity and determine what is and what is not productive.

—Judy Lewent, Chief Financial Officer, Merck & Co. [6]

The high-tech and biotech CEO face many barriers in the attempt to raise money and, once raised, additional problems arise in trying to control costs and manage the "burn rate." This book describes the ways high-tech and biotech CEOs might overcome those barriers and problems.

The book begins with a technology frontier overview followed by an overall discussion of business growth models that encourage others to invest. Succeeding chapters provide insight on how financing is obtained from venture capitalists, the public markets, and corporate partners. Case studies and observations from technology company CEOs are used to demonstrate how key ideas are applied in practice. The book includes a discussion of tax- and equity-based compensation strategies that can be effective in helping companies conserve their cash as they strive to move their new technologies from concept to reality. And this new edition also covers mergers and acquisitions within the biotech arena as well as a discussion of global biotech and the new emphasis on corporate governance since the passage of the Sarbanes-Oxley Act, and ends with a view of technology's future—from the frontier.

FINANCING DECISION TREE

The type of funding to seek depends on the company's stage of development and how it plans to use the financing. Only a few of the various financing sources are appropriate for a given business at each stage of its development. Exhibit 1.1 outlines the different sources of financing available throughout a company's life cycle. Many of these financing alternatives are discussed in later chapters of this book. Of course, since each company is different, so is its business and financial situation. The information contained in this book is intended as a guideline only. Any decision to seek and accept financing from a specific source should be made only after consulting with legal and financial advisors.

NOTES

[1] Ray Kurzweil, *The Age of Spiritual Machines* (New York: Penguin Books, 1999), 2.

[2] Ibid., 3.

[3] Nicholas Galakatos, "What's New in Biotechnology Funding," Presentation at the annual meeting of the New York Biotechnology Association, October 1995.

[4] Nancy A. Nichols, "Scientific Management at Merck," *Harvard Business Review* (January–February 1994): 98.

[5] Erik Christenson, "Profits, Promise, and Positive Results: Biotechnology at 20," *Fortune*, September 30, 1996 (Biotechnology Industry Organization's Special Supplement): S1–7.

[6] Nichols, "Scientific Management at Merck."

CHAPTER 2

Growth Models That Encourage Investment

The key difference between successful and unsuccessful companies is an initial strategy that marries technology and the financial plan. Over the years, I've come to the conclusion that the single most important lesson is that as you conceive it, so it is likely to be.

—William A. Haseltine, Chairman and CEO,
Human Genome Sciences, Inc.

The model I think many people fall into is what I call the "Prayer Model." It's what people do when they get very absorbed on doing all the things you do when you start a biotech company. They choose a hot area of science and develop a first-class team. They go out and get their first and, hopefully, their second corporate alliances. People understand they need to do all those things, but what they overlook is the structure after all that. By default, they end up in the prayer mode.

—Charles M. Hartman, General Partner, CW Group, Inc.

IMPORTANCE OF CHOOSING AN OVERALL BUSINESS MODEL

Entrepreneurs can be attracted to cutting-edge technology for any number of reasons. Often they are scientists or engineers whose passion is pushing the boundaries of technology. A biotech company founder may be interested in achieving a humanitarian objective, such as developing an AIDS vaccine. A software or network engineer's focus may be to develop a product that makes a new technology available to everyone; for example, to bring the Internet to every home television. There may be a wonderful humanitarian or democratic intent, but once a company gets beyond the earliest rounds of private financing, it becomes difficult to find investors interested in achieving these objectives as ends in themselves. Investors may appreciate these goals, but they have a business objective—they need a clear path to a return on their investment in order to consider investing in a company.

For the start-up enterprise, carving out such a path is formidable. Company founders with a new technology face a daunting number of decisions. They must plan for the time and money it will take to bring a commercially viable product to the marketplace. In the case of biotechnology companies, the process of clinical trials and regulatory approvals often takes 10 years or more. There is little chance the company will make money during that time, and the business model must recognize that reality. Consideration also must be given to who will manufacture, distribute, and sell the product. In some cases, the technology may be developed and then licensed to a larger corporation, which will bring it to the marketplace; in others, the founders may decide to handle all of this within their own company. Last, consideration should be given to a likely exit strategy for investors. In most cases, venture capital firms receive their return on investment at the time of an initial public offering.

The manner in which a chief executive officer (CEO) conceives of the company creates a context that can be used as a measure and guide for each individual step in its business development. Unfortunately, founders often fail to recognize the importance of developing a clear business model for the company. As a result, the company encounters great difficulty in finding investment money, or it gets off to a fast start with seed money and then hits a difficult phase in its growth and stalls for lack of additional capital.

BUSINESS MODELS FOR HIGH-TECH AND BIOTECH COMPANIES

Venture capitalists talk about models all the time: what's hot, what's not. One of the fundamental problems with models is that the models you know about are the older models, and you've discovered things you don't like about them. But the new, hot models—you actually don't know anything about. There just isn't any information each time you contemplate doing a deal.

—Charles M. Hartman, General Partner, CW Group, Inc.

Entrepreneurs who are planning new ventures tend to model themselves after existing successful companies. In the high-technology sector, where the focus is on the cutting edge, businesses tend to follow an established pattern. Those models can range from a fully integrated research-to-product-to-market company—known in the biotech industry as a fully integrated pharmaceutical company (FIPCO)—to a virtual company with a handful of employees linked to a wide network of outsourced contractors and strategic partners.

Fully Integrated Companies

A fully integrated company is one that controls all aspects of bringing a product to market, from research and development (R&D) to the manufacture, marketing, and distribution of the final product. In the mid-1990s, many new biotech ventures believed that it was desirable, even expected, to become a FIPCO. In fact, relatively few companies have achieved that goal. Small companies found they simply could not be as efficient as the global pharmaceutical giants in manufacturing and distributing product and therefore could not produce their product at a cost that was acceptable to the marketplace.

Building a fully integrated company takes enormous amounts of capital: money that is difficult, if not impossible, for early-stage companies to raise, particularly on favorable terms. In some instances—for example, in the microchip industry—such a company model can work if the challenge is in establishing *manufacturing* efficiencies through technology, as well as research efficiencies. As technology sectors mature and the number of competing companies increases, the resulting pressure to reduce or maintain product cost containment by managed care organizations places additional burdens on biotechnology and pharmaceutical companies. Establishing a start-up as a fully integrated company capable of dealing with both research and manufacturing imperatives is very difficult.

Virtual Companies

At the other end of the spectrum is the virtual company. The profile of this model would be cautious spending and the outsourcing of internal services to delay capital requirements. At its most extreme, a virtual company would consist of one person managing the company and contracting out everything. More typically, in its early stages, a virtual company seeks to limit fixed costs by keeping a low employee head count. A virtual biotech company makes arrangements with a contract research organization (CRO) or academic university laboratories for development and testing of its compounds. If its roots are within an academic institution, its core team of engineers or scientists will remain there, paying no rent and benefiting from the institution's strong administrative support network, until the company has some scientific success.

This company model is not sustainable in the long term, however. A virtual company has difficulty attracting interest from the financial community because it meets few of the venture capitalists' criteria, such as an experienced management team, one or more corporate partnerships, and proprietary products, tools, or technology with the potential to capture large market share (see Chapter 3).

A number of virtual companies do receive venture funding, but the investors may not choose to continue investing in the start-up company until it is ready for an initial public offering (IPO). This is often the case in the biotechnology sector in particular, where the timing of an IPO has been pushed back to the late development stage, necessitating mezzanine financing or funding through a corporate partnership agreement before an IPO exit. Venture investors may decide they can maximize the return on their investment if they avoid having to give away the mark-ups to middle-round investors. In this case, they may arrange for an earlier exit by finding a buyer for the company. Such was the case for the gene delivery company Targetech. This virtual company start-up within the University of Connecticut grew for two and a half years under the sponsorship of a venture capital firm. The venture capitalists arranged for the company's acquisition within six months after the company founded its own laboratory and realized a very profitable return on their investment.

A virtual company operating outside of academia focuses management on areas in which they add the most value. It may appear to be fully integrated in that it seems to be responsible for research, manufacturing, and marketing. In fact, the company consists of a small central core of key company executives and personnel (usually involved in research or product development). Most company activities are outsourced to business partners in a network of strategic alliances.

Lateralizing Products

Under this model, a company creates a broad-based technology with a myriad of applications, or "lateral" products, in other industries. The objective is to invest once in an intellectual property base of some substance and then spread the results across multiple centers of capitalizable value.

In one example, the chief scientist of Biocompatibles, plc (now a publicly traded company in the United Kingdom), identified and synthesized outside of the body a substance called phosphorylcholine (PC), which is found on the surface of all cells. The first use of this new product was in human healthcare, to coat catheters, cannulae, syringes for diabetics, cardiovascular stents, and various other medical devices to mitigate blood clotting and other problems that arise when devices are inserted into the body.

As it turns out, PC is very inexpensive to produce, and a little goes a long way [a kilogram (2.2 pounds) will coat Europe's annual supply of catheters]. But PC has potential applications on a much wider scale, and this has enabled Biocompatibles to evolve from a company focused on healthcare into a materials technology company whose first application happens to be in healthcare.

Today it holds over 37 patents and has corporate partners in every area of endeavor. As a paint additive, PC prevents barnacles from forming on ships. As a skin care ingredient, it can be used to improve moisture retention and reduce wrinkles. It also can be used to coat windshields and protect furniture and fabric. Biocompatibles has been successful in extending its underlying intellectual property beyond the regulator structures that are required for human health considerations.

Jump-Start

Another structure is modeled on the jump-start method of roadside assistance. The idea is to wire together two or more batteries in the hope of generating enough power to get something moving. Sugen, Inc., was created when the two largest biotechnology laboratories in a certain area of signal transduction-related kinases pooled their resources. When Sugen opened its doors for business, it employed more than 100 scientists in two laboratories working in the area.

The problem in using this approach is that there are not many ways to jump-start something. The universe of experts in a highly focused area of technology is usually small; because of this, it can be difficult to find the necessary critical mass of knowledgeable people to get the company going.

Discovery Platform

A number of companies are based on a discovery platform model; that is, developing a new process for drug or technology discovery. For example, Geron Corporation used a particular area of biology as its discovery platform: the biology of how cells age. Some cells, mainly cancer cells, do not age, and important questions arise as to how these cells remain immortal. Geron's business model is to use cell aging as a platform to discover new drug products.

Information

Companies can adopt the information model plan to create and market information. The form is best typified by the genomics companies, which generally are involved with mapping the human gene sequence.

This information is sold to other companies for use in their R&D efforts. So far the market has not shown that it believes this model represents a long-term success strategy.

Corporate Spinout

It is often more efficient to develop certain technologies in a small, "scrappy" company than within the confines of a large corporation. Large companies that wish to build an entrepreneurial team around a new technology, or that seek a way to handle R&D issues, may choose to create one or more "spinouts," subsidiary companies formed to develop and commercialize a promising technology. This strategy can help preserve shareholder value in the parent company by shifting R&D costs to the spinout, while offering the promise of future value if the technology is successful.

ThermoElectron Corporation has used this model to build an organization with worldwide sales of nearly $3 billion and one of the most diverse and advanced technology portfolios in the country. Founded in 1956 by Dr. George N. Hatsopolous, the technology company's first focus was on the creation of products and services that would answer emerging needs in society. By the 1980s the company had become what one Wall Street analyst called "a perpetual idea machine" by encouraging entrepreneurial ventures through its majority-owned public subsidiaries.

By the late 1990s ThermoElectron had created more than 18 of these publicly traded subsidiaries. By spinning out new technologies and services into subsidiaries and offering a minority share in the newly created companies to the public, ThermoElectron was able to raise capital to support growth, provide an entrepreneurial climate in which employees could pursue their own ideas, bring new technologies to the marketplace, and provide value for its shareholders. Recently, however, ThermoElectron underwent a major reorganization and has consolidated into one publicly traded company, TMO, on the New York Stock Exchange.

DEVELOPING A DETAILED BUSINESS PLAN

A start-up company needs to push to create a realistic plan, because very often no one is forcing it upon them. Many times a company can have an excellent product and first-class management and still fail, because they didn't do their homework on what really is the nuts and bolts of their business.

Detailed planning is extremely difficult. Even more difficult, however, is trying to raise another round of investment when you don't have a credible business plan. That's especially true when you haven't created a plan because you hadn't really thought out the business very well to begin with.

—Dean C. Gordanier Jr., Partner,
Testa, Hutwitz & Thibeault, LLP

Developing a business model will allow the company to answer overarching, large-scale questions such as:

- How will the company minimize the "burn" of equity money until it builds the value of its technology sufficiently for nonequity corporate partner deals?
- How will the company manage the effects of the lead time, especially long in the case of pharmaceuticals, on the company's ultimate profitability? That is, how will it compensate for losses over the period of time it will take to create a product that customers will pay for?
- Is there a defined strategy that builds value for investors and will ultimately generate a good rate of return for their investment?

Once a company decides on a business model, it must then create a detailed business plan from that model. Creating and managing this business plan is not fraught with mystery or complications; many good guides are available that explain the process in detail. It is not something, however, that should be delegated to the financial people alone.

Instead, it is advisable, perhaps even mandatory, that the CEO of the company take responsibility for the plan. In some instances, the company's financial executive, a consultant, or even the outside accounting firm assumes responsibility for compiling the plan. This approach may seem expedient at first, but ultimately the CEO must dive in, take control, and assume ownership of the underlying assumptions behind the plan. If the CEO does not become involved, the plan may be doomed from the start by faulty assumptions.

A successful business plan serves two purposes. First, it is an important management tool—a detailed blueprint that shows where a company intends to go and how it intends to get there. But it is also a selling document that conveys the exciting prospects and growth potential of the company to prospective investors and partners. In a straightforward, organized, and detailed way, a business plan should not only emphasize the strengths of a company, it also should be realistic about its problems, risks, and obstacles— while offering solutions to these issues. In short, the successful business plan must do three key things in about 20 to 40 pages:

1. Discuss the company's plans for the near-term and long-term future.
2. Show that these goals can be achieved.
3. Demonstrate that realization of the plan will satisfy the reader's requirements.

Although different business models will lead to different business plans, certain elements are common to all plans, regardless of the company's overall model.

Assumptions of the Business Plan

It is vital that the company's business plan be based on reasonable assumptions. The primary risk of the plan is that if the assumptions are too optimistic, the money the company works so hard to raise will not be enough. If the money raised is not enough, the company will be forced to go back into the marketplace or back to its investors for additional funds. Chances are, it will be tougher and more expensive to raise money the next time around.

Assumptions generally fall into two categories—time and dollars—with plenty of overlap between the two. In most emerging high-tech and biotech companies, the problems that come up time and again typically relate to the *time* assumptions: what's going to happen when. There is a strong tendency for entrepreneurs to be overly optimistic about how long things will take.

Companies must be realistic with their projections. It is wise to build in extra time for the slippage of key events such as product launches, benchmarks, and approvals, especially if they involve a Food and Drug Administration (FDA) or other regulatory process.

On the *dollar* side, a key assumption is sales. A major issue for the company, and certainly to potential investors, is the nature of the company's market. Key questions to consider include:

- Will revenue come from the sale or licensing of existing products or new products?
- What will these products be competing against?
- What slice of the marketplace will the company get?
- How much will the product sell for?

Particularly with groundbreaking high-tech or biotech products, many of these questions can be difficult to answer, but management must give them some thought and come up with a plausible response if they want to continue to attract investors.

> We had an unfortunate investment a couple of years ago in a high-tech company that had spent two years developing a database product. They were flat out of cash, and it was the night before the CEO was making his pitch to a group of investors to raise additional money. The question was raised, "What are you going to sell the product for?"
>
> "I don't know," the CEO said. "It may be $99 shrink-wrap. Or it may be several thousand dollars. We'll sell it through consultants."

Quite frankly, that was the end of the investment discussion. We pulled up and walked away because we felt certain that the company should have been a lot further along in their strategic thought process than to answer the question like that.

—Daniel J. O'Brien, General Partner, J.H. Whitney & Co.

Key dollar assumptions—such as sales—can be more refined, depending on the company's stage of development. Sales by month, by customer, and by product, for example, should be built into the plan.

Cost of sales should be detailed by labor, overhead, and materials. The R&D function should be run out in terms of the number of people the company will need and exactly when those people will be hired. The cost of materials should be included, if applicable. Outside testing and other services that might be required should be included, as well, along with consideration of their availability and lead time.

A similar analysis should be performed for general and administrative costs. The hiring of personnel will be phased in over time as the company achieves benchmarks, and estimates of general and administrative costs should consider who gets hired when.

The plan should be detailed, not just along product and customer lines, but also in terms of milestone benchmarks the company will achieve. The plan should be divided into time segments by benchmarks or by major projects, or something similar. As the company moves through the time line, management should examine its cost structure and distinguish between fixed and variable costs. Many people think most of their costs are fixed, but in fact, when problems crowd into the picture, most of their costs really are variable.

All this excruciating detail is for management decision-making purposes, not for dissemination to the company's investors. Investors admit they do not want too much confusing detail, but they also clearly expect that the plan presented to them will be built on these kinds of details, which are necessary to answer any in-depth questions they may have.

Sometimes it is helpful to come up with two versions of the plan: one to serve as an internal stretch plan and the other to be shown to third parties. The internal plan might be more optimistic in order to push company personnel to shoot for more ambitious goals. The external plan should be more conservative, with built-in cushions to make sure performance does not disappoint the investors and others interested in the company.

Key Elements of a Successful Business Plan[1]

It is critical to create a document that lays out a road map for the CEO and the management team describing where the company wants to go and how it intends to get there. But it is equally important to create a document that provides all the information possible to attract positive attention from prospective investors and partners. Here are the key sections required for an effective business plan.

Executive Summary   The executive summary is the most concise form of the plan, briefly covering all the key points to follow. A preliminary draft may be prepared in advance as a guide for the more detailed writing of the full plan, but it should be finalized after the full plan has been completed, to be sure that it has captured all the results of research and planning. The executive summary is what potential outside investors typically review first to determine whether they want to read further. Therefore, it is the single most important section of the plan and must suggest a promising business proposition for funding in an enticing and convincing manner.

Company Description   The company description covers the company, its mission, and its history. This section should describe the company's current status, its strategies, and its plans for the future. It answers such questions as: What business is the company in? What is the purpose of the business? How does its products or services relate to its mission? Why is this company uniquely qualified to be in this business? What distinguishes this company from the competition? What stage of development is the company currently at? What are the company's weaknesses, and how are they being addressed?

Key data required: company name; legal form; location(s); financial highlights; shareholders.

Management and Organization   For many potential investors, the management team is the most important predictor of a successful business. This section should describe members of the management team and their backgrounds, as well as the company's needs for additional key people. Key outside advisors and consultants also should be discussed here. This section answers such questions as: Why is the CEO qualified to lead the company? Does the management team have both technical and business acumen? Are compensation programs competitive enough to attract and retain the best people? Do the directors or advisors bring relevant experience to the management team?

Key data required: organization chart; key management; board of directors; consultants and advisors; compensation and other employee agreements; other shareholders, rights, and resolutions.

Market and Competitors   The market and competitors section identifies the current and future potential buyers of the company's product(s) or service(s). It must answer a number of fundamental questions, such as: What is this market? How large is it? Where is it headed? In what industry or industries will the company operate? What are the industry trends? What does the competition consist of? The plan should explain the key factors for the market in terms of how buying decisions are made, how the market is segmented, what kind of market position is planned, and what sort of defensive strategy is envisioned to fend off competitors. How will changes in technology affect the industry? Who are the company's customers today? Have competitors' strengths and weaknesses been analyzed honestly? Is the market price sensitive?

Key data required: market statistics; competitor data; market and customer surveys.

Product or Service   The product or service section is where the features, components, production process, and quality of the product(s) or service(s) are described in detail. Issues that must be addressed are the amount of research and development remaining to be completed, how the product or service will be produced and at what cost, and how the crucial activities of quality control and after-sale service will be performed. Key regulatory considerations also should be addressed. This section will answer such questions as: What are the key milestones in the R&D process? When will the product be ready to sell? What are costs to complete the development of the current product? How much manufacturing space will be needed? How will quality be monitored? How can customers contact the company if they have comments or problems?

Key data required: product literature and technical specifications; contracts and/or purchase orders; competitive advantages; patent, license, and trademarks; regulatory approvals or industry standards; operations plan; research and development plans.

Marketing and Sales   Marketing and sales functions are central to business success because without them, everything else becomes irrelevant. The marketing plan will be based on the results of market research and the value proposition of the product or service. Effective marketing, often through advertising and public relations, also must be described. The plan should describe the company's selling methods (e.g., direct sales, mail order), how sales staff is trained, and how support is provided. Because of the substantial expense associated with business development, the plan should consider and present the most cost-effective options. This section answers such questions as: How is the firm positioning the product or service? What are the key messages the company wants to convey in marketing materials? What types of media will be used to promote the product or service? Do the company need its own sales force, or will it use dealers or reps? What is the company's commission structure?

Key data required: marketing plan; marketing vehicles; marketing materials.

Financial Information   The most important parts of the financial information section are the financial forecasts, presented in balance sheets and statements of cash flow and income. If these are to be believable, they must be consistent not only with the company's past performance trends and the data presented in other sections of the plan, but also with each other, in terms of sales, inventories, sales costs, and other factors. If the plan is intended to raise financing, this section also should include a funding request that states how much money is needed, why it is needed, and how it will be used. Finally, the section must consider the likely return for the investor as well as exit strategies. This section will answer such questions as: Have the firm's current and historical financial statements been carefully analyzed in order to explain the results to prospective investors and to form the foundation for the projections? What type of investment is being sought? How does management plan to finance future company growth? What is the exit strategy for lenders and investors?

Key data required: financial statements for up to past five years; financial forecasts and projections and assumptions; amount and timing of needed funding.

Monitoring the Feedback   Running any business, but especially one on a tight shoestring budget, requires an early-warning system. Management must have access to timely and accurate financial information, which is formatted in a way that facilitates the comparison of actual results to the detailed budget. Management should review this information (which is based on cash receipts, disbursements, invoices, or other data) at least weekly, if not daily. Waiting until the end of the month to look back and see how the company performed is not good enough.

In this monitoring process, the balance sheet sometimes is overlooked, when in fact it can be the source of revealing and useful data. Management tends to overlook the balance sheet because it seems so simple: Receivables are receivables, payables are payables; what else is there?

The balance sheet is useful for detecting slipping timetables and leaking capital. For example, consider the payment terms the company plans for when it enters relationships with customers. Often the actual collection cycle is longer than originally planned. The company may require collection within 40 days, but in reality customers are taking 60 or 70 days to pay. On the production side, the buildup time to get the materials in stock and converted and out the door may be 30 or 40 days longer than originally expected.

Variations between original assumptions and actual results will have a significant impact on the amount of capital the company needs in the early stages of its development. A CEO should build in a cushion for the company's sake, not just for the sake of outside investors.

Remember that the CEO is responsible for the plan and eventually will be forced to answer to the company's third-party audience as to why the targets were or were not met. The company is going to try to raise additional cash in part based on past performance, and that performance will be judged largely against what the company said in its plan that it would do.

INDUSTRY DYNAMICS AND MIDCOURSE CORRECTIONS

A group came to me with an idea for a corporate spinout. The plan they came up with had one idea, one pathway to the market. I said, "Your plan makes no sense." They asked why. "Because it isn't going to happen." Again, they asked why. "Just because it's not."

It's not that I could tell them how I know it won't happen because of X, Y, or Z. I just know it won't happen because that's life.

So I told them they should model their business in a variety of ways, thinking about what would happen to the little business, to the parent, if things didn't work out. I would suggest that everybody do the same thing: be prepared, because you'll have to make midcourse corrections all the time.

—Frederic D. Price, Chairman and CEO of
Biomarin Pharmaceutical, Inc.
(Former President and CEO, AMBI, Inc., now Nutrition 21, Inc.)

When you pick up that fallen signpost, it is not important to know where you came from, because the road may be the wrong road and you may be following the road to doom. The key is only to point the road in one direction: What is the goal, where is the end line? It's financial success. How do I get there? It doesn't matter how I started. If I started in technology and technology's not working, don't become so blind, so limited, so passionate about that which you developed, that which you believed would take you to that ultimate destiny, so as to blind you to the fact that it will not work and you have to choose other courses.

There must be multiple paths because if there aren't multiple paths, what you are essentially doing is taking every shareholder and subjecting them to the ultimate risk of one avenue, and rarely in life does one avenue turn out to be the successful one.

—Jack Nelson, Former Chairman of the Board and CEO,
Advanced NMR Systems, Inc. (now Caprius, Inc.)

It is important for management to carefully consider and choose a model for their business and create a detailed plan for how the company will survive during the many years it may take before it can generate revenues from its products. But of course, no one really knows what will happen 5 or 10 years down the road. Markets may change—the entire industry might change—and management needs to be prepared to make midcourse corrections to adapt the company to those changes.

Chapter 4 presents a case study on Magainin Pharmaceuticals (now Genaera Corporation) and its efforts over a five-year period to raise capital in the public market. The company's president at the time, Jay Moorin, had a strategy for raising capital. This financing plan was tied closely to the company's business model. Two unforeseen events changed everything: The company's lead product failed its Phase III clinical trial, and the market for biotech stock issues went into a three-year slump. As a result, Moorin had to reconsider his financing plan. The business model for the company remained essentially the same, but the financing strategy was completely revised.

Chapter 7 presents a profile of Advanced NMR Systems (now Caprius, Inc.), a company whose original model was built on production of its sole technology through a corporate partnership. Under this model, Advanced NMR would perform basic research and then transfer the resulting technology to the corporate partner, who would integrate it into products for sale.

After working with the partner for a year, Jack Nelson, then CEO of Advanced NMR, came to the conclusion that the corporate partner was not interested in incorporating his company's technology into its own product—the partner was developing a competing technology and had partnered with Advanced NMR as a blocking move. In this situation, the key element of the company's business model proved unworkable, and it had no choice but to completely reinvent itself. Nelson came up with a new business model that involved the spin-off of a product that could function independent of the former partner's host system and the purchase of a service company in a compatible area of technology. In effect, Advanced NMR ceased to be a high-technology business and became a service company. Today Caprius provides some 24,000 breast care service procedures annually through its Strax Institute, but its main activities are centered around therapeutic drug monitoring through the Innofluor line of diagnostic assays of its subsidiary, Opus Diagnostics.

Worst-Case Scenario

During the planning process, company management should anticipate a worst-case scenario. This is not something anyone likes to do, but it is better for a CEO to work his or her way through worst-case planning at the beginning, rather than to do it later, when the worst comes crashing down. An unpleasant but healthy exercise is to take the basic plan, define what those worst-case scenarios may be, and decide what steps to take to get through it.

Many of those worst-case scenarios tend to be time-based. For example:

- The company did not get regulatory approval when it thought it would.
- The product is not coming along as expected.
- The company loses some key people or a key account.
- A corporate relationship falls through.

Thinking through these and similar scenarios, the CEO should realize quickly that cash flow will shrink and that the company's primary goal is survival. What goes first?

The CEO should list all of the company's expenses and all of its people, and decide an order of priority. What would get cut first? Next? Then the CEO should continue all the way down to the end of the list. Such an exercise will prepare the CEO mentally to make these decisions if, in fact, one of these worst-case scenarios should become a reality.

TECHNOLOGY COMPANY CASE STUDY

WorldWinner.com

Founded in December 1999, WorldWinner.com is an online gaming destination that allows participants to compete against other players in games of logic, skill, and dexterity, and win real cash and merchandise prizes based on their performance. Headquartered in Los Angeles, with an office in Newton, Massassachusetts, the company received initial funding from Boston-based Zero Stage Capital, a top venture capital firm, and a collective of distinguished individual investors called CommonAngels. It has been called the first legal alternative to online gambling for U.S. Internet users.[2]

WorldWinner.com has almost 20 games available, including chess, checkers, solitaire, crosswords, and Trac-man (similar to popular video games of the 1970s) that can be played, tournament-style, among 2 to 1,000 players for a small entry fee. The top scorer in the tournament wins a cash or merchandise prize. Unlike casino games, where the odds of winning depend on a player's ability to outplay his or her competitors, luck plays no part in WorldWinner.com's games, where skill is the key qualifier.

The company has over 1 million registered users and over 70,000 "Pro Players" who compete from all over the world. On a typical day WorldWinner.com pays out over $75,000 in tournament prizes to Pro Players. Entry fees start at around $1.00 per game and are pooled to pay for the winners' cash or merchandise prizes. Players do not make any other payments, nor do they pay a monthly subscription fee; accounts may be closed at any time, and players may withdraw their money from their accounts. WorldWinner.com makes its money by taking a percentage of the tournament entry fees and by being the cash tournament partner for sites like Yahoo! Games, Lycos Gamesville, Shockwave, and hundreds of others.

The company's revolutionary business model exclusively uses skills-based games and asks players to pay entry fees via credit card to enter its tournaments. A pioneer in the "skilling" arena, the site has been experiencing revenue growth of over 100 percent per month, a testament to the model's concept that skills-based gaming may be the wave of the future. How to get around the legal issues? Online gambling, while not specifically illegal, is considered by the U.S. Department of Justice to be a violation of the Interstate Wire Act, a 1961 law banning gambling by telephone. WorldWinner.com walks a fine line by offering games of skill, not games of chance. In addition, players can practice for free, and special software ensures that no player gets "dealt" a hand that is impossible to complete. In the 10 states whose laws do not distinguish between games of skill and chance, WorldWinner.com will not permit players to bet and win money. And, of course, all players must be 18 or older.

The company says that the average returning player puts more than $33 each day on its tournaments—which now number in excess of 7,000 per day—and that it books about $25,000 a day in revenue, a figure that is growing rapidly each month.

In July 2001 WorldWinner.com signed a strategic distribution agreement with Flipside, Inc., the world's largest Internet games and entertainment destination, to distribute its skill-based games. It will help Flipside expand into the skill-based pay-for-play arena by offering 16 games in Flipside's iWin.com section for real cash prizes and will handle all aspects of back-end fulfillment including customer service, credit card processing, and prize disbursement.

Uproar, Inc.

Uproar, Inc., proves that old game shows never die—they just find new homes on the Internet. Founded in 1995, Uproar offers a wide variety of online games, including such favorites as *Family Feud, Name That Tune,* and *To Tell the Truth*, to online players in the United States and Europe who compete in single- or multiplayer games for cash prizes at sites in their own language. In its original iteration, Uproar attracted some 12 million unique players each month and also operated an e-commerce site. Originally located in New York City, Uproar, Inc., had offices in Budapest, London, Tel Aviv, Los Angeles, and San Francisco.

In March 2000 Uproar completed a public offering of 2.5 million shares of its common stock on the Nasdaq exchange, netting the company about $79 million. Also in 2000, the company acquired iWin.com, a games-for-prizes and Internet lottery site; Traffic Marketplace.com, an online advertising brokerage service based in Los Angeles; and ibetcha.com, which was later discontinued. That same year the Uproar Network was rated in the Media Metrix Top 20 and ranked as the fifth largest gainer among the Top 50 Web sites rated, with a 34 percent increase over the previous year.

Uproar was acquired in March 2001 by Vivendi Universal Publishing's

Flipside, Inc., also headquartered in New York City, comprising the Flipside Network and Traffic Marketplace. Today Flipside targets players and advertisers with specific "channel" offerings—Uproar, iWin, and Virtual Vegas—and has almost 20 million registered members. It attracts over 7 million unique users every month. Traffic Marketplace is a leader in innovative online advertising solutions for performance-based marketers. Its ad network spans over 80 sites across the Internet and provides advertisers with a true broadcast solution to online advertising.[3]

Unlike WorldWinner.com, which makes its money from players' fees, Uproar, Inc., makes its money primarily from its family of advertiser-supported interactive entertainment sites, which comprise the backbone of the Uproar Network, an extensive entertainment-based Internet advertising platform.

Whether venture-backed or publicly financed, whether a game originator or a game distributor, whether the model is play-for-pay or advertiser-supported, someone is poised to hit it big in the online gaming market. According to the River City Group, a Missouri firm that tracks the interactive gaming industry, worldwide revenues are projected to go from $3.1 billion in 2001 to $6.3 billion by the year 2003.[4] Is there room for both models in the field? It is anyone's bet.

NOTES

[1] *Writing an Effective Business Plan,* Deloitte & Touche LLP, 2001.
[2] "WorldWinner.com Creates First Legal Alternative to Online Gambling for U.S. Internet Users," *Business Wire,* February 20, 2001.
[3] Tom Kirchofer, "Site Knows It's Not Gambling . . ." *Boston Herald,* April 2, 2001.
[4] Ibid.

CHAPTER 3

Where to Find Capital— Part I: Venture Capital

Investing in high technology has never been suitable for the faint of heart. On the other hand, for the long-term investor, it is a classic area of investment. It's obviously risky, but I think we are in an extremely exciting time today, where years of sustained investment— if somewhat erratic and changeable—have advanced technologies on many fronts, ones that will continue to open up new areas for potential investment.

—Patricia Cloherty, Co-Chair and General Partner, Apax Partners

UNDERSTANDING THE VENTURE CAPITAL BUSINESS

Venture capital funds provide financing to start-up companies and emerging businesses. Generally these funds are organized as limited partnerships, with a venture capital firm serving as the general partner, which receives a management fee and a percentage of the profits earned on any deal. The limited partners supply nearly all the funding while the general partner usually puts up about 1 percent. Limited partners may include institutional investors, such as insurance companies or pension funds, as well as corporations or wealthy individuals. A percentage of the venture capital fund may also include the venture capitalist's own money. Return on venture investment is realized either through an initial public offering (IPO) or the acquisition of a company.

Obtaining some form of venture capital funding is critical for the survival of most emerging high-tech or biotech companies. To be successful in obtaining venture capital funding, an entrepreneur must understand the nature of the venture capital business, as well as the specializations of individual venture capital funds and the investment criteria they use as a guide in their decision making.

In general, the venture capital industry serves a narrow area of the investment business. Venture capitalists put a tiny fraction of a society's savings at high risk in order to create the next generation of large capital values. They do this by taking equity positions in small companies that promise but do not always achieve these ambitious value-creating goals.

Such opportunities occur from time to time on various scales, and when a technology offers the potential to transform society, investors see the potential for high value. For example, the growth of the computer industry over the last 45 years continues to offer multiple and very large opportunities, but the introduction of the World Wide Web and commercial online services on the Internet offer "transformational" opportunities. The potential earning power of companies that are involved in developing new ways to communicate, entertain, and transact business on the web has triggered a wild financial ride for investors and entrepreneurs alike. Similarly, the deregulation of communications in the 1990s opened up an entire industry to technology-based companies that are using fiber optics, cellular technology, digital networks, and other advances to transform the way society communicates. Here, too, are significant opportunities for investment in tomorrow's highly valued companies.

> *The first thing venture capitalists are looking for in high-tech and biotech companies is an investment that meets their criteria. This may seem obvious, almost moronic, but it's remarkable how many deals are misrouted within the venture capital community.*

> —Jeffrey R. Jay, M.D., General Partner, Whitney & Co., LLC

MATCH THE DEAL TO THE INVESTOR

One of the popular misconceptions about venture capitalists is that they are risk takers. Actually, almost the opposite is true. Venture capitalists are paid to *minimize* risk. To accomplish this, they conduct a great deal of due diligence to become familiar with the target company, its proprietary science or technology, and its industry. Buck French, a general partner in the venture firm J.P. Morgan Partners, says his firm looks for three kinds of risk when evaluating a new deal: (1) technology risk (is it unique, breakthrough, proprietary, easily replicable?), (2) team risk (are these the right people to make the deal succeed?), and (3) market risk (is it growing?).

The emerging company searching for venture capital financing should do its own form of due diligence to fully understand the venture capital firm it is planning to approach. Doing this will save a considerable amount of time and effort by eliminating those who are predisposed to reject their deal because it does not match their investment criteria. Due diligence also helps senior executives assess the varying management styles among the firms—crucial information, since they will be trading away a measure of control over their company in exchange for venture capital funding.

Venture capitalists often tend to turn to a select group of other venture capitalists for co-investment opportunities. From the venture capitalist's point of view, this provides an assurance that if the business turns sour for an investee company, the reaction of the co-investors will be predictable. What it means for the company's management is that if these other venture capitalists are not in the first round of financing, they eventually will be in the second, third, or fourth round. If management's due diligence has identified a potential problem with one of the venture capitalists, it should know up front if that venture capitalist is likely to participate in a later round of financing.

It is important for a company to choose its investors as carefully as the investors choose the company. There are many ways in which senior management of an emerging company can perform its own due diligence. Managers can start by asking for referrals. Attorneys, accountants, and bankers usually have strong connections to the venture capital community. A company looking for funding should be interested in learning about the types of deals the individual venture capitalists have backed in the past. For example, have they provided seed money to start-up enterprises, or invested only at the second or third rounds of financing for companies with more proven technologies? Additionally, company management should seek to gain a feel for how the venture capital firm thinks, how it works, and how it interacts with the companies it backs.

Exhibit 3.1 illustrates the rates of return required by venture capital investors for investments at various stages of development and the time period that venture capitalists expect to hold those investments.

Venture capitalists constantly seek out new investment opportunities. They attend industry conferences and often perform a great deal of industry research. They look at the frontiers of today's technology for the ideas and scientific advances that will create tomorrow's technologies. From there they try to identify the companies that fit into that framework.

For example, in biotech, a venture capitalist might focus on the drug discovery process and predict how this process will work in the future. An emerging biotech company then would be evaluated based on how it fit into the model of how drugs will be discovered in the future.

In the mid-1990s, PC-based, real-time, multiplayer computer games were

EXHIBIT 3.1 Annual Rate of Return

Stage	Annual Rate of Return (%)	Typical Expected Holding Period (Years)
Seed and Start-up (A Round)	50–100 or more	Can exceed 10 years
First Stage (B Rounds)	40–60	5–10
Second Stage (C & D Rounds)	30–40	4–7
Expansion	20–30	3–5
Bridge and Mezzanine	20–30	1–3
Leveraged Buyouts	30–50	3–5
Turnarounds	50+	3–5

Source: Timmons, *New Venture Creation: Entrepreneurship for the 21st Century,* 4th ed. (1994): 512.

Holding Period	Multiple	Compound ROI
3 Years	3X	44.2%
	5X	71
	10X	115.4
5 years	3X	24.6
	5X	38
	10X	58.5
6 Years	3X	22
9 Years	5X	22
10 Years	3X	11.6
	5X	17.5
	10X	29.5

thought to be the next big thing in the computer industry. Different venture capitalists with an interest in computer entertainment each developed different scenarios for how this trend would develop.

Long-term average portfolio rates of return for VCs have been estimated to be in the range of 17–22 percent. The following table gives approximate compound rates of return over 3-, 5-, and 10-year periods for various multiples of investment return, and also shows how long a VC would have to hold an investment to achieve a particular multiple and a 22 percent ROI.

Institutional Venture Partners, a firm based in Menlo Park, California, believed that game companies would play a central role in bringing the technology to the market. For that reason, the firm invested in a company that developed an open platform technology enabling game developers to launch their own proprietary, interactive, real-time, online games.

Kleiner Perkins Caulfield & Byers, another Menlo Park venture capital firm, was also bullish on PC-based real-time computer games. Under its scenario, millions of consumers would become subscribers to online services that offered entertainment options such as games. Rather than the game manufacturer being central to commercializing this new technology in the market, Kleiner Perkins believed that online providers would play the critical role, and it subsequently invested in a company that offered over 30 popular games for which it acquired Internet rights from their developers.

Originally created in 1985 as Total Entertainment Network (TEN)—a site for committed game players who would pay $20 per month to play "shoot-'em-up" games—Pogo.com is part of the Kleiner Perkins Caufield & Byers "keiretsu" (word used to refer to an interwoven, symbiotic web of business relationships among industrial companies, banks, and the government that exists in Japan) of companies. In fact, Kleiner Perkins also helped pay the bills, separately, for game sites Excite and @Home in their early days. Today Pogo.com is an advertiser-based site offering free family-oriented games drawing in excess of 4 million visitors a month and is part of Electronic Arts (EA), the world's leading independent developer and publisher of interactive entertainment software for PCs and advanced entertainment systems.

Gaining an Understanding of the Venture Capitalist

The senior management of an emerging company should try to obtain as much information as possible about the venture capitalists from whom they are seeking financing. Questions to ask include:

- What companies has the venture capitalist backed in the past?
- Does the venture capitalist specialize in a particular industry or type of company?
- When venture capitalists say they invest in "start-ups," exactly how do they define a "start-up"?
- Has the venture capital firm added value to investee companies with experienced management and business advice?
- With whom does the venture capitalist co-invest?
- How many of the companies in which the venture capitalist has invested have completed successful IPOs?

WHAT VENTURE CAPITALISTS LOOK FOR

It's remarkable how many deals are misrouted within the venture capital community. We get calls all the time from people at other firms who say, "You know, I saw this really interesting deal, but we just don't do this sort of thing." I probably get one to two, sometimes three, calls in a given day with that same lead-in. It's very important to understand the investment criteria of the firms that you're interacting with.

—Jeffrey R. Jay, M.D., General Partner, Whitney & Co., LLC

Over the past several years, venture capital firms have segmented themselves considerably—not just in terms of industries, but also in terms of the company's stage of development—so it is extremely important for company management to know which firms are funding which kinds of deals. Some firms want to get in very early and are interested only in seed-stage investments where companies have no revenues. Others will look only at companies that meet the "Three P.O. Rule"—that have lined up at least three customers for their product or service.

The two fundamental aspects of the venture capital biotechnology business model today is that every available equity dollar must go to technical risk reduction and reduction of time to market. No more building laboratories. The early days were one of great expenditures on new lab space . . . but that's not true anymore.

—Patricia Cloherty, Co-Chair and General Partner,
Apax Partners

Companies with good technologies and good management, with proprietary products in markets that meet unmet needs, are going to get funding.

Most companies aren't there. They don't have all those pieces in place. For them, the world is very different. [Ten] years ago, we used to joke that a Nobel laureate and an entrepreneur could go out and raise $40 million on an idea. Those days are gone, and hopefully they'll never come back because a lot of bad deals were done.

Today you need a proof of principle. You need to show that you have a management team that understands the process. That's true, I think, for any investor.

—Philippe L. Sommer, formerly Managing Partner,
Alsacia Partners, Inc.

We're quite interested in—and have been limiting our investment in—the companies we create, to focus only on those opportunities in science that will contribute to the overall reduction in healthcare costs, rather than to increase healthcare costs.

—James H. Cavanaugh, Ph.D., General Partner,
HealthCare Ventures

Before a venture capitalist decides to invest in a particular company, he or she will make a detailed review and analysis of the investment opportunity (this process is often called "due diligence"). Venture capitalists emphasize that the most important determinants of the success of a venture (and their investment decision) are the management team, followed by the market or market segments for the company's products or services, the uniqueness and proprietary nature of the company's products or services, and the company's strategy.

The venture capitalist also has to be convinced that the valuation of a company supports the required financial return. To the venture capitalist, the company's valuation is important because it determines whether the investment can generate the return required. Meanwhile, to the entrepreneur or a growing company's management, the valuation determines the percentage of the company's equity that must be given up to raise the required capital.

Venture capitalists become good venture capitalists based on how well they can decipher business cases, how well they can raise funds and, in large part, on who they know. What I frequently see is that venture capitalists over-rely on their personal contacts for validation of a business case, rather than on the due diligence expertise of unbiased professionals.

Take the world of biotechnology. Making an investment in genomics or proteomics or stem cell research is a very tricky business and venture capitalists are kidding themselves if they think that within three weeks of looking at a business case they'll know everything they need to know to make a valid judgment. But there are firms out there that are paid to assess these things. They don't own the company, they don't manage money, they don't own any interest in your fund; all they care about is being right. And it's not just the venture capitalists who should be looking at this commitment; the entrepreneur who approaches a potential investor with this kind of due diligence will make a huge impression.

Some of the bigger firms are well known: Gartner Group and Forrester Research in the pure technology area and Cambridge HealthTech Institute on the genomics side. But there are more of us out there, like Decision Resources or DataMonitor. As the world of investing becomes more and more difficult, I think people will come to rely on us more. Solid due diligence is the only way to approach the business plan in today's environment—to prove the case and to prove that you can create a product or service and sell it profitably.

—Hugh Jones, Managing Director, DataMonitor, PLC

All venture capital firms have well-defined investment criteria they use to determine whether to fund a particular company. The specific investment criteria may vary, but most venture capitalists consider six factors:

1. Company management and personnel
2. Growing companies in large markets
3. Proprietary products
4. Science and technology
5. Liquidity
6. Leverage

Company Management and Personnel

There is a saying in the venture capital community that "you can't due diligence the future." In other words, an investor can perform all the due diligence in the world about the company, its technology, the industry, and markets in which the company operates, but while that information is useful, it is limited as an investment criterion because it is based solely on historical results and current conditions.

Business conditions will change. An investor wants to back a company that is run by an experienced management team that will know how to react when changes occur.

There is another saying in the venture capital community that investment companies "would rather back an 'A' management team with a 'B' product than an 'A' product with a 'B' management team." In general, the venture capital community, given its druthers, looks for people with track records, people who have successfully managed a business before, and people the venture capitalists have invested in successfully before. These people are not limited to entrepreneurs, but may include successful *intrapreneurs,* as well—that is, senior executives who have built a division of another company or created a new business or product line within a larger organization. Venture capitalists will likely invest earlier with someone with a successful track record. However, they know that new talent bubbles up all the time; they will not turn away a first-time entrepreneur who has bootstrapped beyond some technical hurdles merely because he or she is a first timer.

"Management" generally means a *management team.* Venture capitalists tend to shy away from the company founder or CEO who thinks he or she is the jack-of-all-trades, an expert in every area. Venture funding usually tends to go to companies that have a team of qualified people in key positions.

This team includes scientists in the case of a biotech company or technical experts such as developers or programmers in a computer-based or other technology company, as well as members of the board of directors. These experts should be people who are among the best in their field, people who can outinnovate or outthink the competition and thus create a competitive advantage by putting the company one step ahead of its competitors. Board members should be those who can lend their expertise and time to help management build a strong business. Experts and board members should be uniquely qualified, with the credentials and reputations that give the company credibility in the eyes of potential investors and strategic corporate partners.

Growing Companies in Large Markets

Venture capitalists are looking for companies with the potential to operate in large, highly profitable markets. To attract the interest of venture capital funding, the total (global) market opportunity must be in the hundreds of millions or billions of dollars. Some venture capitalists measure profitability in terms of after-tax profit. Others may define their profitability criteria in terms of profit before interest and taxes or gross margins. For example, Whitney & Co., LLC looks for companies with 18 to 20 percent earnings before interest and taxes or that offer 50 to 80 percent gross margins.

It is also vital that the company is growing in a way that establishes it as a dominant player in its market. Doing that usually requires rapid revenue growth. A company that can carve out and maintain significant market share will make up for a lot of the problems encountered by emerging-stage companies.

Given the long lead time to a marketable product, venture capitalists will look at the potential for a biotech company's product or service to gain desirable market share. Until they are close to commercialization of their product, biotech companies usually need to show significant progress through success in clinical trials, obtaining proprietary patents, Food and Drug Administration (FDA) approvals, or significant corporate partnerships.

Most venture capitalists will not be interested in investing in a company that is the third, fourth, or fifth one to enter a particular field, with a product or service that offers only a slight, incremental improvement in price or performance.

Proprietary Products

The company must focus on real products.

I'm amazed sometimes. You talk to people about the model for their company. They take you through issues like controlling the equity and attracting good people and getting the proprietary position and managing the efficiency of the project, moving along through the different science stages, but they don't actually focus on a real project.

They just seem to think that it's too far out and what they've got to do is focus on the science and the selection of the delivery system.

But if you're not talking about a product, I don't know why you would call it a business model versus an academic model. At the end of the day the project is not a research project. It's a product project.

—Charles M. Hartman, General Partner, CW Group, Inc.

An emerging company must be focused on developing a product and not simply on conducting research.

Additionally, venture capitalists like companies with *proprietary* products. These companies are able to create a sustainable competitive advantage, which over the long term allows the company to be valued at a premium.

Proprietary advantages can mean patents, for example, on composition of materials, processes, or devices. Typically, strong patents provide the best kind of competitive advantage, but patents are not the only way to achieve a proprietary edge. A company may achieve a proprietary edge even though a product does not have patent protection, if its engineering is too difficult for others to replicate and bring an identical or comparably effective product in the market.

An example is Premarin, manufactured by Wyeth-Ayerst Laboratories, a division of American Home Products Corp., one of the most prescribed pharmaceuticals in the United States.* The drug has been off patent for close to 20 years, and yet there is no competing generic drug because no other company has been able to make a bioequivalent version and obtain FDA approval.

Science and Technology

One prerequisite for any company in the high-tech or biotech industry is that it must be based on good science or technology. Corporate partners will be alert to the opportunity offered by a breakthrough technology, but will commit their money in the form of a joint venture of strategic partnership only after their own due diligence confirms it. According to one venture capitalist, the true measure of the commercial potential of a company's newest

---

*Premarin® is a registered trademark of Wyeth-Ayerst Laboratories, a division of American Home Products, Corp.

scientific discovery or technology advance is that "after they get 35 to 100 people to work on it for one or two years, it's got to be good enough for a large corporate partner to invest in it at a significant level."

Liquidity

Venture capitalists need liquidity, that is, a means to sell their investment for cash within a reasonable period of time. A basic tenet of venture capital financing is that the venture capitalists must have a right to exit their investment. Typically, that liquidity is provided by an initial public offering, although it may also come through the sale of the company. Chapter 4 focuses on the process of obtaining funds from capital markets.

Leverage

Venture capital generally is considered to be the most expensive source of financing a company will receive. For their own self-interest as well as that of the company, venture capitalists like to minimize the additional equity dollars that are required and to stretch the equity provided by the venture capital firm to go a little further. For that reason, venture capitalists tend to favor companies that have a strategy for controlling the "burn rate" of that money and thus leveraging their high-cost equity dollars. Strategies for leveraging venture capital funding include:

- Obtaining additional funding through corporate partners and strategic alliances (discussed in Chapter 6).
- Obtaining lease lines for equipment instead of outright purchases.
- Using debt financing with warrants. Many venture companies will be willing to consider this type of funding vehicle.
- Exploring mezzanine sources of capital—prepublic organizations that are looking to invest at just below the IPO price as a bridge to the initial public offering. Typically, mezzanine financing is provided by institutional sources such as corporations or pension funds.

VALUATION PROCESS

In order to approach a venture capital financing intelligently, a company should have some understanding of the methodologies by which venture capitalists determine valuations. In discussing the venture capital valuations for new and emerging companies, one commentator has stated that "while there is no standard valuation formula employed by all venture capitalists, in its simplest form, company valuation will be based upon the present value of the expected future valuation, computed at the anticipated date of future liquidity."[1]

Under this approach, the venture capitalist first determines the future or terminal value of the company at the point in time he or she plans to exit the investment. Future value generally is determined by multiplying the net income of the company at the time of exit by the price-earnings multiple of comparable companies.

The projected net income of the company will be based on the projections presented by the entrepreneur and the venture capitalist's view of those projections. The appropriate price-earnings multiple to apply to the company's projected net income generally will be based on the price-earnings multiples of public companies that have characteristics similar to those of the company.

Once the future value of the company has been determined, the venture capitalist will then discount that value by his or her required rate of return on that investment to arrive at the estimate present value of the company. The required rate of return will depend on the company's stage of development, the risk analysis of the company, and the projected future capital needs of the company.

The last step in the valuation process is to determine the percentage of ownership required by the venture capitalist. This simply is a function of the amount of the venture capital investment divided by the estimated present value of the company prior to the investment under consideration.

The valuation process is not a one-time exercise. In all likelihood, a new or emerging company will go through a number of rounds of financing during its life cycle. Each time the company raises equity financing, the value of the company will be determined. The company's founders, directors, and officers should appreciate that their percentage of equity of the company will be reduced with each successive round of financing. However, if the company is growing and achieving its milestones, and market conditions are favorable, its valuation will increase, and therefore less equity will be given up in order to raise the same amount of capital in later financing rounds.

Similarly, although the founders' equity stake may be less as a percentage of the company's total equity, the value of that stake likely will be greater than if venture capital had not been raised. The company seeking venture capital also should be aware that, due to the ongoing nature of this process, a balance must be achieved between the desire to raise as much money as may be available against the fact that the company will give up less to raise the same amount in the future if it is successful and the money is then available. A good rule of thumb is that the company should raise enough capital to take it to its next stage of business development. This is sometimes referred to as the next "risk inflection point." It is, in other words, a point in which some aspect of risk has been overcome or lowered. In a drug development company, an example would be FDA approval of a particular phase of clinical trials. The amount raised also should include a cushion in the event the company does not perform according to its plan.

POSITIONING A COMPANY FOR VENTURE CAPITAL BACKING

We receive about 1,000 business plans every year, and from that we invest in maybe six, The other 994 are a lot like those characters in The Wizard of Oz.

Some don't have a heart, some don't have the brains, and some are simply afraid.

—Howard Anderson, General Partner, Battery Ventures[2]

Early-stage companies that seek venture capital financing should work to position themselves to make their pitch to the venture capital community. All (or most) of the elements described in the previous section of this chapter should be in place. The company should have an experienced management team, a proprietary product with the potential to dominate in a large market, and strategies for leveraging equity investment.

Before approaching potential investors, company management has one final step to accomplish to pitch their company: They need to develop a realistic expectation of how much of the company they will own after all the fund-raising is done.

This is one of the basic truths of the venture capital business: Whoever puts up the money controls the company. If the business requires extensive capital or a lot of expertise from venture capitalists, the company's founders will find themselves trading control for cash. Contrary to the intuition of many first-time entrepreneurs, this can be a very positive experience for the company, which may not have any other means to attract the seasoned industry, business, and scientific advisors that can mean the difference between success and failure.

Many deals get hung up because the company's founder is unwilling to part with small percentages of ownership. Management would be wise to consider that, at the end of the day, owning 6 or 10 percent of a $200 million company is much better than owning 100 percent of a $1 million company that is going nowhere.

MAKING THE PITCH

The person or team that makes a pitch to potential investors should consider a number of dos and don'ts.

Have the Right Attitude

Do not have an ego. I can't stress this enough.

—Peter J. Crowley, Managing Director, CIBC Oppenheimer Corp.

Before making the pitch to the investment community, company management needs to cultivate an approach to which investors will respond favorably. Investors quickly tire of management that brings an oversized ego to the negotiations. Likewise, investors generally will not be impressed by the novelty of the company's concept. They are not swayed by management's assurances that there are barriers to entry that are prohibitively high for would-be competitors, that the return will be outrageous, and that the person making the presentation has the breadth of experience to create such a business.

Investors like credible presentations with realistic statements. They will understand the technology quickly and usually are more interested in determining whether the opportunity meets their investment criteria. Unfortunately, the management teams of too many young companies get off to a poor start by offering a sales pitch rather than a realistic presentation of the company's potential earnings.

Along the same lines, the company should avoid including in its business plan any press clippings and endorsements from local newspapers stating how revolutionary the company is. This is a fairly common ploy that most venture capitalists find meaningless—they are not interested at all in what the local paper thinks about the company or its technology.

Know (Don't Ask) How Much Is Needed

It sounds trite, but there are lots of people out there who walk into my office and aren't quite sure how much money they want to raise. They start out saying they need $500,000. If you say, "We'd really like to invest at a million dollars," they'll say, "No problem, we can take an investment at a million dollars." Well, that doesn't work.

—Philippe L. Sommer, former Managing Partner,
Alsacia Partners, Inc.

Before managers of the emerging company begin seeking venture capital funding, they must determine the amount of money necessary to make their business viable and get it to the next stage. They should *not* start out asking the potential investor how much he or she can afford to invest. That approach will only make the venture capitalists wonder whether management really knows what it is doing.

Know If the Firm Is a Whole Company, a Product, or a Product Line

Management should understand whether they have a company, a product, or a product line. There is a distinction. A *company* has a technology that allows the entity to create and market multiple products. Technology that is not broad enough for several products in the pipeline does not support a company. That type of technology describes a *product line*. A *product* is basically something that someone else should be able to sell that is based on a technology specific to the individual product.

Having one or the other is not necessarily good or bad—investors can do well with a company, product line, or individual product. But when seeking funding from venture capitalists, management should be sure to understand the difference.

Have Realistic Projections

The magic number for a lot of people is $100 million. It seems like every business that comes over my desk will be, in five years, a $100 million business. It's totally unrealistic. It doesn't work that way in the real world. It's far more important that you have a credible business plan that shows how the capital you are trying to raise gets you a thriving and viable business than to make an unrealistic statement that the business is going to be $100 million.

—Philippe L. Sommer, former Managing Partner,
Alsacia Partners, Inc.

In general, business plans that show realistic growth projections will be more successful in raising capital. Investors always assume a growth rate far below that reflected in the stock market. A conservative, realistic approach to future earnings enhances management's credibility with potential investors.

Do not ask the early stage investor, "How big do my forecasts have to be to get money from you?" Perhaps no one ever poses the questions quite so directly, but many times entrepreneurs in essence ask the same thing. Again, this does not bode well for management's credibility in investors' eyes.

Carefully Plan the Presentation

Be prepared with a handout that summarizes the key points of the presentation. Plan several versions of the company's story and rehearse them. It is easy for an enthusiastic presenter to talk too long, and even the most dynamic slide show can put people to sleep eventually, so it is wise to ask the investor(s) *before starting the presentation* if they want the 10-minute version, the 20-minute version, or the full-length version. Most initial meetings with prospective venture capitalists last an hour or less. Plan the presentation accordingly. Leave time for questions. The author teaches a live session which demonstrates that a complete first meeting presentation can be achieved with about 12 slides.

Learn from Rejections

If a venture capitalist declines to fund the company, management should find out the reason why. It can then make changes to the business plan to improve the chances with the next potential investor.

Peter Crowley, managing director of CIBC Oppenheimer Corp., even suggests going *first* to the venture capitalist who will deny funding. "If you go to people who you know are going to say no first, it's going to help you for those people you want to say yes," he explains. "So there's nothing wrong with going to meetings, gaining information as to why they don't want to invest with you."

DECISION-MAKING PROCESS

Each venture capitalist has chosen one or more industries or technologies in which to concentrate investments and has a clear model for the companies that are attractive investment candidates. The decision-making process at individual firms will vary, but generally they follow a similar approach.

Most venture capitalist firms have partners with expertise in a particular industry. This allows for two basic advantages:

1. It helps the firm to better evaluate their opportunities for investment.
2. Over time the firm will build a portfolio of companies with similar customer bases. This allows the venture capitalists to figure out creative ways, perhaps through joint marketing or other collaborations, to have their portfolio companies work together.

The partner with specialized industry expertise is responsible for championing a deal in his or her segment. That partner leads the due diligence, which consists of industry and technology analyses, management references and background checks, and computer financial analyses. A second partner may get involved to review the analyses and serve as a quality control check.

Periodically (perhaps even weekly) all the partners will get together to review the proposed deals. Even though one partner champions the deal, at many venture capital firms all the partners have some understanding of the deal and what the company does.

CORPORATE VENTURE CAPITAL FUNDS

Most venture capital firms manage the money of pension funds, along with the money of foundations and wealthy individuals. While pension funds operate under the strict rules of ERISA (Employee Retirement Income Security Act), a handful of venture firms manage *corporate* rather than ERISA money. These firms are said to manage *strategic* funds, and generally they have two goals: (1) to assist the fund's limited partners and (2) to earn a good rate of return. They are run by managers who tend to have extensive corporate experience as well as good venture capital track records. Strategic fund managers work closely with their counterparts in corporations to identify potentially winning deals, provide advice, and introduce new technologies and contacts.[3]

But there is yet another kind of corporate involvement in the world of venture capital financing. During the mid-1990s, when it seemed that technology companies were making breakthroughs almost weekly—and investors and entrepreneurs alike were making enormous profits as a result—many corporations launched their own in-house venture capital arms to get a piece of the pie (see Exhibit 3.2). Senior corporate managers saw dollar signs when it came to early-stage investments and funded in-house venture capital firms in unprecedented numbers. Although popular in the 1980s, in 1999 more than 50 corporations contributed close to $100 million each to new in-house venture capital funds, and some firms—including EDS, Intel, and Accenture—each committed to a $1 billion venture fund. Such "direct investing" seeks to find qualified opportunities that are aligned with the parent company's strategic technology or that provide synergies or cost savings.

The Nasdaq Composite Index, which measures all Nasdaq domestic and international based common-type stocks listed on the Nasdaq Stock Market, rose every year from 1995 through 1999—at a minimum of 20 percent annually—fueling enthusiasm for initial public offerings and creating great wealth for those in the game. According to Harry Edelson, general partner of Edelson Technology Partners, a venture capital firm that manages corporate, rather than pension, money for 10 multinational companies: "Emerging companies with little or no revenues (e.g., Cerent, Chromatis, Xros, Arrowpoint) were being acquired for billions of dollars by companies whose stocks were selling at exorbitant multiples of revenues, much less earnings."[4]

As the bubble began to burst in early 2000 and Internet and telecom-

EXHIBIT 3.2   Growth of Corporate Venture Capital Funding

Year	Funding
1980–1996	$ 85–542 million
1997	$ 1.1 billion
1998	$ 1.6 billion
1999	$ 8.6 billion
2000	$ 16.5 billion

Source: Harry Edelson, "The Downside of a Corporate VC Fund," Directors & Boards (Spring 2001).

munications stocks—once the darling of many venture firms—plummeted, the wiser fund managers took their profits and got out. But most of the corporate funds stayed in and, in fact, continued to spend, because commitments of this sort are hard to turn off.

> *"Companies such as Intel, which has made 400 or so VC investments, are becoming conglomerates, spreading themselves thin, exposing themselves to problems and lawsuits, and burdening top management not with one company but with many. Independent VCs distribute holdings and are finished with them. Corporations usually retain their holdings for too long because it is not comfortable to sell the stocks of "strategic partners."[5]*

> —Harry Edelson, General Partner, Edelson Technologies

The typical distinction between corporate venturing and independent venture investment vehicles is that corporate venturing usually is performed with corporate strategic objectives in mind while other venture investment vehicles typically have investment return or financial objectives as their primary goal. And while several large in-house corporate venture arms have folded (e.g., Exxon, Xerox, Gulf & Western), some still exist and may be worth pursuing.

PRIVATE INVESTORS

In some instances, when a company is not yet ready for venture capital financing, it may seek funding from private sources, often called "angels." Angel investors generally make investments in the range of $100,000 to $1 million to promising emerging companies. Increasingly, these private sources are to be found overseas, and increasingly, they are not individual investors, but groups of investors (see Chapter 5 for more about angel investors).

In general, private investors are not looking for research and development companies. They are looking for companies with proven technology or those with a corporate partner. Private investors may not possess the same in-depth industry knowledge as a venture capital partner, but they may be able to appreciate the emerging company and its technology on a more personal level.

This ability to value a company's product on a personal level can provide a private investor with a built-in motivation for investment, which companies should use to their advantage. For example, a biotech company researching a product related to ulcers or gastric cancer would be wise to look for investors in Japan, where the incidence of these problems is high.

Communications technology that does not rely on existing telephone infrastructure will be attractive to third world countries that lack that infrastructure. Companies looking for wealthy individual investors would do well to try to match their technology to people who can see its application in their own personal or societal context.

CASE STUDIES: HOW VENTURE CAPITAL FIRMS WORK

HealthCare Ventures

HealthCare Ventures (HCV) is one of the world's largest venture capital funds specializing in healthcare. Its mission is to create, finance, and manage early-stage and emerging growth healthcare companies with exceptional growth potential. HCV's six funds make investments in privately held early-stage and emerging companies, with the criterion that it will develop and market only those products and services that reduce healthcare costs. It is committed to creating new biopharmaceutical companies by effectively linking important advances in medicine with successful and experienced management teams. (See Exhibit 3.3 for a snapshot of HCV's investment criteria.)

HCV adds substantial value to new ventures through the active participation of its general partners, business advisory boards, and scientific advisory boards in the strategic development and management of its portfolio companies. From the initial business concept through the formative years, they work closely with each portfolio company's management on strategy, planning, recruitment, collaborative deals, and commercial development.

EXHIBIT 3.3   Venture Snapshot: HealthCare Ventures

HCV Investment Criteria
■ Opportunity to achieve rapid and substantial market share
■ Potential liquidity in 3 to 5 years at a valuation in excess of $100 million
■ Markets in excess of $500 million worldwide
■ Initial investment of $500,000 to $10 million in the form of equity or debt convertible to equity
■ Annual revenue potential of $50 to $100 million at a minimum 15% after-tax profit
■ Opportunity for HCV to add value through its capital resources, management, and scientific experience

Since its inception, HCV has created leading biopharmaceutical companies in strategically important fields such as genetic therapy, genomic sciences, drug discovery and delivery, neuroscience, cancer therapy, and organ and cellular transplantation. One distinct advantage is the firm's ability to assess quickly and accurately the commercial value of a scientific discovery. HCV typically makes investments in companies created from its own concepts; in concepts or technologies brought in by scientists and entrepreneurs that can be built into healthcare companies; or in private or public healthcare companies that offer an opportunity for HCV's scientific, marketing, and business skills to turn a low-valuation investment into a high-valuation company.

From 1987 through 2001, HCV has created and developed some 46 successful biotechnology-based healthcare companies, including Avant Immunotherapeutics, Inc., Bio Transplant, Inc., Human Genome Sciences, Inc., MedImmune, Inc., and Versicor, Inc. The majority of HCV's portfolio companies have successful corporate partnerships with global leaders in the pharmaceutical industry, including SmithKline Beecham, Bristol-Myers Squibb, Johnson & Johnson, Warner-Lambert, Merck KGaA, Hoffman-LaRoche, and Rhone-Poulenc Rorer.

An example of HCV's hands-on approach to its investments is Genetic Therapy, Inc. (GTI), a company founded in 1986 by HCV Fund I. The company was formed around concepts that were initially developed within HealthCare Investment Corporation, then the venture firm's parent, with the intent to become the first and foremost developer of products in the field of genetic therapy.

HCV actively sought out and worked with one of the pioneers in gene therapy, W. French Anderson, who was then at the National Institutes of Health (NIH). It also recruited the first CEO for the company and then worked with him to form a scientific advisory board, recruit the scientific staff, and fund the company.

As a way to attract equity into the company, HCV helped develop an initial research and development (R&D) collaboration with Sandoz Pharmaceuticals Company. By 1991 Genetic Therapy was ready for an initial public offering, and HCV worked with the company and its underwriters to develop the offering.

In 1994 HCV helped develop a second corporate collaboration with Sandoz, this one covering specific R&D in the field of cancer, which also gave Sandoz the marketing rights to any products that it might develop outside of Genetic Therapy in that specific field.

In 1995 Sandoz acquired Genetic Therapy for $304 million. At that point, HCV had returned $50 million to its limited partners, from an initial investment of $5.2 million. In December 1996 Ciba-Geigy Ltd. and Sandoz Ltd. merged to form Novartis AG, a global leader in the life sciences. Genetic Therapy is now an indirect, wholly owned subsidiary of Novartis and is established as the Novartis Center of Excellence for gene therapy. In January 2002 it was reported that Geron Corporation announced a licensing agreement with Genetic Therapy that gives GTI nonexclusive rights to Geron's human telomerase (hTERT) promoter for the development of therapeutic products targeting cancer.

Whitney & Co., LLC

Whitney & Co. (formerly J.H. Whitney & Co.) was founded in 1946 with capital from the Whitney family and as such was the first venture capital partnership in the United States. It has evolved from a $10 million venture capital fund to a global manager of over $5 billion in alternative assets for some of the world's most respected institutional and high-net-worth investors. Whitney's private equity activities are focused on growth capital investments in transforming companies poised for expansion in five sectors: communications, financial services, information technology, healthcare, and growth industrial. (See Exhibit 3.4 for a snapshot of Whitney's investment criteria.)

Whitney views its role as helping entrepreneurs to build high-quality companies with the help of the general partners' insight and direction. The firm's partners, associates, and staff are all industry specialists; some are focused on the Internet, others are focused on communications, software, biotech, healthcare services, or medical devices. Each is responsible for knowing his or her area exceptionally well. A typical partner has been investing venture capital for 15 years.

As a result, the firm is very active with the companies in which it invests. It may be involved in recruiting key executives or financing an acquisition to fill in a key piece of the company's product line and to improve its competitive position. One aspect of the company's business in which Whitney does not become involved is operations. The firm relies on its portfolio companies' CEOs and management teams to make the operating decisions.

EXHIBIT 3.4   Venture Snapshot: Whitney & Co., LLC

Whitney & Co., LLC Investment Criteria
■ High-quality companies capable of achieving rapid growth
■ Large markets and highly profitable market opportunities
■ Experienced management teams in companies with a proprietary edge
■ Average initial investment of $5 million to $50 million, with a minimum of $1 million
■ High probability of an initial public offering

The central themes of all of Whitney's companies are rapid growth and industry leadership. If a company is not growing rapidly or does not have the potential for rapid growth, or if it cannot be first, second, or possibly third in its market segment, it will not meet Whitney's investment criteria.

Whitney provides equity capital as well as subordinated debt for the companies it finances. Because of its extremely large capital base (Whitney V, the most recent private equity fund, closed to new investors in the summer of 2001, having raised over $1 billion), Whitney is capable of providing all of the capital a company typically needs. Its preferred role is as a deal originator, although at times it does invest in deals created by other venture capital firms when those firms have expertise in a particular area. In most of its investments, Whitney has a minority position, and management has control.

The firm has an impressive record for bringing its portfolio companies to the public market. In the 10-year period from 1986 to 1996, 27 of Whitney's portfolio companies became public companies, with a combined market value of approximately $24 billion in 1996. In any given year, Whitney brings an average of 7 to 10 companies public.

The investment decision-making process at Whitney & Co. begins with the firm's individual partners. Each is responsible for championing a deal in his or her industry segment and leading the due diligence process. A second partner serves as a quality control check, reviewing the data and financial analyses. Write-ups on the potential deals are circulated to the full partnership prior to their weekly meetings, so that all partners have an understanding of the companies involved. Global partnership approval is required for every deal in order to maintain the consistency of the firm's investment process and the quality of its portfolio companies.

JPMorgan Partners

JPMorgan Partners (JPMP), the direct private equity organization of J.P. Morgan Chase & Co., is a global private equity firm that provides equity and mezzanine capital financing, primarily to private companies. Established in 1984, JPMP focuses primarily on three areas: venture capital (28 percent of its business; see Exhibit 3.5 for a snapshot of JPMP's areas of venture capital interest), growth equity (27 percent), and middle-market buyouts (45 percent). With $24 billion under management, 150-plus investment professionals, and nine offices around the world, JPMP has closed more than 1,000 individual transactions and holds a diversified portfolio that includes board seats in over 300 companies.

The direct private equity (venture capital) portion of the business is in excess of $13 billion; the company's average annual investment of approximately $1 billion makes it one of the largest venture capital firms in the world. And its global presence and other equity activities give it a leverage that is unique in the industry.

EXHIBIT 3.5   Venture Snapshot: JPMorgan Partners

JPMorgan Partners: Key Areas of Investment
■ Telecommunications/Media/Technology: 35%
■ Industrial Growth: 30%
■ Consumer, Retail & Services: 18%
■ Life Sciences & Healthcare Infrastructure: 11%
■ Financial Services: 6%

Buck French, one of the firm's general partners, is responsible for JPMP's software ventures investments. A seasoned entrepreneur himself—he cofounded OnLink Technologies, which was acquired by Siebel Systems in August 2000—French says that the firm looks at a broad spectrum of opportunities within its focus area. In technology, it is primarily software. In the media area, it could be publishing or it could be cable assets, both on the content and the infrastructure side. Telecommunications could mean either services or equipment.

In the software area, the firm looks at postproduct development, postrevenue types of products, while on the bio side, it looks at much earlier stage ventures, often companies in the conceptual, pre-FDA approval stage. Venture firms know that in biotech, that is where the high risk/high reward investments are made.

JPMP is bullish on the software business, especially as the industry goes through a platform shift from the client/server environment to a web-based environment. With that shift still in the early days, good investment opportunities are out there, in areas that range from systems management and security to customized, downloadable composite applications.

When reviewing plans and speaking to entrepreneurs, JPMP looks for three core requirements:

1. A growing market
2. A product that addresses the market
3. A team that can execute in the market

Of these three, the most critical component is the team and its experience or—even more important—its passion. "If you don't have passion to do a start-up, you won't be successful," warns French. "And the passion isn't necessarily for the product or service—it stems from an innate desire to win." After the team and its passion, comes the market opportunity, and last comes the product.

What does it take to be an entrepreneur? JPMP understands that entrepreneurship is a cyclical state of being, whereby business founders can go through peaks and valleys several times in a single day: Sign a large contract in the morning and learn that a customer is furious by lunch. Be assured that products will ship midafternoon and then learn that the company's funding has fallen through by the end of the day. Being successful surely takes resiliency and optimism—with a healthy dose of skepticism—and a true team spirit.

On the flip side, JPMP understands very well the venture capital life cycle. The first job of the venture capitalist is to develop a deal pipeline and be assured, through reputation and relationships in the business community, that the firm is seeing the highest quality investment opportunities in the marketplace. Second is the ability to structure a deal that is a win-win for everyone involved—the new investors, the entrepreneur, and the current investors. And the third job is to work hard for the success of the portfolio company. How that differs from firm to firm is the added value that each venture group can provide.

For JPMorgan Partners, the added value is its robust global network. As one of the largest private equity firms in the world, and given the diversity of its investments—from buyouts to growth equity to venture capital—the synergies that JPMP can create for its clients are enormous.

With over 100 companies in its portfolio with revenues of at least $100 million, JPMP can easily facilitate introductions among its holdings, creating customers for one company while solving a problem for another. Leveraging this globally integrated network is a unique value proposition for the firm. It is truly world-class networking.

Like others in the industry, JPMP is seeing fewer deals in the post-September 11 business environment, but they tend to be high-quality deals. It predicts that the quantity game of the 1990s is over and that business is back to its prebubble realism: more thorough and thoughtful evaluations, and an exiting time horizon that will take a few years, not a few months.

Apax Partners

Formerly Patricof & Co., Apax Partners was founded by Alan J. Patricof in 1969 and is one of the world's largest venture capital and private equity investment firms. Major areas of investment are technology, (including communications, new media, software, computers, networking, and the Internet), biotech, and healthcare. In 2001 the company reported that it had more than $11 billion under management, on behalf of major institutional investors in the United States and abroad.

Guided by the investment philosophy of investing in products and services that people need, the firm has participated during the last 33 years in the financing and development of public and private companies that span a wide range of technologies, from Apple Computer to Office Depot and from America Online to Park 'N View, a young company that provides entertainment and communications services to long-haul professional truck drivers in the privacy of their own cabs.

The firm looks for companies with outstanding management teams that have defined high-growth opportunities and are leading well-planned efforts to exploit those opportunities. Apax's dozen or so partners actively participate in the management of their portfolio companies, collaborating on strategic, operating, and recruiting issues, and often serve on their boards of directors long after the company has become public (see Exhibit 3.6).

Apax Partners' investment strategies evolve as industries mature. The firm's biotechnology investment policy changed, for example, to accommodate three key events in the biotech industry: (1) the development of monoclonal antibodies; (2) advances in genetic engineering as a common tool; and (3) the improvement in physical methods of conducting scientific R&D. The firm's biotechnology investment strategies have more or less paralleled developments in the field and can be divided roughly into three phases.

Phase I occurred during the early 1980s and is referred to by Patricia Cloherty, co-chair and general partner, as the "clearing away of the cobweb phase." During this time, the firm—like many others—focused exclusively on human health. Its handful of early-stage investments backed leading scientists with potentially beneficial insights. For example, Apax (as Patricof & Co.) funded Creative Technologies in the hard- and soft-tissue growth area and Liposome Technology (now Sequus Pharmaceuticals), one of the two national leaders in liposome encapsulation (the delivery of important site-specific therapeutics).

The companies today are fine ones, with much of their potential still to be realized. As is true in the biotech field (and in other technology-driven fields during the early years), they took longer and cost more than initially forecasted to fully develop the technology into proven products. Only later in the decade did the days of corporate partnering, shorter time to market, and emphasis on technically grounded but managerially seasoned entrepreneurs enter the picture.

Phase II of Apax's investing strategy spanned the late 1980s and early 1990s. Cloherty refers to it as "the time for real criteria period." The firm adopted formal investment guidelines, which it modifies at healthcare group

EXHIBIT 3.6   Venture Snapshot: Apax Partners

Apax Partners Biotech Investment Criteria
■ Companies positioned for strong growth in revenues and profits
■ Initial investment of $5 million to $20 million, with a minimum investment of $1 million
■ An intellectual property base that has more than one center of capitalizable value

meetings approximately every quarter. While still concentrating in human health applications, the firm also considered criteria that included the stage of clinical development, the size of the therapeutic or diagnostic category, the number of competitors in the market, the direction of federal policy, and already established and clear intellectual property rights. The firm was no longer interested in "one-shot" therapeutics. Instead, it was looking for broadly enabling technologies. In every instance the firm worked to bring in corporate partners at the appropriate time, and structured the deals to protect against the "downside" of its investments.

Phase II investing played out in several different scenarios, much like the following ones. In 1989 the company invested in Agouron Pharmaceuticals, Inc., which uses rational drug design (i.e., X-ray crystallographic) and other methods of drug development to shorten the time (and therefore the cost) of drug discovery. These new methodologies were applied to antiviral, antifungal, and antitumor compounds for the treatment of cancer, AIDS, and other diseases. Thus, Apax had based its investment both on an *enabling technology* and on *specific therapeutics*. Agouron's corporate partnerships have been mutually beneficial to both parties and have been critical in seeing the publicly held company through the inevitable ups and downs of the stock market.

During this time, Apax also invested in PPL Therapeutics, with a slightly different strategy. PPL Therapeutics is a Scottish company that makes high-value pharmaceutical proteins in the milk of genetically altered sheep. The company focuses on such compounds for the treatment of genetic emphysema and hemophilia. PPL Therapeutics' technology—rather than *removing* genetic material from nature—is focused on *inserting* it back into plants, animals, and humans.

The premise of this technology is that nature makes proteins—especially complex ones—better, more efficiently, and more cheaply than scientists do by synthetic means. For Apax Partners, the opportunity to invest in PPL was, in effect, a low-cost production opportunity.

Phase III of the firm's investment strategy emerged in the mid-1990s when it started to fund companies that looked to expand the application of biotech beyond human healthcare. In addition to evaluating a potential portfolio company for basic criteria such as management expertise and market potential, the firm paid great attention to costs and price for the end user.

During this phase, the company invested in Recombinant Biocatalysis, Inc. (now Diversa Corporation), a company that harvests genetic material from microbial life that grows in extreme environments, such as the inside of a volcano. The company clones this material and grows it in common media to create new and robust classes of enzymes for use in industrial and chemical processes. In contrast with portfolio companies in Apax's (Patricof's) earlier investment phases, the company developed its initial revenues (from contracts) within 90 days of the initial venture capital investment.

Over the last 20 years, the healthcare group at Apax Partners has gradually come to pay greater attention to costs and price-to-user issues. In all biotech applications that do not relate to treatment of a life-threatening condition, the firm spends a great deal of effort to analyze the cost of the product to the user and the productivity improvement to be achieved. Companies under consideration for investment must demonstrate the technological path to continuous cost reduction. Early-stage companies often resist performing this type of analysis, instead making their presentations to venture capitalists on the strength of their science and a proposed new application. However, such analysis is a prerequisite before Apax Partners will consider investment in an emerging biotech company.

Over the same 20-year period, the healthcare sector has shifted enormously. If we consider the field of "life sciences" as a whole, the view from mid-2003 is one of dramatic ups and downs. In the public markets, biotech, which had been long out of favor, has rallied in the public markets; consolidations on the pharmaceutical side are commonplace; medical devices are performing better than the overall market; diagnostic labs are generally struggling, although there are a few exceptions; and pharmaceutical benefit managers (PBMs) have seen consolidation completed.

What lies ahead? It is a safe guess that private equity investors will come back into the market, as will strategic buyers who will continue to use their stock as currency for transactions. Hospitals and health maintenance organizations (HMOs) will continue to be active and, while government intervention should be minimal for the remainder of 2003 and through the 2004 election cycle, 2005 and beyond could be the years the feds look hard at those segments of the life sciences arena that are making good margins.

NOTES

[1] Alan Salzman and John Doerr, "The Venture Financing Process," *Start-Up Companies: Planning, Financing, and Operating Successful Businesses*, McGraw-Hill/Irwin, first edition, 7.02 [5] (1985).

[2] Michael Osenger and Skip MacAskill, "Venture Capitalists Sow the Seeds of Future Nets," *Network World,* October 17, 1994: 10.

[3] Harry Edelson, "The Downside of a Corporate VC Fund," *Directors & Boards* (Spring 2001), p. 10.

[4] Ibid.

[5] Ibid.

CHAPTER 4

Where to Find Capital—
Part II: Public Markets and
Private Placements

In the hands of talented people, capital is the ultimate competitive weapon.

—Alfred Berkeley III, Vice Chairman,
The Nasdaq Stock Market, Inc.

NEED FOR PUBLIC FINANCING

Early in a company's life, management must decide whether to position the company for a future initial public offering (IPO) or acquisition, because this choice will influence the company's financial and operating structure. If the plan is an eventual public offering, the company should focus on and emphasize strong quarterly comparisons of revenue and profitability growth. If management adopts a merger or acquisition strategy, it can focus more exclusively on developing its customer base of core technologies at the expense of short-term results.

There are many benefits to be derived from going public. First, the growth of high-tech and biotech companies—from development-stage enterprises to companies with successful products in the marketplace—is capital-intensive and can take many years. An IPO of securities enables the company to raise a large amount of cash in a single transaction, enhances the company's net worth, provides access to future capital, and creates a "second currency" consisting of liquid tradable stock. The increase in its net worth may enable a company to borrow on more advantageous terms. For the long term, the public equity markets can offer a sizable source of funding for years; if the stock price performs well, there are opportunities for follow-on and secondary offerings.

An equally important consideration is the liquidity provided by the public markets for stockholders. Liquidity provides an opportunity for the company's early-stage investors and founders to exit from their investment. Additionally, offering publicly traded shares or stock options as part of its compensation package can enhance the company's ability to recruit and retain key personnel. Many companies use the funds derived from a public offering to consummate mergers and acquisitions. Alternatively, companies whose securities enjoy a public market may use their authorized but unissued securities as a second "currency" to complete acquisitions. In short, companies that have the ability to raise funds at a reasonable cost in the public markets usually enjoy a significant competitive advantage over those that do not.

The IPO is a landmark event in the development of any company—and a major distraction for senior management. The success of a company in both the IPO and "after market" depends significantly on whether the company and its management team are prepared for the IPO process and for life as a public company. Success is not merely a question of whether a company has a history of revenues and earnings and/or growth potential to entice the investment community. It is also a question of whether management has the experience, resources, and professional advisors to properly prepare for and endure the lengthy IPO process and the many regulatory and reporting requirements of living as a public company.

The management team of any company contemplating an IPO should begin the planning process early. Early planning helps to ensure that the team can move quickly to undertake an offering when the company has developed into a viable IPO candidate and the market conditions are right for companies of similar size, potential, technology, and industry. When contemplating an

---

WHY GO PUBLIC?[1]

Whether in a bull market or a bear market, there are many reasons why a company decides to go public:

- To obtain expansion capital
- To generate currency in stock for future acquisitions
- To gain prestige
- To guard against the drying up of small-business financing that could result from bank megamergers

IPO, the management team must consider the business and financial goals, the strategic direction of the company, regulatory requirements for a publicly held entity, and relations with investors and investment banks. Going public is not a one-time event; it's a way of life.

Being a public company has its share of drawbacks, and making the transition from private to public can be difficult. The management team of a company contemplating an IPO should consider carefully whether they are prepared to live up to the increased responsibilities, problems, and expectations inherent in the IPO process itself and of being a public company. These may include issues such as loss of confidentiality, loss of control (with the addition of outsiders to the management team), an increased risk of liability, and an expanded scrutiny of short-term results to the exclusion of a longer-term focus.

Public companies are required by the Securities and Exchange Commission (SEC) to disclose extensive information in the offering prospectus—and later in periodic quarterly and annual disclosure documents—that ranges from revenue and executive compensation to an analysis of the competitive market. This information will be available not only for analysts, investors, and corporate partners, but for competitors, as well.

The immense time commitment of management in the IPO process necessarily will mean that management is diverted from the first order of business: running the business. Without a quality organization of superior middle managers, the business of the company could suffer during the IPO registration process. The time to market of key products might be lengthened. Hence, possible competitive advantages can be diluted.

Small companies accustomed to working with private investors such as venture capitalists, wealthy individuals, or corporate partners are used to dealing with knowledgeable investors who have realistic expectations about a company's likely performance. Public buyers often have more unrealistic expectations, and yet company management is expected to be responsive to those expectations. Shareholders hold different standards about financial performance, operating results, technology milestones, and market price. If shareholders or analysts perceive the company to be underperforming, the stock price may suffer and management will be under pressure to apply a "quick fix," even while long-term goals remain intact.

When contemplating an IPO, management rightfully focuses on the brass ring in sight: preparing the registration statement, closing the IPO, and getting the proceeds into the bank. However, there is a major responsibility waiting for the company's chief financial officer: complying with all of the requirements of the SEC and the applicable stock exchange and/or Nasdaq. This is not a chore to be taken lightly. Living as a public company affects all facets of the company's public exposure, from marketing brochures and press releases to annual reports and proxy statements. The company's scientists, programmers, or other technical personnel also will need to be cautious about the information they share in publications, exchanges of data on the Internet, and at conferences and symposiums.

SELECTING AN INVESTMENT BANK TO UNDERWRITE THE DEAL

Just as a company's management team expends a great deal of time in analyzing potential venture capital firms, equal care should be taken before approaching an investment banker to underwrite the company's public offering. The underwriter's primary initial role is to sell securities to the public. A follow-on and equally important role is market-making activity in the aftermarket once an offering is completed. As part of the IPO team, the underwriter also will advise management on financing opportunities, the structure of the transaction, and the timing of the offering.

The selection process often begins a year or more before the actual offering, as management begins to build relationships with key investment bankers. Venture capital investors may facilitate the introduction of their portfolio company to investment bankers who have underwritten offerings for others in their portfolio. At the same time that the investment banking firm investigates the company before making its decision to underwrite an IPO, the company's management should be conducting its own due diligence to determine whether the qualifications of the investment banking firm make it the right match for the company.

UNDERSTANDING THE INVESTOR BASE

Selling at the cheapest price or going public as quickly as possible is not necessarily the best thing. What's most important is that you

---

QUALIFICATIONS TO CONSIDER WHEN EVALUATING AN UNDERWRITER

- Experience in comparable underwritings in terms of number of shares and dollar value
- Knowledge of the company's industry
- Ability to communicate the IPO opportunity to investors and provide investment analysis to support the aftermarket
- Market-making ability that translates into attracting a sufficiently large number of investors and sustaining interest in the stock after the IPO
- Additional services after the IPO, including financial counseling and assistance in identifying future public or private capital sources and possible acquisition candidates

bring a deal to the public at a time when you're ready, when you can appeal to the core long-term buyers in this sector who will be with you for the long term.

Realistically, if you're going to lose money, you'll have to finance over and over again. Inevitably you're gong to have to go back to the well in a difficult market period, and you need those buyers to be there at those times.

—Jeffrey W. Casdin, former managing director,
Life Sciences Hambrecht & Quist

Before approaching an investment banking firm, it is useful to understand its distribution system of shares to its investor base. In general, investors will fall into two classes: individual *retail* investors or *institutional* investors, which generally encompass mutual funds, pension funds, and other private investment funds. An investment banker usually has a distribution system that assigns a certain percentage of shares to each. For example, healthcare offerings at investment banking and brokerage firm Tucker Anthony (now RBC Dain Rauscher) typically are distributed with 60 to 70 percent going to institutional investors, and the balance to retail investors.

There are advantages and disadvantages to having a large percentage of a company's shares concentrated in either class:

Retail investors: Having a strong base of retail investors can provide greater liquidity in the aftermarket because individual investors as a rule generate higher trading volume than is usual with institutional investors. In addition, shares are spread over a wider number of investors who will not have the same level of interest in the company's day-to-day management as institutional investors. Although this may seem to work in management's favor, the downside is that retail investors can be quick to sell their shares at the first sign of bad news from the company.

Institutional investors: Portfolio managers for institutional funds have the expertise to understand and evaluate investment opportunities in higher-risk technology companies. If they hold a significant block of shares, institutional investors may decide to act as partners or advisors to the company, paying close attention to its business and financial management.

The mid-to-late 1990s saw explosive growth in the amount of money under management by institutional investors, particularly through the tremendous growth in mutual funds. As investors in these institutional funds sought higher rates of return, investments in healthcare and high-tech companies also grew. The flip side to the cycle of institutional investors increasing investments in a particular industry is what happened to many technology groups as institutional investors exited and stayed out of these segments over the last 3 years. Companies in these groups saw their stock prices crushed. And until institutions return to investments in out-of-favor

SPHINX PHARMACEUTICALS CORPORATION

Lacking an Investor Base

In its early years, Sphinx Pharmaceuticals was an example of a company without a solid institutional investor base. This proved to be a problem during the company's subsequent financing efforts. Initially its IPO in 1992 exceeded expectations and was oversubscribed 10 to 15 times. Looking back, the underwriter admits that "we basically lost control of the deal," and as a result, small pieces of stock were distributed to the clients of the firm as a favor. No single investor got enough stock to have any influence, and because the major institutional investors could not get the large blocks of shares they wanted, they stayed out of the deal.

Within weeks, the market headed down and continued straight down for three years. Sphinx lacked a solid group of core buyers who knew the company and its technology and who had a large enough stake in it to continue to provide financing through a difficult market. In September 1994 Eli Lilly and Company acquired the company, which now operates as a division of Lilly Research Laboratories.

companies, these prices tend to stay down, even in the face of improved operating results.

It is important to note that the favorable distribution of IPO shares to clients of underwriters has come under intense scrutiny in the last few years, and has been the subject of proceedings against major Wall St. firms.

FOLLOWING THE MARKET CYCLES

With regard to raising public capital, our rule of thumb is to raise public capital when you can. There are times when the market allows companies to go public earlier—some would say earlier than they should. If that's the circumstance, we generally advise our companies to take advantage of it, because a year or two later, they could be ready to go public. Some people say that even in a bad market you can raise capital. That's close to being true, but not entirely. You can have a very fine company where the process and the valuation are going to be so punitive that it's just better to wait.

—Jeffrey R. Jay, M.D., General Partner, Whitney & Co.

Companies that rely on public markets as a source of financing must follow and understand the market cycles for their particular industry segment.

The nature of the market at any point in time will affect the amount of money raised, its cost, and the structure of the offering necessary to raise that money.

A company can keep current with the public markets and try to gauge the best time for seeking public funding in a number of ways:

- *Track cash held by mutual funds.* Many mutual funds specialize in the high-tech and biotech sectors, and the companies in these fields should track the inventory of cash maintained by these funds. Rallies in the marketplace (which create opportunities to raise capital cheaply) are almost always preceded by large supplies of cash within the technology mutual funds.
- *Compare stock indexes.* Stock indexes exist for many different sectors. Fluctuations in these indexes can be compared to other broad-based indexes such as the Standard and Poor's (S&P) 500 to gain an understanding of the relative strength of high-tech and biotech issues.
- *Track the level of financing activity.* Tracking the financing activity for high-tech and biotech companies—both in terms of the number of deals and dollars raised—is a way to gauge overall market activity. This information is available in industry publications. For example, biotech industry publications such as *BioWorld* compile such statistics on a quarterly basis.

In addition to these quantitative measures of market activity, company management also should be aware of the qualitative nature of the market offerings. Two changes usually occur to mark the end of a speculative period and the beginning of a slowdown in the market:

1. *Weaker companies begin to make offerings.* The end of a highly speculative market is marked by weaker and weaker companies registering to go public. "Weaker" is relative and may be measured in terms of revenue size, operating history, management qualifications, or the number and quality of corporate partnerships. The bursting of the dot-com financing bubble in the late 1990s could be viewed as directly resulting from the large number of Internet start-ups that went public with virtually no product and fewer revenues.

2. *Offering terms made more attractive to investors.* In order to attract investors to these weaker companies, the terms of the offerings start to change. Look for these signs, which may signal the peak of the speculative market and foreshadow the end of a cycle:
   - Hybrid securities and various "kickers" such as warrants, designed to attract speculators
   - Significant drops in the price per share
   - The emergence of penny stocks targeted to speculators
   - An increase in fees ("spreads") offered to underwriters and in the

number of deals that are offered on a "best efforts," as opposed to afirm underwriting, basis

Since early 2000, with the end of the dot-com–fueled speculative bubble, the IPO cycle has slowed to a near-glacial pace.

BIOTECH: AN ONGOING STUDY IN MARKET CYCLICALITY

The public equities market for biotech companies during the five-year period from 1991 to 2001 illustrates how changing market conditions can affect a company's ability to raise capital.

Exhibit 4.1 compares the Nasdaq Biotech Stock Index to the Nasdaq 100 and the S&P 500 Index. After peaking in 1991, biotech stocks underperformed these indices for several years until rallying into 1996. Another down cycle hit biotech stocks in 1997–1999. Then the bubble rally took over in late 1999 into the first half of 2000. Once the bubble burst, biotech trended down throughout 2001 and 2002 until beginning what has developed into a sustained rally in 2003. The IPO window, however, remains closed.

Exhibit 4.2 tracks the amount of money that went into public biotech companies during the period 1998 through 2002. Starting from a base of

JUST WHAT IS BIOTECH, ANYWAY?[2]

Over the last 10 years, the definition of biotechnology has changed. It used to be that "biotech" meant recombinant genetic engineering—the art and science of using biological processes to develop products. Today the term is broadly expanded and encompasses all of the life sciences—driven by a new set of enabling technologies (e.g., genomics, combinatorial chemistry, proteomics)—to affect the discovery and development of products for:

- Human healthcare (therapeutics, diagnostics, drug delivery, cell and gene therapy, and even moving toward some devices and drug/device combinations)
- Agriculture (food, feed, fibers, transgenics)
- Environment (bio-remediation)
- Bio-based industrial processes
- Bio-based energy
- Supply (reagents, biologicals)

EXHIBIT 4.1 Comparison of Nasdaq Biotech Index versus Nasdaq 100 and S&P 500 Indices since 1994

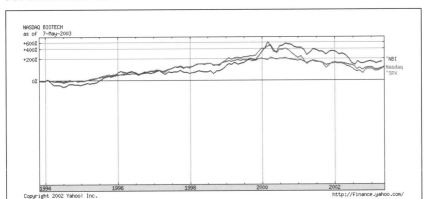

under $5 billion raised in 1998, money raised by the biotech industry surged to nearly $30 billion in 2000, before backtracking to $10 billion in 2001 and nearly $15 billion in 2002. Despite an inability to sustain the "bubble" level of 2000, the biotech industry was still able to raise a significant amount of equity. In 2002 biotech IPOs numbered below 10 compared to over 50 in 2000 (see Exhibit 4.3).

EXHIBIT 4.2 Capital Raised by Public Biotech Companies, 1998–2002

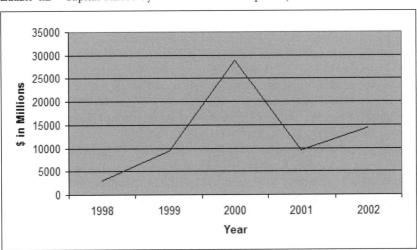

EXHIBIT 4.3 Capital Raised through Biotech IPOs by Year

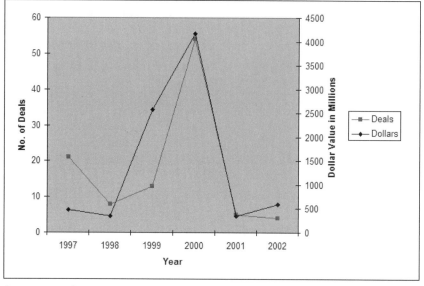

Source: www.hoovers.com/ipo/view

Analyzing the Market Cycle

The year 1991 marked the first significant peak in market opportunity, which was driven by the four Ps: products, patents, partners, and processes. Several key events coincided with this peak. For example, Amgen, Inc., achieved significant product approvals and product sales from EPOGEN® and Neupogen®, and Biogen, Inc., received product approval from the FDA for Alpha interferon. In addition, the FDA announced that it would streamline the drug approval process to make it easier for companies to get their products to market. The net effect was that Tier I biotech companies began to generate products and demonstrate a clear path to the commercialization of those products.

During the 1991 market, the hurdles a company had to clear in order to go public were relatively low. It was not unusual to see an IPO for a company that had a single product and one corporate alliance that offered a few years of guaranteed funding—as long as the company had a management team with the right credentials and a sophisticated, scientific advisory board. During this time, companies were successful in attracting public financing even without programs that showed efficacy data or results of any kind.

Sphinx Pharmaceuticals' IPO illustrates what occurred at the very peak of the 1991 market. Originally priced at $12 per share, the offering ended

KEY EVENTS: 1991 AND 2001

These events—over two 12-month periods—played a key role in creating favorable market conditions for biotech and healthcare companies.

1991	2001
■ Genetechs Actimmune was approved by the FDA.	■ First complete map of the genome of a food plant (rice) was completed.
■ Amgen received a favorable ruling on appeal in its EPO patent dispute with Genetics Institute, which was blocked from the U.S. market.	■ Scientific journals publish the complete human genome sequence.
■ Amgen's Neupogen was approved by the FDA for chemotherapy treatment.	■ The European Commission issues rulings requiring labeling of all foods and animal feed derived from GMOs (genetically modified organisms).
■ American Home Products acquired Genetics Institute.	■ Chinese National Hybrid researchers report developing a "super rice" that could produce double the yield of normal rice.
■ Centocor was granted a patent for Centoxin®.	

up selling 5 million shares at $15 each and was 10 times oversold. The company raised $75 million on the basis of one corporate collaboration, $13 million in R&D (which could be canceled within a few years), and a $4 million equity investment. It had two products for which investigational new drug (IND) applications were promised within the calendar year and three other products in discovery. Its pre-IPO revenues were $1 million.

In 1992 the market for emerging biotech companies cooled considerably, due primarily to:

■ *Product failures.* The failure of high-profile products to make it to the market when originally anticipated had a negative impact on investor confidence. For example, in April 1992 the FDA notified Centocor, Inc., that there was insufficient efficacy data on Centoxin. Two months later the FDA informed XOMA Corporation that additional clinical tests were required for E5.

■ *Presidential elections.* In November 1992 Bill Clinton was elected president with an ambitious, far-reaching plan to reform the nation's healthcare system. Uncertainty about the direction of these reforms caused investors to retreat from healthcare and related biotech stocks.

As a result of these and other events, investors pulled out of the biotech sector and shifted their investments to cyclical and durable stocks. The ensuing depression in the biotech market lasted until 1995.

By 1995 the president's proposed healthcare reform plan had failed, removing the uncertainty from one of the Ps—namely, process. Additionally, the two other Ps helped revitalize market activity.

During 1995 a number of human growth hormone products were approved by the FDA. At the same time, several companies released positive data, including Cephalon's announcement that Phase III trials for Mycotrophin were positive in treating amyotrophic lateral sclerosis (ALS), also known as Lou Gehrig's disease.

Partnering also played a role in the market resurgence, as a number of pharmaceutical companies began to collaborate with emerging biotech companies on a much larger scale, particularly in the genomics and combinatorial chemistry areas.

In contrast to Sphinx Pharmaceuticals' position prior to IPO in 1991, Millennium Pharmaceuticals, Inc., is an example of the requirements necessary by 1996 for a company seeking to go public. At the time that its IPO was registered in May 1996, Millennium had three corporate partners. These deals gave Millennium combined pre-IPO revenues of approximately $41 million, with the potential for up to $170 million more in financing over the next five years, based on achieving milestones in research and product development. About $120 million of this was guaranteed by licensing fees and research funding.

During the five-year period from 1991 to 1995, the factors driving success in the biotech industry became more complex. Today they are more complex still. Over that time period investors came to focus more closely on products, whether these products were proprietary, and how the products would get to market at a reasonable cost and be salable at a reasonable price. They also focused on the competition facing the company from other products and technologies. By 1995 investors were looking for companies that had products in clinical trials, strong corporate collaboration agreements, and product news that could be announced almost immediately.

As the biotech industry has matured, investor attitudes have changed. Investors are willing to fund a company once, but they have become less inclined to fund a company three or four times. As a result, when evaluating potential investments, underwriters and investors also consider:

- *Burn-rate management.* Many companies are going public based not on the potential of their technology, but rather on how much of their future burn rate is covered. A company that is unable to implement cash-conserving strategies will be penalized or possibly excluded from the public market.
- *Quality of corporate partnerships.* Companies are judged by the number

and size of extended alliances with multiple corporate partners. Not only do these partnerships validate the company's technology, they also provide up-front cash and continuing cash infusions as certain R&D milestones are reached.

Biotech market cyclicality has continued to demonstrate a pattern of fat and lean times. After a financing resurgence in 1995, availability again slowed until a huge financing window opened during 1999, which carried into the first quarter of 2000, apace with the dot-com bubble. Valuations of biotech companies surged, and those biotech companies that were quick to bring deals out benefited from a receptive market. This financing window closed quickly when the stock market turned bearish in the second quarter of 2000. Not until 2003 did valuations begin to recover, but IPO availability remains nearly nonexistent at this writing.

STRATEGIES FOR RAISING MONEY IN BEAR MARKETS

In terms of creative financings, they almost must have sound economic rationale. Basically, if you can give somebody a discount, they're apt to buy. In terms of capital structure, simple is still preferred.

—Peter J. Crowley, Managing Director, CIBC Oppenheimer Corp.

Three factors, singly or together, provoke the onset of a bear market: a policy of monetary restraint by the Federal Reserve, a sudden loss of market liquidity, or the outbreak of war. [Today] we are in a bear market in S&P 500 stocks in general, and Nasdaq stocks in particular. . . .

—David Edwards, Portfolio Manager and President,
Heron Capital Management[3]

Even during bear markets, high-quality companies are usually able to raise capital in the public markets. However, in order to attract investors, they may need to be more creative in how they structure their deals and in being realistic about the valuations set by the market. The key thing to remember is that what goes up usually has to come down. The stock market of the 1990s was, by most accounts, extremely overvalued; it was a bubble waiting to burst. And like all bubbles, it eventually comes back down to earth. Bear markets are part of a bigger picture, part of a historical trend. They are not the end of the world. But they do require special strategies and, sometimes, a tightening of the seat belt (see Exhibit 4.4).

EXHIBIT 4.4 Comparison of 1992 Bear Market Offerings

	LIGAND Class A Convertible Common Stock	CORTECH Common Stock Units
Offer Date	November 18, 1992	November 24, 1992
Price	$11 per unit	$8 per unit
IRR Target	20%	31%
Size	3,750,000 shares (25% increase)	4,000,000 units (33% increase)
Separation Date	N/A	45 days after closing
Conversion	Automatic into Class B at 1.000 to 1.444 times 60-day average	Automatic into 0 to .5 shares of common based on 40-day average
Time to conversion	2 years	* 18 months
Target price	$15.84	* $12.00
"Meltaway"	NONE	After 40 consecutive days trading at or above $12.00
Corporate Buyers	Allergan (13% of deal) and Glaxo (6%)	NONE
Antimanipulation	No Class A purchases by company during determination period	NONE
Liquidity Provisions	25% of predeal capital stock converted to Class A but no active market for Class B shares prior to Class A conversion	NONE
Stage of Company	Preclinical	Phase II trials
Premoney Valuation	$166 million	$107 million

Performance Guarantees

Performance guarantee deals (guaranteed return offerings) in which the company's corporate sponsors may participate sometimes can jump-start the market for a company's stock. These products involve the sale of a unit, a part of which depends on how well the stock performs. In effect, the company guarantees that at some future date (usually a year or two later), it will provide its investors a specified return on the money. This may involve, for

EXHIBIT 4.5   Bear Market Comparison: Case Study 1993—PIPES

SELECTED PIPE TRANSACTIONS
- Private investment in public equity
- $ 10 million–$ 20 million raised
- Simultaneous registration of stock with funding

Issuer	Offering Date	Amount Raised ($M)	% Sold	% Discount[a]
Alpha Beta	6/3/93	$20.0	10.3	8.2
Celtrix	6/7/93	10.4	16.7	23.4
ReoRx	6/26/93	9.0	13.2	12.3
Cantab	7/22/93	4.8	9.1	11.9
MedImmune	8/13/93	20.7	6.3	13.0
Creative Biomolecules	8/24/93	16.0	15.6	22.0
Cyto Therapeutics	9/13/93	18.8	24.0	18.8
Magainin Pharmaceuticals	9/27/93	19.3	16.6	12.0
Univax Biologies	11/19/93	10.7	10.0	8.7
T Cell Sciences	11/23/93	18.0	17.3	14.3
Isis Pharmaceuticals	11/24/93	17.6	14.8	13.2
Somatic Therapy	12/2/93	11.7	13.1	18.8
Alliance Pharmaceuticals	12/6/93	16.4	10.3	11.6
Interneuron	2/24/94	15.8	6.5	14.4
Cytogen	3/1/94	12.9	9.1	4.7
Cambridge Neuroscience	3/11/94	14.2	19.6	13.3
Trimmed Average		$14.8	13.3	13.8

[a] 20-day average

example, giving investors in the units additional shares at a specified future date to enable them to achieve the pre-agreed rate of return.

Private Investment in Public Entities Transactions

In a private investment in public entities (PIPE) transaction, investors are interested in existing stocks, but they want to pay a discount to the bid price, rather than full market, which allows them to lock in a guaranteed return over a short period of time. The structure is simple: Selected investors receive a discount, and the company agrees to register the stock within a specified period, usually 30, 60, or 90 days after the close. The investor pays simultaneously with the close.

In the biotech industry, these transactions were successful for a period of time during the bear market of 1993 and 1994 (see Exhibit 4.5).

One of the drawbacks to PIPE transactions is the possibility that a company might pull its prospectus during critical events. This is an extreme disincentive to PIPE investors, because it exposes them to market risk and results in a longer period of illiquidity than planned.

Directed Placements

Investors want liquidity; because of that, they are tending to shy away from straight private placement offerings. A directed placement is similar to a private placement in that it targets specific institutional investors, but unlike a private offering, it offers liquidity, as well. With a directed placement, the company and its underwriters go directly to the large institutions and offer them a discount on stock, after which the stock is publicly traded.

An example of this approach to raising capital was Guilford Pharmaceuticals Inc., a public company with three separate business lines and an attractive valuation. The company had assets to monetize, having committed a fair amount of capital for facilities, and was looking for sponsorship to raise money for R&D. This company was an excellent candidate for a directed placement, and that was the direction it took, ultimately raising $20 million.

PRIVATE PLACEMENTS OF SECURITIES

Private placements offer privately held companies a means of obtaining financing from investors through the sale of stock without the regulatory burdens, delay, and expense of a public offering—and without regard to the prevailing conditions in the public securities market.

U.S. securities laws generally prohibit the offer and sale of securities unless they have been registered under the Securities Act of 1933 and the securities ("blue sky") laws of the states in which they are offered. Nevertheless, these laws permit the offer and sale of securities without registration upon compliance with one of the currently available express exemptions from registration.

Private placement exemptions are among the most commonly used exemptions from registration. They allow a company to raise money privately without publicly soliciting investors. In preparing for a private placement, the company prepares offering materials containing information about the company and the securities being offered. The company then approaches a limited number of investors who satisfy certain suitability standards, so-called accredited investors—without general solicitation or advertising. Last, filings are made with the SEC and with the appropriate state securities commissions.

The company selling the securities does not become a public company by reason of the private placement and does not become subject to the periodic reporting and ongoing disclosure requirements under the securities laws. Resales of the securities sold in a private placement are restricted, and typically no trading market in these shares develops. Shares acquired in such transactions are stamped with a legend stating that such shares have not been registered in a public offering.

Private placements can be structured in various ways, but most are designed to comply with one of the three alternative provisions of Regulation D of the Securities Act of 1933, depending on the amount of financing sought and the type of investors to be solicited.

Rule 504

Rule 504 allows a privately held company to raise up to $1 million within a 12-month period. The securities may be offered to an unlimited number of investors, and no specific type of disclosure material is required to satisfy the exemption. In some instances, Rule 504 offerings may be made through public solicitations and the securities sold are not subject to resale restrictions and investor accreditation standards. While no federal registration is required, state governments also regulate offerings. In Alaska and Montana, for example, companies may raise up to only $500,000 by the sale of securities to investors residing in those states because they have no disclosure laws applicable to the offering. And while a private placement memorandum is not required, it is probably a good idea to create one to minimize legal liability.

Rule 505

Rule 505 allows a company to raise up to $5 million within a 12-month period. Rule 505 may not be used by an investment company or a company that is disqualified due to prior misconduct relating to the securities laws by the company or its officers, directors, principal shareholders, or other affiliates. The securities may be sold to an unlimited number of "accredited investors" and up to 35 nonaccredited investors. Specific types of disclosure must be given to nonaccredited investors, similar to that which is required for Rule 506 offerings, under $7.5 million.

Rule 506

Rule 506 does not limit the dollar amount of the securities that may be sold in a private placement. As with Rule 505, the securities may be sold to an unlimited number of accredited investors. However, each nonaccredited investor must, either alone or with a purchaser representative, have such knowledge and experience in financial and business matters that the investor is capable of evaluating the merits and risks of the prospective investment (or the company must believe at the time the securities are sold that each nonaccredited investor satisfies this requirement). Rule 506 requires detailed disclosure of relevant information to potential investors; the extent of disclosure depends on the dollar size of the offering.

State Blue Sky Laws

Exemptions from private placements under state securities laws vary from state to state, depending on the structure of the offering and the number of

---

ACCREDITED INVESTORS

Accredited investors are individuals who, by reason of their financial situation, experience, or knowledge of the company selling the securities, are considered not to require many of the protections afforded by the securities laws. Accredited investors include:

- An individual whose net worth, or joint net worth with his or her spouse, exceeds $1 million at the time of purchase
- Individuals whose income exceeded $200,000, or joint income with his or her spouse exceeded $300,00 in each of the two most recent years and who has a reasonable expectation of reaching that income level in the current year
- An institutional investor, such as a bank, an insurance company, or a qualified pension plan with assets in excess of $5 million
- Certain trusts with assets in excess of $5 million
- An executive officer, director, or general partner of the company selling the securities, or any director, executive officer, or general partner of that company
- Any entity in which all of the equity owners are accredited investors

investors solicited. Most state securities laws limit the number of offerees and/or purchasers, prohibit public solicitations, and require a filing with the state securities commission as well as payment of a fee.

Although private placements are exempt from the registration requirements of applicable securities laws, they are not exempt from the antifraud or civil liability provisions of these laws. Management of a company that offers and sells securities in a private placement, therefore, must take care to disclose material information about the company and the securities being offered. This is usually accomplished by the preparation and delivery of a private placement memorandum.

Careful consideration should be given to the types of investors to whom securities will be offered and sold in a private placement, Standards of investor suitability usually are established by the company selling the securities because, in general:

- Privately placed securities are risky investments offered by companies that are not yet ready to go public.
- The securities may not be resold unless they are registered under the Securities Act of 1933 and appropriate state securities laws, or unless an exemption from registration is available.
- Even if an exemption from registration can be found, it is unlikely that a trading market for the securities will develop without market makers in the stock.

Since privately placed securities are not liquid investments and must be held for an indefinite period, the company is not obligated to provide the investors with periodic financial reports and ongoing disclosure, and the risk of loss could be substantial.

Private placements can be offered and sold directly by the issuing company through its directors and officers or through an intermediary placement agent, such as a securities broker or investment banker, which charges a fee analogous to an underwriter's commission. Although a private placement made without an intermediary is generally less expensive, its likelihood of success depends on the ability of the company's directors and officers to identify the appropriate investors, approach them through private solicitations, and then persuade them of the merits of the investment. These barriers, in addition to the constraints of time and resources available to company directors and officers, and the restrictions on the number of investors who can be solicited, frequently limit the amount of financing that can be raised in this manner.

Investment intermediaries, such as securities brokers and investment bankers, often have an identifiable pool of prospective investors who satisfy the accredited investor standards. Intermediaries, therefore, may be essential in raising the large amounts of capital required by emerging high-tech and biotech companies.

Using intermediaries also can be advantageous because they are experienced in structuring private placement offerings and valuing the securities to be offered, and they can decrease substantially the amount of management time devoted to the selling effort. Commissions or selling fees paid to intermediaries are generally based on the dollar amount of the securities sold. The size of the fees usually range up to 10 percent plus expenses, depending on the type of securities offered and the nature of the investors being solicited. As a rule, only securities brokers and investment bankers who are registered with the SEC may accept a commission or selling fee for soliciting investors.

Some private placements are negotiated directly between the company and the investors. Often the company retains a broker or investment banker to identify investors and assist the company in its negotiations. The investors in these private placements are typically institutional investors or sophisticated accredited investors who undertake their own due diligence investigations and who require specific representations, warranties, covenants, and undertakings on the part of the company selling the securities. These institutional private placements are feasible for companies that can demonstrate the likelihood of providing excellent returns to investors over a relatively short period of time.

CASE STUDY ON ACCESSING PUBLIC MARKETS

Genaera Corporation

If we decided to do an offering tomorrow, we could have it at the SEC within three hours. We are always prospectus-ready, always ready to take other people's money. We lose over a million dollars a month, and so we need to do that.

—Jay Moorin, Former President and CEO,
Magainin Pharmaceuticals (now Genaera Corporation)

Genaera Corporation (Nasdaq: GENR) is a biopharmaceutical company committed to developing medicines through genomics and from natural products for serious diseases. The company isolates and develops compounds from the host-defense systems of animals and uses molecular techniques, such as gene identification, to understand the pathogenesis of disease. Its R&D efforts are focused on anti-angiogenesis, obesity, and infectious and respiratory diseases.

The company was incorporated in the State of Delaware in 1987 as Magainin Pharmaceuticals, Inc., and began operations in 1988. The company name was changed to Genaera Corporation in March 2001; its headquarters and laboratory facilities remain in Plymouth Meeting, Pennsylvania. Since its founding, the company has been a development-stage company, receiving no revenue from product sales.

By 1991 the company had been through three rounds of venture financing and began a series of public financings with its IPO on December 12. By 1996 the company had attempted seven public financings and had been successful with five.

Jay Moorin, then-CEO of Magainin, explained his philosophy on obtaining financing:

I never think about financing as a financing per se. I think about financing in five-year blocks, in one-year blocks, and in a current time frame. And in my head, when I'm selling a share of Magainin stock, I'm always cost averaging. I never look at the deal that I just did and say, "Oh, that was a good one because it was $10. Or that was a bad one because it was $6." In fact, it's gone so far as to affect the way I define good deals and bad deals. Good deals are ones that close and bad deals are ones that don't close.

For Moorin, the primary objective of a financing is to keep the company moving forward, to provide it with the necessary capital to make a product and launch it. From this point of view, quibbling over minor differences in price can be self-defeating if the company holds out for so long that it fails to raise the necessary financing.

According to Moorin, the company never enjoyed a completely smooth financing, though ultimately it has been successful several times in closing deals. One of the keys to the company's success in raising capital was that Moorin stayed in close contact with the company's shareholders. Over the years this strategy allowed Magainin, in subsequent financing rounds, to retain many of the same investors who participated pre-IPO. In 1992, with the benefit of these close shareholder relationships, Moorin recognized that key shareholders were not interested in a private placement and would much rather have Magainin do another public offering. The shareholders felt it was in their best interests to have other research analysts communicating broadly about the company. These arguments were persuasive, so rather than do a private placement as originally planned, the company completed a second, or follow-on, public offering in February 1993.

By the middle of 1993, the company decided that it was time for another round of financing, this time through a PIPE transaction, a process that worked so well the company subsequently tried a second PIPE.

This second PIPE transaction was scheduled for the spring of 1994. In two days the company sold another $18 million worth of stock, but for the first time, the SEC decided to review the S-3 filing. During this review period the company released negative clinical data. Its stock plummeted to $5 per share on the news, and eventually to $1.75. Meanwhile, the company already had a PIPE commitment to sell shares to seven investors at $15 per share.

A conflict soon developed. The seven investors were unwilling to pay

$15 per share for stock in free fall with a current value of only $5. Magainin agreed to renegotiate. That strategy did not sit well with the company's existing shareholders, who insisted the company try to collect the original contract price of $15. Eventually the deal fell apart.

At that point, the company had a low stock price, but high cash balances. It cut its burn rate and took other steps to conserve cash before it was ready for another financing attempt. The company conducted another study, began new clinical trials with the same drug candidate, but aimed at a different disease end point, and this time the clinical trials showed positive results. In the summer of 1995 Moorin considered another public offering, but was concerned because the company's share price had been recovering based solely on data.

Instead of a public offering or a PIPE, the company chose a registered direct placement and planned to sell 2 million shares at $7 per share. It held a one-day road show in Boston, visiting eight major institutions. The smallest order taken was $100,000. Interest was high. The share price went from $7 to $10, and the company raised $35 million at $10 per share 16 days later.

In the summer of 1996, the company prepared to announce pivotal Phase III data on its lead compound, and Moorin was cautiously optimistic that the results were going to be good. He decided it was prudent to go out and raise some more money before the company received the data.

His thinking was as follows: If the company raised money first, and if the news was good, the company's balance sheet would be in a strong position. In any negotiations with corporate partners, Magainin would have the leverage, secure in the knowledge that it had the money to do what it wanted to do, perhaps even launch the product and take all the value for its shareholders.

If the data was bad, the stock might go down again, which was all the more reason to finance before the data were released, to make sure the company could support all the things it was doing. In the end, Magainin did another direct registration before the release of critical data. The financing was completed in a week and a half and raised approximately $12 million.

During the five-year period from 1991 to 1996, Magainin received financing from the public market on five separate occasions, raising over $100 million. By the end of this period, the company was much stronger and more developed than it was in the beginning, and it was on the verge of becoming commercial.

Since the summer of 1996, Magainin completed clinical trials on its initial product, Cytolex™. It also entered into a distribution agreement in February 1997 with SmithKline Beecham, which garnered $5 million paid up front and another $5 million as a milestone payment in June of that year. Ultimately, the agreement could have brought the company another $225 million in milestone payments, as well as a share of profits from any future sales of Cytolex. Ultimately, however, Cytolex, was not approved, the project was halted, and Magainin changed its name to Genaera.

Today Genaera's lead drug candidate is derived from squalamine, a substance found in the tissue of certain sharks that have a natural immunity to cancer and infectious diseases. It is a potential anti-angiogenesis therapy for ovarian and non–small-cell lung cancer, as well as age-related macular degeneration. Additionally, Genaera and MedImmune are working together on Lomucin™, a treatment for asthma based on hCLCA1, a gene that regulates the production of mucus.

CASE STUDY OF A PRIVATE PLACEMENT

Nymox Pharmaceutical Corporation

Nymox Pharmaceutical Corporation (Nasdaq: NYMX) is a biopharmaceutical company that specializes in research and development of therapeutics and diagnostics for the aging population, with an emphasis on Alzheimer's disease. It is based in Maywood, New Jersey, and Saint Laurent, Quebec, and has two subsidiaries, Nymox Corporation and Serex, Inc.

Nymox was incorporated in 1989 and became a public company in 1995. It is the first company to have successfully developed an accurate peripheral test for Alzheimer's disease, AlzheimAlert™. The company currently markets its AlzheimAlert™ test to physicians in the United States and its NicAlert™ test for tobacco exposure in the United States and in Japan. Its strong scientific relationships have led to the development of at least one major new product initiative every year. Nymox has a pipeline of drugs in development and a proprietary antimicrobial treatment against deadly *E. coli* contamination. It also has a line of other "Alert" products—such as OsteoAlert™ for osteoporosis—in development, as well as a unique proprietary diagnostic platform technology.

Nymox has funded its operations and projects primarily by selling shares of its common stocks. Since 1998 a small portion of the funding has come from service revenues. However, these service revenues have not been—and may not be, in the foreseeable future—sufficient to meet the company's anticipated financial needs. Nymox has been funding its ongoing R&D work as well as it marketing and sales functions through private placements of its shares.

On December 1, 1997, Nymox shares began trading on the Nasdaq Stock Market. Nymox's common shares also traded on the Montreal Exchange from December 18, 1995 through November 19, 1999.

Since December 1995, Nymox has completed at least nine private placements, for a total of approximately $20 million, with about 200,000 warrants still open. Its most recent offering was announced on August 2, 2002, for in excess of $760,000, to be used for general corporate purposes.

Nymox recently announced that is has filed an investigational new drug (IND) application with the FDA for its drug NX-1207 for the treatment of benign prostatic hyperplasia (BPH) in men and was rated bullish on technical evaluation by Standard & Poor's Stock Report in July 2002.

SUMMARY

Technology companies have seen several wide swings in financing sentiment over the past 20 years. In biotech, the early 1990s were a golden age, when very early stage companies were able to raise both private and public financing. The mid 1990s saw a huge falloff in the market's appetite for life science companies. Once again, this trend reversed in 1999 and early 2000, while valuations soared.

Internet companies had a huge bubble in the late 1990s, during which capital was nearly free and easily available. That situation seems a distant memory now, after a three-year bear market. As of this writing, the broad market has rallied over 20 percent from its lows, biotech stocks have rallied more than that, many tech stocks have yet to rally, and IPOs are still rare. History teaches us that cycles reverse. However, timing those reversals is a fool's errand.

NOTES

[1] "A Cold Look at Going Public," *Business Week,* November 10, 1998.
[2] G. Steven Burrill, "Life Sciences: State of the Industry," presentation given at BIO2002, June 2002.
[3] David Edwards, "Portfolio Manager's Toolbox: A Brief History of Bear Markets," June 2, 2000, special to The Street.com

CHAPTER 5

Creative and Alternative Financing Strategies

What financing alternatives are available for a company that is not yet positioned to attract the attention of venture capitalists, or that needs to supplement funds received from venture financing? The alternatives described in this chapter range from a new way to look at old-fashioned bootstrapping all the way to government-sponsored and philanthropic agency programs available for small businesses.

ANGEL INVESTORS

According to an informal poll of the delegates to the 1995 White House Conference on Small Business, the primary problem for financing innovative growth companies was obtaining equity capital in the range of $250,000 to $5 million.[1] That is still true at this writing. For amounts below $500,000, entrepreneurs often turn first to their personal resources and raise money through second mortgages, credit cards, or from family, friends, and colleagues. But there is a substantial gap in equity capital available for rapidly growing companies needing between $500,000 and $5 million.

Twenty years ago even the largest venture capital funds often invested from $250,000 to $1 million in small entrepreneurial operations. However, the success of venture capital partnerships in raising significant amounts of capital—in particular from large pension and other institutional funds—has made smaller investments much less attractive. In large part this is because venture capitalists do not see the utility in spending as much due diligence time as every investment requires for these microinvestments. But it also stems from the fact that today's very large venture partnerships are sustained economically largely through individual investments in excess of $10 million.

Thus, small funding transactions for early-stage companies generally do not emanate from venture capital funding or broker/dealer-led private placements, but instead from private individuals—so called angels. Angel investors are most often wealthy (high-net-worth) individuals who are looking to invest between $250,000 and $5 million of seed and start-up capital in small businesses.

In 1995 the Center for Venture Research (CVR) at the University of New Hampshire was commissioned to prepare an updated analysis of the angel marketplace. Published in 1996, the report's conservative estimate was that the total investment per year by angel investors was approximately $20 billion. That figure was almost twice the annual amount invested by institutional venture funds.[2] Today conservative estimates put the U.S. angel network at nearly 3 million strong, investing in excess of $60 billion per year. Principals of early-stage growth companies have heard about his angelic trough and are eager to access it.

In the vast majority of cases, entrepreneurs seek angels for a very compelling reason: Theirs is the only source of available money. Either the amount sought is too low for the venture fund investor, or it is too early in the development of the entity to attract even the very few early-stage venture funds in their region. In such cases, what remains available is relatively limited: a strategic alliance with a corporation that has deep pockets, an angel, friends and family, or the entrepreneur's own pocket.

In a minority of cases, an experienced entrepreneur with a following in the investment community chooses to tap individual investors, even when venture money is otherwise available. Some entrepreneurs believe that venture funds are more demanding and intrusive on management, or that they will achieve a better valuation with an angel—although this may or may not be true, depending on the venture fund and the angel.

Some very early stage entrepreneurs who have track records with prior successful ventures have little difficulty in raising money from scores of angelic investors, without help from a broker. Given a choice, some would still welcome the value-added involvement of a venture fund, but others eschew it as unnecessary or have identified an angel with contacts or industry experience, which they believe to be even more valuable.

An angel is simply any individual who can be motivated to invest. Company founders with track records usually find it is easier to generate that motivation. The inexperienced entrepreneur has a far more difficult quest. One way he or she may start is by talking to people who would be naturally motivated by knowledge of the entrepreneur's capabilities or by specific industry knowledge. Such people can include former bosses, successful colleagues, or others who have achieved success in their industry, as well as successful friends and (of course) family, for whom the motivation is the most natural of all. These approaches all benefit from a knowledge or bias concerning the founder's capabilities, which in some cases meshes with a sense of personal obligation. Of course, some founders are unwilling to take advantage of the familial sense of obligation and cannot tolerate the possibility of having family members risk their capital.

The next angel possibility is the wealthy stranger to whom access can be obtained in a manner that will produce the motivation to invest. While the angel universe includes family members and acquaintances, the term is most often used to describe "accredited" investors, as defined under federal and state securities laws and regulations. In general, accredited investors currently are identified as "natural persons whose net worth (with or without spouse) is more than $1 million and whose individual income exceeds $200,000 for the most recent two years ($300,00 including spouse's income)."[3] The characteristics of accredited, or angel, investors (according to the CVR report) are:

- Investments typically are concentrated in markets and technologies with which the angel is familiar.
- Angels, as a rule, invest within their own state or region (within one day's drive).
- They seek active participation, either by serving on the company's board of directors or by providing guidance as an informal mentor or consultant to the company.
- As a group, private investors prefer to invest at the venture's seed and start-up stages.
- Angels are patient investors, with long-term exit horizons of 5 to 10 years or more.
- Angel financing rounds are most often less than $1 million and in most cases less than $500,000.
- Angels tend to co-invest with trusted friends and business associates.
- They are "adventure" investors—prepared to take higher risks or lower rewards when attracted by nonfinancial aspects of the venture.
- Angels' investment terms and conditions tend to be brief and less formal than those of venture capitalists, although the dot-com bust has stiffened the terms required by angels and driven them to seek preferred stock rather than common.

There exists a growing network of nonprofit and governmental organizations, including the Internet-based Access to Capital Electronic Network (ACE-Net, formerly the Angel Capital Electronic Network) whose mission is to help connect investors with companies. Entrepreneurs also turn for introductions to lawyers, accountants, and business advisors who specialize in emerging growth companies. These professionals often come into contact with potential backers who have supported similar ventures or who have a desire to support a particular kind of business.

These referrals can help establish credibility for the new venture. By staying alert and doing industry research, the founder also may identify investors who have achieved success in the same industry or with the same kind of technology. On occasion, a start-up company has gotten the ear of an investment advisor who administers pension plan dollars for angelic physicians who are interested in some high-risk/high-growth diversification.

Angels also can be found in networking groups and venture fairs.

Organized groups of angels have formed in recent years to look at deals. Examples include the Pennsylvania Private Investors Group, the nation's first formal investor-angels network, and the New Jersey Private Investors Network, which is administered by the South Jersey Entrepreneurs Network. Venture fairs provide an opportunity for companies to present their business or technology to a wide range of attendees, who usually include private investors or angels.

Angels outside of familiar circles are elusive. Finding them and then getting them interested in an investment requires resourceful research, networking, patience, and boldness. Angels usually have little appetite or attention span for long meetings or convoluted business plans. Once a founder gets in front of an angel, the presentation should be crisp, should be carefully rehearsed, and should give explicit reasons why the angel should be motivated to invest. Once the angel is interested and begins the due diligence phase, he or she can be provided with the more detailed information necessary to evaluate the venture.

Most angels look for competent, credible entrepreneurs. Since angels ordinarily do not perform the kinds of independent technical and market due diligence that are performed by venture funds, the entrepreneur's goals should be to convince the angel to believe in the venture and its founders.

There are obvious opportunities and challenges (including securities and tax law implications) in structuring and offering angel fundings. If a company is considering an angel investment, it would be wise to consult its legal and financial advisors to ensure that structured opportunities are maximized and legal pitfalls are minimized.

According to an Angel Advisor Angel Network Activity Survey, on average, angel groups funded 235 percent more companies in 2000 than were funded in 1996, a steady annual compounded growth rate of 35 percent—in spite of the market downturn in the broader capital markets. In a typical round of financing, reports the survey, a start-up company received an average investment of $350,000—about one-third of the total round.[4]

Angel investor networks are easily found today on the Internet. Exhibit 5.1 presents just a few such networks.

A Closer Look at ACE-Net

The Access to Capital Electronic Network, sponsored by the U.S. Small Business Administration's Office of Advocacy until its privatization in 2001, is a secure Internet-based listing service that provides information to private accredited angel investors, Small Business Investment Corporations (SBICs), and institutional venture capitalists on small, growing businesses nationwide seeking to raise up to $5 million in equity financing. But its sweet spot is companies seeking up to $1 million, because such capital raises are exempt from SEC Regulation D Rule 504. A direct outcome of the recommendations

EXHIBIT 5.1   A Sampling of Angel Investors[5]

Name of Angel Group Activities	Description of Group's Activities
Access to Capital Electronic Network (ACE-Net) https://ace-net.sr.unh.edu/	Nationwide Internet-based listing service that provides information to angel investors on small, dynamic growing businesses seeking $250,000 to $5 million in equity financing. Sponsored by the Office of Advocacy of the U.S. Small Business Administration.
Catalyst LLC (formerly Amis Ventures) www.catalyst.com	Addresses the private equity financing needs of entrepreneurs by providing an efficient early stage funding process. Also enables qualified investors to locate, assess, and co-invest in prescreened high-potential start-ups. Focused on Northeast and Mid-Atlantic regions.
International Capital Resources *www.icrnet.com*	The oldest for-profit business introduction service in the U.S.; developers of a database of accredited business and angel investors in North America.
New Vantage Group *www.newvantagepartners.com*	Manages early stage venture funds for active angel investors including the Dinner Club, LLC, The eMedia Club, LLC, and The Washington Dinner Club, LLC.
www.angelinvestrors.org http://angelinvestors.infopoint.com	A non-profit corporation whose goal is to facilitate information and profitable investments through an International League of Angels, among other activities.

of the delegates to the 1995 White House Conference on Small Business, ACE-Net provides a precedent-setting solution to the problem of raising capital for small companies seeking investments in the range of $250,000 to $5 million.[6]

Private offerings through ACE-Net differ from traditional private placement stock offerings and offer a potentially larger pool of investors. Traditional private placement exemptions allow companies to circumvent the costly registration process, but companies are prohibited from engaging in general solicitation and advertising of offerings. This leaves an extremely small pool of investors, since entrepreneurs can approach only those investors with whom they have previous relationships. ACE-Net, on the other hand, is limited only to "accredited investors," as defined by the Securities and Exchange Commission (SEC), so subscribing entrepreneurs can make use of Accredited Investor Exemptions. These allow an entrepreneur to make offerings to subscribers in several states without being required to complete the registration process in those states.

The people responsible for creating ACE-Net have been extremely careful to structure the network, the information displayed on its Web page (https://ace-net.sr.unh.edu), the management of the listings database, and the administrative functions of the network operators so that its business cannot be construed as offering advice or issuing reports on securities listed on the network, or effecting any transaction in a security.

The system is administered by regional Network Operators—each a not-for-profit university- or state-based entrepreneurial development center. The selected Network Operator will be the entrepreneur's or investor's direct contact with the ACE-Net system. Network Operators have experience in all aspects of economic development in their regions and have, to date, helped small companies raise over $4 billion. The database itself is maintained by the CVR at the University of New Hampshire.

Once registered as an ACE-Net subscriber, accredited investors who visit the Network's homepage are able to search a password-controlled database of early-stage small-company stock offerings and can download offering circulars. Search criteria include:

- The state in which to invest
- The type of business/industry
- The amount a company is seeking to raise
- The amount the investor wishes to invest

The search engine notifies the investor via the Internet when a company listing on the Network matches any of the specified search criteria. If an investor wishes to purchase stock from a small company listed on the Network, he or she must contact the small company directly.

Before being given a password, each investor is required to provide certification as an "accredited investor" within the meaning of Rule 501 of Regulation D under the Securities Act of 1933. In other words, the investor must have a net worth of $1 million or have an annual income of more than $200,000. Before completion of any sale, it is the responsibility of the offering company to determine independently whether the investor satisfies the criteria for "accredited investor" within the appropriate jurisdiction.

For a small company to qualify for listing on the Network, it must have a qualified or registered offering pursuant to federal and/or state securities laws and regulations, or be qualified for an exemption from registration.

According to ACE-Net's enrollment information published on its Web site, participation is limited to companies that:

- Have a registered or qualified small corporate offering pursuant to either (a) regulation A of the federal securities regulations (and the corresponding state securities laws/regulations), or (b) Regulation D, Rule 504 of the federal securities regulations (and the corresponding state securities laws/regulations, known in many states as a Small Corporate Offering Registration [SCOR]).
- Have completed the SCOR form or Registration Form U-7.
- Are not disqualified under the disqualification provisions set forth in Part IV of the North American Securities Administrators Association's "Statement of Policy Regarding Small Company Offering Registrations," adopted April 28, 1996 (the policy statement can be viewed at http://ace-net.sr.unh.edu/).

Entrepreneurs of small companies are advised by ACE-Net to go through five steps before submitting an enrollment application:

1. Thoroughly research the applicable federal and state securities laws and develop a securities law compliance strategy.
2. Determine a range for how much will be sought in investment—as a general rule, there are two cutoff limits for registration exemptions: at $1 million and at $5 million.
3. Identify the states in which investors will be sought.
4. Develop a securities law compliance strategy.
5. Prepare an offering circular, if a SCOR offering or private placement memorandum has not already been completed.

Small, rapidly growing early-stage technology companies should consider a listing on ACE-Net as part of their capital-raising campaigns if they are looking for equity financing in the range of $250,000 to $5 million and are ready to sell shares of their stock in exchange for an infusion of capital.

ACE-Net is a fee-based service with a maximum annual fee of $450 at this writing. It is not available to sole proprietorships, general or limited partnerships, joint ventures, "blank check" or development-stage companies, or those companies involved in oil, gas, or other extractive interests.

ACE-Net has recently formed a partnership with California State University at San Bernardino to advance its educational and training programs, which are expected to be available by late 2003.

BOOTSTRAPPING

Probably the most common method of initial financing for entrepreneurs—whether by design or not—is bootstrapping. When a management team makes a conscious decision to finance the company without raising equity capital or taking loans from traditional resources, it plans to rely largely on internally generated retained earnings, second mortgages, credit cards, and customer advances for capital.

Venture capital firms and other private investors often cannot commit to helping very early stage companies in need of small sums of money because of the firms' specific investment criteria and the high costs of due diligence and monitoring. Because of this, some companies are forced into the bootstrapping scenario, but it actually has some distinct advantages for entrepreneurs and is probably the best method for positioning the company for later rounds of equity capital. Investors are always impressed to learn that management teams have invested their own capital and have made use of creative financing techniques before coming for the serious money.

Some bootstrapping techniques are obvious:

- Delayed or reduced compensation
- Use of personal savings
- Working from home or seeking out space at below-market rent
- Taking home equity loans
- Negotiating with service providers for favorable deals
- Buying used equipment instead of new
- Hiring contract employees instead of permanent employees
- Getting credit lines from suppliers

Others are less obvious and can include everything from barter arrangements for needed space, services, or equipment, to special deals with customers.

The key to bootstrapping is to use the company's resources wisely and creatively to get operations up and running, to keep growth and outside financial resources in check, and to get to the market with cash-generating products or services as quickly as possible.

VENTURE PHILANTHROPY

There are biotech companies out there with good ideas, good science, good intellectual property, for whom a $500,000 PRI [Program-Related Investment] would mean a great deal, not only in terms of their survival, but also in terms of their advancement and their subsequent ability to attract venture capital and progress in their work.

—Dr. Howard M. Fillit, Executive Director,
Institute for the Study of Aging

One of the more interesting financing models available to some high-tech and biotech companies is in the area of venture philanthropy. While the term "venture philanthropy" is used in different ways—most commonly to describe nonprofits providing infrastructure funding to other nonprofits—the focus of this discussion is on philanthropies that help young companies raise financing for purposes of commercialization.

This type of venture philanthropy is strictly a mission-driven model. Companies that obtain funding from such an entity must work toward outcomes that are strategically aligned with the mission of the organization. For example, the Institute for the Study of Aging (ISOA), a New York City-based Biomedical Venture Philanthropy established by the Estee Lauder Trust, provides grants and program-related investments to young companies that are involved in preclinical and clinical research in the areas of normal cognitive aging, Alzheimer's disease, and related dementia. Their mission is to support drug discovery for their targeted diseases, and they fund companies that are aligned with that mission through a vehicle called a Program-Related Investment (PRI).

According to Dr. Howard M. Fillit, founding executive director of ISOA, foundations and government agencies have traditionally funded *basic* research in academia, while the actual *production of new drugs* traditionally has been done by the large pharmaceutical companies. So there exists a gap today between the academic world—which receives vast amounts of money from governmental agencies such as the National Institutes of Health (NIH)—about $23 billion in 2002—and the smaller companies working toward the discovery and delivery of new chemical compounds and new drugs. Venture capitalists sometimes will fund projects along the drug discovery continuum that are certainly earlier than where most investment banks and public markets dare to tread. But since the primary goal of venture investing is to make a profit, few of them will throw their hat in so early in the process as to fund young biotech ventures without proof of concept. ISOA is one organization that is helping to bridge that gap in its particular disease area.

Since the process of getting a drug to market takes anywhere from 12 to 15 years and, according to the pharmaceutical industry, costs about $800 million when costs are averaged out over that time period, it is a hugely time consuming and expensive proposition—and a risky one.

If academia is interested in basic research that typically does not lead to a pill or an injection for a specific disease, where are the new drugs going to come from? One answer is a direct result of the Bayh-Dole Act of 1980, which encouraged commercialization at the university level. So now, with the advent of new technologies that allow for computerized modeling work at the desktop level and increased activity in technology transfer—whereby academic institutions such as Columbia and Harvard and Stanford can make enormous amounts of money every year from royalties on discoveries that their scientists make that are ultimately translated into new drugs—the stage is being set for a change in the way academic institutions view their research behavior.

TYPICAL FAILURE RATES IN THE DRUG INDUSTRY

The pharmaceuticals industry, which has been developing drugs for some 100 years now, estimates that:

- Only 1 in 10,000 compounds makes it to market—and with new technologies, that number can go as low as 1 in 1 million.

- Only 1 in 5 drugs that make it out of a lab and into clinical development ever get FDA approval.

- Of the group of drugs that gets approved by the FDA, only 3 out of every 10 drugs ever make a profit and only 1 becomes a "blockbuster," actually contributing significantly to the pharmaceutical company's bottom line.

However, what the Bayh-Dole Act also engendered was a vast number of academicians wanting to start their own biotech companies. But there is precious little financing available for such risky businesses, especially in these tough economic times. Today, in large pharmaceutical companies, the business model has been to wait, let the early-stage investors take the risk on small biotechs, and simply buy the companies that succeed. The large pharmaceutical companies are not likely to drive new hypotheses into new drugs.

Fully 25 percent of all new drugs approved by the FDA in 2001 came from the biotech industry. But with this financing gap, the question remains: Where are the drugs of tomorrow going to come from? And that is the basis of ISOA's venture philanthropy model.

The vehicle for the venture philanthropy model is called the Program-Related Investment. Created by an Act of Congress in 1968 and pioneered by the Ford Foundation during the country's War on Poverty, PRIs are a way for nonprofits to achieve social missions while funding the for-profit businesses they work with to help achieve those missions. ISOA pioneered the use of the PRI in the biomedical field because the need is tremendous and PRIs help the institute achieve its mission.

ISOA functions much like a venture capital firm, in that it provides strategic management assistance to select young biotech companies, and it may even take an observer's seat on a company's board. The institute conducts scientific and business due diligence, it approves each PRI, it negotiates a return on investment (ROI)—albeit at a lower rate than venture capital rates—and it has accountability. All the grants made by ISOA are negotiated with an ROI built in, but the primary purpose of the grant is not for profit—it is to advance the institute's mission.

"Our money is in many ways more attractive to these early stage

A PRI AT WORK

In the late 1960s and early 1970s, the Ford Foundation took on a mission of building housing and businesses in economically deprived areas as part of its work with the War on Poverty. While the foundation wanted to use tax-exempt dollars to achieve its social mission, it needed help from real estate developers, housing contractors, building contractors, and so on—all for-profit businesses.

What the PRI enabled the foundation to do was use a variety of financial instruments, including equity investments and loans—at half of the prime rate—to fund its for-profit contracting partners to help achieve their mission.

Over the years, the PRI programs have been used by family foundations that give out loans of $1,000 all the way up to major foundations that give out millions of dollars this way each year. The PRIs are enormously successful and have been used by many entities to further social and economic development.

companies than venture money is because our rates are lower and we're not as intrusive in their business as venture capitalists," explains Fillet. "On the other hand, a venture capital firm might have a better ability to raise additional dollars and its management assistance might be more sophisticated."

Of course, all these early-stage companies want to get venture capital funding, but most of them will have to wait. ISOA's Biomedical Venture Philanthropy provides the gap financing and keeps early-stage biotech focused on its disease area. And because it does such excellent scientific due diligence, companies that achieve ISOA funding also bring a kind of "Good Housekeeping Seal of Approval" to their future fund-raising efforts.

> *We sit at the intersection of venture capital, economic development, and socially responsible investing. We invest in early stage technology companies, always alongside a lead venture capital investor. And we look for companies that are likely to generate benefits for New York City and its communities—job creation, revitalization of distressed areas, and innovative ideas or products that position New York at the cutting edge of growth sector industries.*
>
> —Maria Gotsch, Senior Vice President,
> New York City Investment Fund

Companies in the greater New York City area have another kind of venture philanthropy to turn to: the New York City Investment Fund (NYCIF), a private fund with a civic mission. Established in 1996, the fund was the vision of Henry R. Kravis, founding partner of Kohlberg Kravis Roberts & Co., who still serves as its chairman. Mobilizing the city's financial and business leaders to help build a stronger and more diversified local economy, the fund comprises a network of experts from the investment and corporate communities who help identify and support the city's most promising entrepreneurs in both the for-profit and not-for-profit sectors.

NYCIF is capitalized at more than $100 million, with individual investments typically ranging from $250,000 to $3 million. It is an evergreen fund, in which realized gains are reinvested into other projects, and is viewed by venture capitalists as an "additive," strategic investor, not a competitor. The fund provides both equity and debt funding, structured to meet the needs of the specific project. It will invest at any stage of development, but expects to exit in about five years.

"We don't just put money into companies," says Maria Gotsch, senior vice president of NYCIF and president of Civic Capital Corporation, a public charity established to administer tax-exempt contributions donated to NYCIF. "We are about marshalling the intellectual capital resources of the City of New York, which are vast, and putting them to work for companies that fit with our mission."

The fund has more than 250 industry experts—many of whom are investors—volunteering their time and institutional resources to develop its investment strategies, conduct due diligence, monitor portfolio projects, and sit on the company's boards when investments are made. So a company that has a training, education, environmental, or community revitalization component to it—and that is backed by the NYCIF—might find itself working with one of New York's preeminent business leaders. It will get money plus great contacts and a lot of credibility.

The fund carries out its investment activity through industry sector groups, including Retail and Tourism; Healthcare and Sciences; Education and Information Services; Media and Entertainment; Communications; and Finance, Insurance and Real Estate.

RESEARCH PARKS

What brings bioparks and research parks into prominence now is the fact that universities are getting involved in their development. As the knowledge-based economy accelerates, the fuel to fire innovation comes from the intellectual capital of universities and colleges. In addition to everything else that's talked about in this book, a key component is: Where are the innovations going to come from? They're going to come from a person first. You need the concept. The secret ingredient in having research parks or university affiliated research parks succeed is to have an entrepreneurially focused university, one that is accepting of the university-industry collaboration.

—Michael J. Donovan,
Assistant Vice President for
Administrative Services, BioSquare

Something is happening near many major universities and hospitals these days—the establishment of research parks. Some are dedicated bioparks, while others are more broadly based business incubators, while still others concentrate on any number of very specific research topics, according to the expertise of the sponsoring institution.

The Association of University Research Parks describes a research park or technology incubator as a property-based venture that has:

- Existing or planned land and buildings designed primarily for private and public R&D facilities, high-technology and science-based companies, and support services
- A contractual and/or formal ownership or operational relationship with one or more universities or other institutions of higher education and science research
- A role in promoting R&D by the university in partnership with industry, assisting in the growth of new ventures, and promoting economic development
- A role in aiding the transfer of technology and business skills between the university and industry tenants

The association further explains that the park or incubator may be either a not-for-profit or a for-profit entity, owned wholly or partially by a university or a university-related entity. Alternatively, the park or incubator may be owned by a nonuniversity entity, but have a contractual or other formal relationship with a university, including joint or cooperative ventures between a privately developed research park and a university.

The first research park was created by Stanford University in the 1950s. With acres of land available and a vision to use that land productively (i.e., bring in revenues to the school), Stanford put together a real estate development plan to lease the land to research-based businesses. Over the years Stanford discovered that it was a good idea to have universities in close proximity to businesses because of the gain sharing that could happen between the institutions. That basic plan appears in multiple models around the country (and the world) today.

This book features two of those models, one in Boston and one in New York City, which both focus on biotechnology, but in slightly different ways.

RESEARCH PARK CASE STUDIES

Boston: BioSquare

BioSquare was established in the early 1990s as a way to provide space for the expanding research program at Boston University (BU) Medical Center and is today Boston's preeminent biomedical research and business address. It combines state-of-the-art, built-to-suit facilities that include a comprehensive list of tenant amenities all within easy reach of the world-renowned academic, medical, and research facilities of the BU Medical Center. By allowing innovative biomedical research companies and businesses the opportunity to work in tandem with leading principal investigators from the BU Schools of Medicine, Dental Medicine, and Public Health, BioSquare represents an academic/industry collaboration at its best.

> *The thing about these university-affiliated and located research parks is that it's a learning experience for both universities and companies. And I think it's where companies are headed. They need to plug into the academy, and that takes vision and leadership at the university level.*
>
> —Michael J. Donovan,
> Assistant Vice President for
> Administrative Services, BioSquare

BioSquare's intent was to diversify BU's research interests and activities, so that by bringing corporations into its midst as tenants, it could facilitate university/industry collaborations. Today, not only does the Medical Center collaborate with its tenants, it also extends faculty rank to the leading scientists of these tenant corporations, allowing them to tap the intellectual capital of the school's departments and allowing the schools to pick the scientists' brains. It is a win-win for both sides.

The 16-acre facility comprises a $600 million real estate development project that provides 2.5 million square feet of state-of-the-art research, office, conference, hotel, and retail space right in downtown Boston. The research facilities can be built to incorporate everything from basic bench research all the way up to BL3 (Bio Safety Level 3) testing. Facilities include:

- Center for Advanced Biomedical Research (CABR), a 200,000 square-foot research facility that opened in 1993. This building, BioSquare's anchor, contains many of the important advanced biomedical core services that are available to outside corporate tenants of BioSquare.
- Evan Biomedical Research Building, a 192,000 square-foot research and office facility that opened in 2002, containing state-of-the-art facilities for any type of biomedical R&D.
- Parking, hotel, and conference centers.

Tenants have access to a range of cutting-edge laboratory and biomedical equipment and services not usually found in research parks of this kind, including:

- A 60,000 square-foot Animal Science Center and Transgenic Facility
- A Cardiovascular Imaging Suite
- A macromolecular X-ray Crystallography Facility
- A Mass Spectrometry Resource Core
- A number of NMR facilities
- On-site access to Medical Center regulatory affairs personnel and Medical Center research committees that are well versed in research protocols and studies involving the use of animals, radioactive materials, recombinant DNA, other biohazardous materials, and human subjects
- A wide variety of other high-end biomedical research facilities and on-site expertise usually found only in major academic medical centers
- The 500-plus-bed tertiary care facility at Boston University Medical Center, directly across the street—an excellent site for clinical research

Since its beginnings in the early 1990s, BioSquare has hosted companies like Amgen, Merck KgaA, Infinity, Combinatorics, Nitromed, Dipighenics, and Antergeon. While these companies were—or became—mature during their tenancy, they began as leaseholders and ended as collaborators, with continuing relationships to BU.

But BioSquare is also available for early-stage companies, providing an "incubator" and a kind of novel financing mechanism for research-driven organizations. Locating mature companies that need space is easier than finding early-stage companies, of course, so BioSquare relies on a time-tested venture capital approach to market it services to young companies. It has created a grassroots network of professional services companies of accountants, attorneys, and law firms that interact with young and start-up enterprises, and regularly attends scientific conferences.

Boston's only life sciences incubator facility, BioSquare's Discovery and Innovation Center, offers a turnkey solution to early stage research-oriented companies looking for space. Only the monthly phone bill is extra. The center provides:

- Individual state-of-the-art biomedical laboratory facilities
- Use of essential lab equipment including cold rooms, centrifuge, autoclave, glass washer, and freezer
- Access to outstanding biomedical research support services, including conventional animal and transgenic facilities, NMR spectroscopy core, mass spectrometry, and macromolecular X-ray facility
- Flexible, short-term space arrangements available from six months to two years

COMMUNITY TECHNOLOGY FUND

Boston University has a constellation of other entrepreneurial initiatives that focus on a number of distinct technology sectors, all of which offer platforms through which the university and industry may collaborate. Among these are:

- The Photonics Center, which focuses on the technology of light
- Fraunhofer Center for Manufacturing Innovation, which focuses on manufacturing
- The School of Management, which focuses on information technology through the Bronner Center

But what happens when faculty members develop a technology as a result of these collaborative activities? The technology can either be licensed out and commercialized by another entity, or it can be spun out and be the genesis of a new company. Using the resources of BU's Community Technology Fund (CTF), either path can be taken.

CTF's venture capital team invests in technology and life sciences companies alongside top-tier venture funds. It also invests in limited partnerships of venture capital funds on behalf of BU's endowment. It is especially interested in early-stage investments in which it can add significant added value by leveraging BU resources. CTF always invests as a strategic part of an investment syndicate of venture capital firms and, in most cases, serves as an active board observer.

CTF typically invests between $500,000 and $1,500,000 initially, depending on the stage and capital requirements of the company. In information technology, the fund looks at promising companies in:

- Communications equipment and components
- Enterprise software
- Internet infrastructure
- Semiconductor technology

In life sciences, CTF will consider business plans in these areas:

- Biotechnology, including genomics and proteomics
- Drug discovery
- Medical devices and instruments
- Pharmaceuticals and drug delivery

For more information about BioSquare or the BU's Community Technology Fund, visit www.biosquare.org.

- All-inclusive price structure with flexible terms that include cost for space, research permits, utilities and taxes—leaving scientific teams free to focus on research activities rather than administrative duties
- Modern office space with Internet connection, security and custodial services, hazardous waste disposal, plus an on-site, service-oriented management team

In the BioSquare model, mature companies have an obligation with their lease to pay market-rate rents. However, early-stage companies have options. BioSquare developed its Discovery and Innovation Center incubator for a number of reasons:

- To bring companies into the facility so they can grow and make good use of the space
- To provide opportunities for collaboration between the company's scientists and the BU faculty
- To give BU an opportunity to secure equity stakes in some new and exciting biotech companies

To that end, BioSquare can be flexible with early-stage tenants: If the companies want to pay full rent with no equity offering, that is fine. But if they want reduced rent in exchange for a small equity stake, that works, too.

Technology Transfer

The resources of BU and BioSquare are invaluable in helping with technology transfer issues, as well. Protectable intellectual property is critical in the process of bringing a new idea to market. Companies will invest in an idea only if they believe it can be protected.

As a research-driven enterprise, a young company's intellectual property can provide additional funding via a sponsored research agreement with outside institutions; can incorporate unique materials and access to specialized equipment into your research program; and can attract highly skilled collaborative personnel. BU's extensive contacts in the venture capital industry and corporate community can provide critical introductions and financial support for new technologies. And BU can guide inventors through the steps of technology transfer, including:

- Grants and patent process
- Disclosure
- Evaluation
- Patent applications
- Marketing
- Forming relationships
- Negotiations
- Policies and forms

Within the BU model, 30 percent of royalty income is distributed back to the inventors of the technology, and the possibility for consulting opportunities is great. The bottom line is that a facility like BioSquare can provide early-stage technology companies with an environment and resources—and, in some cases, the financing help—in which to create, as well as the experience to help bring suitable inventions to market. BioSquare joins other such facilities around the country—in North Carolina, San Diego, Colorado, to name a few—and around the world—in Paris, Cambridge, and Heidelberg—that see a bright future in the university/industry alliance.

New York: New York-Presbyterian Hospital

A slightly different model is taking shape at New York-Presbyterian Hospital (NYPH), the entity created by the merger of The Presbyterian Hospital on Manhattan's West Side and The New York Hospital on the East Side. NYPH is affiliated with two medical schools, College of Physicians & Surgeons of Columbia University and Weill Medical College of Cornell University, together comprising arguably the largest academic medical hospital in the world.

When the merged hospital was getting a new vision statement a few years ago, senior management had as one of its strategic goals to create a new role that involved innovation and the creation of new technologies and avenues for commercialization. Since one of the new managers was Dr. William Polf, who had been in research park development for some 20 years—beginning with the Audubon Biomedical Science and Technology Park at Columbia Presbyterian Medical Center in New York City—the new mission was in good hands.

In January 2003 Polf announced that a Center of Excellence focusing on high-tech medical research would be constructed in White Plains in New York's Westchester County. That center is NYPH's $250 million biomedical research and cancer treatment facility, part of the 384,000 square-foot complex that sits on a 214-acre campus just north of New York City. It will include laboratory space for neuroscience research as well as a $100 million proton-beam accelerator for cancer treatment.

The State of New York has spent $250 million since 2000 to create five Centers of Excellence around the state dedicated to medical research. New York's governor George Pataki recently announced that New York City also will have a research center before long.

The NYPH Center in White Plains will collaborate with its affiliated medical schools—Cornell and Columbia—as well as with New York Medical College; IBM Corp. and General Electric will participate, also. IBM will provide software, computers, software, and technology services, and its scientists will collaborate on life science technology research. General Electric researchers will collaborate to refine the company's molecular-imaging technology, which can diagnose diseases at the cellular level.

While the center will not open for another two or three years, Polf is enthusiastic about its effect on Westchester and environs—in terms of both jobs and improved access to clinical trials of medications and disease treatments—while recognizing the potential tensions that can impact the affiliated entities. Even though the hospital has merged, the two medical schools are separate and could get territorial once grants start being given out and intellectual properties are at stake. In addition, the people who watch the bottom line may balk at the percentage of time that doctors spend on research and teaching versus direct patient care. But NYPH is prepared.

An academic medical center is a unique place where a teaching hospital allies itself to a medical education and research entity, and the synergies between those entities make it. Both sides need each other. The school can do almost nothing without a superb hospital—no clinical research, no access to patient's records, and so on. And the hospital would just be a hotel with good doctors if it didn't have the innovation, the breakthroughs, the research into new kinds of procedures and pharmaceuticals that people expect. We're two important sides of an equation, and we can't forget that.

—Dr. Willam Polf
Senior Vice President, External Relations
New York-Presbyterian Hospital

While not a real estate-driven, "outside company" tenant research park like BioSquare, NYPH's White Plains model provides enormous benefits to researchers both within the hospital and within the medical schools. On the medical school side, it encourages faculty to build their careers by doing science, making discoveries, publishing papers, and teaching students. It also brings in government grants and the indirect costs that come in with these grants—revenues that many schools rely on for their discretionary income.

The hospital side benefits by attracting superb doctors and offering them prestigious faculty positions where they can be doing research and teaching and interacting with their peers in the profession, in addition to patient care. Plus, the hospital gets the benefits of any of the ground-breaking innovations that result from the research and that directly benefit patients. There is no doubt that the availability of new technologies and procedures build a hospital's prestige in the marketplace, and since much of the research being done at Columbia and Cornell has to do with improving outcomes and reducing medical errors, the hospital also earns a direct bottom-line benefit.

Polf's vision for the Westchester campus is to create a biomedical "knowledge park" where NYPH can experiment with new models of partnerships. The first Center of Excellence is geared toward helping the two schools expand in areas in which NYPH has interest in growing: medical informatics, medical imaging, and zero science research, to start. With the participation of outside collaborators, such as IBM and General Electric, the two schools will be able to come together with the hospital and develop a wide range of biomedical technologies.

Moreover, the Columbia side of the equation has a great deal of experience in the commercialization process and in bringing new businesses to the table. Ownership of intellectual property, sharing of proceeds, and who belongs to which entity within this rather complex model, will need to be worked out, but NYPH is well versed in the patenting process and technology transfer negotiations. And it is also, by sheer size and the amount of technology it uses, able to attract significant R&D agendas that will keep the partners going.

Certainly the research park paradigm has changed over the last 20 years. According to Polf, the focus has shifted from information technology to biomedical businesses, and the idea of having commercial enterprises next to academic enterprises is no longer abhorrent, as it once was. In fact, in today's environment, hospitals have a hard time recruiting ambitious young bioscientists if there is no incubator nearby in which they can work on ideas and invent new products and processes.

Today's doctors and scientists understand very well the benefits of commercialization, and some of them will undoubtedly go on to found their own companies. Research parks also are creating synergies between companies—remember that the Research Triangle project in North Carolina began primarily as a real estate venture and has become a center of intellectual ferment. These biomedical research parks and incubators are facilitating the creation of the innovations of the future while enhancing patient care today. And they are doing it in a way that allows small companies and individual research scientists to have the tools, resources, and financing that they need to make it happen.

RESEARCH AND DEVELOPMENT FUNDING FROM FEDERAL PROGRAMS

The U.S. government, through the Small Business Administration (SBA) and other federal agencies, has several programs for funding emerging businesses. Perhaps the best known of these is the SBA loan program, which guarantees loans to small businesses with fewer than 500 employees.

The government is also very interested in helping to develop and commercialize new technology. In the last few years the size and number of programs targeted for technology development with the goal of making the United States more competitive in global markets have grown. These programs include grants, contracts, and opportunities for collaboration with federal laboratories.

The savvy entrepreneur who gets support from such programs is essentially partnering with Uncle Sam to fund new product development. Unlike most partners, however, this uncle does not want equity in the company or cash repayment of his investment. The largest and best-established program is the Small Business Innovation Research (SBIR) program, which provides thousands of awards to small businesses for commercializing new technologies.

Government agencies such as the SBA and the many regional and local economic development authorities are a significant source for financing the growth of emerging technology companies. Often these agencies provide more favorable terms and conditions than private financing sources. Given the many changes in policy (lessening of paperwork, larger pools of capital) relating to small businesses, both early-stage and growing companies should review this form of financing.

Small Business Innovation Research Awards

Each year the SBIR program provides highly competitive awards (grants) to small businesses to pursue innovative ideas and provides the incentive to profit from their commercialization. The program's stated mission is to stimulate high-tech innovation by including qualified small businesses in the nation's R&D arena. The SBIR targets the entrepreneurial sector because "that is where most innovation and innovators thrive." The SBIR believes that by funding the start-up and development stage of these innovative small businesses, it encourages commercialization of the technology, product, or service—which, in turn, stimulates the U.S. economy.[7]

Small businesses must meet certain eligibility requirements in order to compete in the SBIR programs:

- They must be U.S.-owned and independently operated.
- They must be for-profit entities.
- The principal researcher must be employed by the business.
- The business may have no more than 500 employees.

Ten federal departments and agencies are required to participate in this program. These agencies include:

Since its enactment in 1982—as part of the Small Business Innovation Development Act—the SBIR has paved the way for thousands of small U.S. businesses to compete for federal R&D awards.

An SBIR award adds value to an emerging company in two ways. First, there is the monetary award—up to $100,000 for six months for Phase I and up to $750,000 over two years for Phase II—which is awarded as a grant or contract (see Exhibit 5.2). Thus, a company can obtain up to $850,000 in grant or contract funds to develop a new product. The second value, often underappreciated, is that SBIR proposals are competitively judged on their commercial potential and technical merit. That means that a company receiv-

Agency	# Awards FY 2001	Web site for Information
Department of Defense (see also DARPA [Defense Advanced Research Project Agency], www.darpa.mil/sbir/)	2,141	www.acq.osd.mil/sadbu/sbir/
Health & Human Services	1,392	http://grants.nih.gov/grants/funding/sbir.htm
NASA	426	http://sbir.nasa.gov/
National Science Foundation	305	http://eng.nsf.gov/sbir/
Department of Energy	311	http://sbir.er.doe.gov/sbir
Department of Agriculture	127	www.reeusda.gov/sbir
Environmental Protection Agency	53	http://es.epa.gov/ncer/sbir
Department of Transportation	23	www.volpe.dot.gov/sbir/
Department of Education	55	www.ed.gov/offices/OERI/SBIR/
Department of Commerce	45	www.oar.noaa.gov/ORTA/SBIR www.nist.gov/sbir

ing an SBIR award has gone through an external review of its technology by experts in the field, typically by a panel of researchers and scientists from academia and industry. This external validation of the technology and its market may add value when seeking investors or corporate collaboration partners.

Getting Small Business Innovation Research Award Information

The first step to securing an SBIR award is to get on the mailing lists for solicitations. The SBA compiles a quarterly presolicitation mailing list containing the titles of solicitations being issued by the various governmental agencies. A request to be placed on this mailing list can be made by calling the SBA at (202) 205-6450 or by visiting the SBA Web site at www .sbaonline.sba.gov/sbir/.

Additional information is available directly from the various agencies,

EXHIBIT 5.2 Total SBIR Awards for 2001

Phase I Awards	Phase I Dollars ($000)	Phase II Awards	Phase II Dollars ($000)	Total Awards	Total Dollars
3,215	$ 317,094	1,533	$ 977,343	4,748	$ 1,294,437

which also maintain their own mailing lists and Web sites. Each agency also publishes a brochure describing the topics for which the agency is soliciting SBIR proposals. The lion's share of SBIRs are provided by the Departments of Defense, Health and Human Services, and Energy, as well as by the National Science Foundation and NASA. Often an agency's topics may be broader than expected. Fr example, a biotechnology company may find that products it wants to develop are of interest to the Department of Defense as well as to the Department of Health and Human Services.

In addition to contacting the individual agencies, SBIR announcements and general information—as well as the latest updates concerning national SBIR conferences—are available through the SBA Office of Technology Web site at www.sbaonline.gov/sbir/.

What Makes a Successful Proposal?

Small businesses that receive awards or grants then begin a three-phase program: Phase I, the start-up phase, for the exploration of the technical merit or feasibility of an idea or technology; Phase II, to expand on Phase I results, during which time the small business evaluates commercialization potential; and Phase III , the period in which Phase II innovations move from the laboratory to the marketplace. During this phase, no SBIR funding is granted; companies must seek funding from the private sector or through other non-SBIR federal agency funding. Only small businesses awarded Phase I grants are eligible for Phase II.

A successful SBIR application meets these three criteria:

1. The proposed work meets a need identified by the granting agency.
2. The proposal contains a sound research program that will be implemented by people with the appropriate training and experience.
3. The proposed work will lead to a commercial product for which there is a demonstrated need.

Many frustrated entrepreneurs complain of the difficulties in obtaining funding from the SBIR program. One problem comes from entrepreneurs who approach SBIR proposals the same way they approach bank loans or investment capital, without realizing that they are targeting a very different audience.

The SBIR proposals, as previously mentioned, are reviewed by a committee of scientists who are used to reviewing research proposals rather than business plans. Although the commercial potential of the proposed research is very important (and should be clearly stated early in the proposal), the research plan will be subject to in-depth scientific scrutiny. Utilizing the resources in the scientific community in drafting a proposal enhances the proposal's credibility, For example, an established scientist at a local university may be included as a consultant, or his or her laboratory may be subcontracted to perform some of the work requiring resources that are not available within the small technology business itself. The majority of the work, however, must be performed by the small business.

SMALL BUSINESS TECHNOLOGY TRANSFER PROGRAM

An important new small business program that expands funding opportunities in the federal innovation R&D arena is the Small Business Technology Transfer Program (STTR). The most important role of the STTR is to foster the innovation required to meet the nation's scientific and technological challenges in the 21st century.

The program hopes to expand the public/private sector partnership to include joint venture opportunities for small business and the nation's premier nonprofit research institutions.

A Competitive Opportunity for Small Business

Like SBIR, STTR is a highly competitive program. It reserves a specific percentage of federal R&D funding for small business and nonprofit research institution partners. While small business has long been where innovation and innovators thrive, the risk and expense of conducting serious R&D efforts can be beyond the means of many small businesses.

At the same time, nonprofit research laboratories have been instrumental in developing high-tech innovations. But since innovation frequently is limited to the theoretical, STTR combines the strengths of both entities by introducing entrepreneurial skills to high-tech research efforts. The technologies and products are transferred from the laboratory to the marketplace. As with the SBIR, the small business profits from the commercialization, which, in turn, stimulates the U.S. economy.

Qualifications for the Small Business Technology Transfer Program

Small businesses must meet these eligibility criteria to participate in the STTR program:

- They must be American-owned and independently operated.
- They must be for-profit businesses.
- The principal researcher need not be employed by the small business.
- The company size is limited to 500 employees.

Nonprofit research institutions also must meet certain eligibility criteria:

- They must be located in the United States.
- They must meet one of three definitions, being a
  - Nonprofit college or university
  - Domestic nonprofit research organization
  - Federally funded R&D center (FFRDC)
- There is no size limit for nonprofit research institutions.

STTR System

Each year five federal departments and agencies are required by STTR to reserve a portion of their R&D funds for award to small business/nonprofit research institution partnerships:

1. Department of Defense
2. Department of Energy
3. Department of Health and Human Services
4. National Aeronautics and Space Administration (NASA)
5. National Science Foundation

STTR's Three-Phase Program

Following submission of proposals, agencies make STTR awards based on small business/nonprofit research institution qualification, degree of innovation, and future market potential. Small businesses that receive awards or grants then begin a three-phase program.

- Phase I is the start-up phase. Awards of up to $100,000 for approximately one year fund the exploration of the scientific, technical, and commercial feasibility of an idea or technology.
- Phase II awards of up to $500,000—for as long as two years—expand on Phase I results. During this period, the R&D work is performed and the developer begins to consider commercial potential. Only Phase I award winners are considered for Phase II.
- Phase III is the period during which Phase II innovation moves from the laboratory into the marketplace. No STTR funds support this phase. The small business must find funding in the private sector or other non-STTR federal agency funding.

The U.S. Small Business Administration (SBA) helps the five agencies implement STTR, reviews their progress, and reports annually to Congress on STTR's operation. It also collects solicitation information from all the participating agencies and publishes it periodically in a Pre-Solicitation Announcement (PSA). The PSA is a single source for the topics and anticipated release and closing dates for each agency's solicitations.

For more information on the STTR Program, call (202) 205-6450 or visit the SBA Web site.

U.S. SMALL BUSINESS ADMINISTRATION LOAN PROGRAMS

The U.S. Small Business Administration was established as an independent federal agency created by Congress in 1953 to assist, counsel, and champion the efforts of American small business. Its mission is to provide perspective to new or established persons in small businesses with financial, procurement, management, and technical assistance. This mission is accomplished through a number of loan programs.

Small Business Administration Loan Guaranty Program

Any new business presents a considerable risk to a potential lender. An SBA guaranty can help the lender reduce the risk and approve a business loan that is based on a solid business plan, but perhaps is weak in other areas. Often the lender can extend a loan on more favorable terms with an SBA guaranty, thus improving cash flow and the likelihood of success for the business owner. SBA-guaranteed loans are made by private lenders, usually commercial banks, and are guaranteed up to 90 percent by the SBA. The largest loan guaranty program is the 7(a) program, named after the section of the Small Business Act that created it.

There are three principal parties to an SBA-guaranteed loan: the small business loan applicant, the lender, and the SBA. The lender plays the central role in the loan delivery system. To obtain an SBA-guaranteed loan, the applicant must submit a loan application to the lender, who performs the initial review and then, if the application is approved, forwards it—along with an analysis—to the SBA office with an application for a loan guaranty. Once approved by the SBA, the lender closes the loan and disburses the funds.

While businesses are encouraged to work with their bank or local lender for an SBA-guaranteed loan, some banks are designated by the SBA as Certified Lenders or Preferred Lenders because of the volume and quality of SBA loan applications they have completed.

The Certified Lender performs the complete processing of the loan application, subject to a review by the SBA. As a result, the turnaround time is much quicker; the total time from receipt of a completed loan application to the notification of the decision is usually no more than three working days. The Preferred Lenders' program is the ultimate designation given by the SBA to an active lender. The Preferred Lender has the authority to process and approve the loan, subject to a limited review by the SBA.

General Eligibility Requirements

The SBA defines a small business as one that is independently owned and operated, not dominant in its field, and meets employment or sales standards developed by the SBA. The general criteria used to determine whether a firm qualifies as a small business are:

- For wholesale operation: not more than 100 employees
- For retail or service operation: annual sales or receipts of not more than $5 million, depending on the particular industry
- For manufacturing operation: not more than 500 employees

SBA approval cannot be granted if the applicant is engaged in gambling or speculation or real estate held for sale or investment.

SBA loan guarantees may be granted for one or more of the following business purposes:

- To finance the purchase of land or buildings for new construction, or for the expansion or conversion of existing facilities
- To finance the purchase of equipment, machinery, supplies, materials, or inventory
- To supply working capital
- For short-term asset-based lines of credit

SBA Credit Requirements

To qualify for an SBA loan, the applicant must:

- Have sufficient capital in the business so that, when combined with the loan proceeds, he or she can operate on a sound financial basis.
- Show that the proposed loan us of sound value.
- Show that the past earnings records and/or future prospects of the company indicate an ability to replay the loan and other fixed debt, if any, out of profits.
- Be able to provide from his or her own resources sufficient funds to have a reasonable amount at stake to withstand possible losses, particularly during the early stages, if the venture is a new business.

Amount and Terms

The actual amount of the SBA's guaranty will vary with the intended loan proceeds. The maximum SBA share of any loan or guaranty usually will not exceed $750,000. The SBA guaranty on a loan of $155,000 or less is usually 90 percent. The SBA expects all loans to be repaid as rapidly as possible.

Generally, the maturity will vary with the proposed purpose of the loan: up to seven years for working capital; up to 10 years for machinery and equipment; and up to 25 years for purchase or construction of plant facilities. Repayment is usually on a monthly installment basis, principal and interest, although variations may be negotiated to meet seasonal cycles of business activity.

Interest rates on SBA-guaranteed loans are negotiated between the applicant and lender, based on the credit merits of the application. The SBA establishes a maximum that bankers may charge, depending on the maturity of the loan.

The time involved for the SBA to process a loan is related to the quality of the application received. If the loan package submitted to the SBA by the bank is complete, the SBA will usually have a decision to the bank within two weeks.

Collateral is not a prime consideration, but the SBA does require that all business assets be pledged to secure the loan. In addition, the personal guarantees of the principals, secured by specific personal assets, may be required. All owners of 20 percent or more must guarantee the loan personally.

SBA LOWDOC LOAN PROGRAM

In response to requests for a simplified process for smaller SBA loans, the SBA has instituted the LowDoc program for business loans up to $150,000. The goal of this program is to provide a rapid response from the SBA, usually 36 hours from when the lender submits a completed application, making small business financing faster and easier. The maximum LowDoc guaranty is 85 percent.

The LowDoc applicant must:

- Have a willingness to pay debts, as indicated by his or her credit history.
- Show historical or projected earnings with evidence of repayment ability.
- Demonstrate that the requested financing provides the business with a good chance of achieving success.
- Understand that the total outstanding balance of all SBA loans to one customer is limited to $150,000.
- Agree that all owners of 20 percent or more of the business will be required to personally guarantee the note.
- Be required to submit credit reports and personal financial statements for the business, the owners, and all guarantors.
- Use loan funds for normal business uses, such as working capital, debt payment, equipment, inventory purchases, construction, and real estate.
- Agree not to use loan funds for distribution to principals for payment of

personal debt. Credit card debt may be refinanced, but the debt must be business-related.

■ Show that the average number of employees for the preceding 12 months did not exceed 100 and that annual receipts over the previous three years averaged no more than $5 million.

SBA Certified Development Company 504 Loan Program

The Certified Development Company (CDC) Loan is a subordinated loan program designed to finance up to 40 percent of the fixed asset portion of a project cost, up to $1 million. Fifty percent of the financing is secured from a conventional first lender, usually a commercial bank. In certain instances, however, various other state programs can be used as a match to the 504 program. A business must provide at least 10 percent equity as an investment toward the project. Loan terms are very attractive in providing long-term fixed-rate financing for up to 25 years.

Acceptable collateral for the program includes land, buildings, machining equipment, lease-hold interests, and personal guarantees. The SBA CDC 504 program is available through certified development companies that provide long-term financing for fixed assets used by a specific small business. Businesses whose net worth does not exceed $7 million and whose profit after tax for the previous two years did not exceed $2.5 million are eligible for the program.

ASSET-BASED LENDING

Asset-based lending has been defined as making loans where collateral substitutes for a partial lack of creditworthiness. While this definition may conjure up visions of last-chance financing for troubled companies, it is not an accurate impression. Companies that benefit most from asset-based lending are financially healthy companies whose financing needs or ownership structure do not fit the traditional bank credit profile.

True asset-based financing began in the 1920s when two brothers who sold encyclopedias decided they could expand their business if they offered their customers financing for their purchases. From that humble beginning, asset-based financing grew to be the method of choice for the entrepreneurs and corporate raiders who engineered the megabuyouts of the 1980s. Asset-based lenders are still very active today. Many major banks have established or expanded their asset-based lending units to take advantage of the very attractive returns and the perceived safety of this type of lending.

Commercial banks supply the bulk of capital for small to-medium-size businesses. Bank regulations, bank size, and the bank's own asset/liability mix and management, among other factors, determine the types of services offered and the amount of risk an individual bank is willing to take. The bank's evaluation of how well the assets (collateral) would cover the loan outstanding if the borrower defaulted is the equalizing factor that determines the size and pricing of each loan.

Traditional institutional lenders usually focus on a company's cash flow and its balance sheet ratios when making the decision to extend credit. Financial statements are, by definition, a retrospective measure of the company. The traditional lender must, therefore, be conservative in how much and to which companies it makes loans.

Asset-based lenders also consider traditional credit evaluation methods. In contrast to traditional bank loans, though, asset-based financing permits a much higher level of funding. Credit approval focuses on collateral, management, and other resources available to the company, instead of solely on the borrower's financial statement position. Asset-based lending relationships are provided under a contract between the lender and the borrower. This contract normally covers a period of one to five years and is renewed automatically unless one or the parties cancels it.

Closely or privately held companies can benefit from the asset-based lender's reduced dependence on the company's financial ratios when evaluating a loan applicant. Asset-based lenders supplement their credit approval with the strength of the collateral's value and their ability to monitor it. The owners can thus maximize their current return from the business by maximizing distributions of the company's earnings and by substituting deductible interest expense for double taxation of dividends.

Costs of Asset-Based Lending

The two major differences between traditional bank loans and asset-based loans are the somewhat higher stated interest rates and the borrower's additional financial reporting to the lender required in asset-based loans. The stated or contract interest rate can be as much as 1 to 2 percent higher than on a traditional bank line of credit. However, the differential has shrunk dramatically in recent years, as more competitors have entered the market.

Also, in an asset-based loan contract, the stated interest rate is not always an indicator of the true cost. One reason is that the asset-based borrower only takes down the amount of loan actually needed at that time. Because all of the company's cash is collected in a lockbox and is immediately applied to reduce the loan balance, the outstanding amount tends to average significantly less than a traditional credit line. A lower loan balance results in lower average interest cost on an annual basis, even at a higher rate.

Asset-based lenders usually require the borrowers to report sales, credits, and collections to the lender at least once a week and to report inventory levels at least monthly. Traditional lenders do not require this extra step.

The increased borrowing capacity and flexibility of an asset-based lending relationship may well offset this necessary evil.

Certain emerging technology companies can benefit from asset-based lending, while others whose businesses are new and unproved may not be attractive to the asset-based lender. Asset-based loans usually are not more expensive than traditional loans. In fact, considering the flexibility they afford and the additional profit opportunities they can open up, such loans actually may be a relatively inexpensive form of capital.

LEASING AS A SOURCE OF FINANCING

A lease allows a user of equipment (the lessee) to use an asset without actually purchasing it. The lessee makes regular payments throughout the life of the lease and, at its conclusion, may have the option to:

- Renew the lease
- Purchase the equipment at a fair market value
- Return the equipment to the lender
- Purchase the equipment for a nominal amount

Leases can be obtained from many sources, including banks, leasing companies, equipment manufacturers, and other companies within the same industry (i.e., high tech or biotechnology).

Leasing is, basically, a form of secured lending. Since the lessor retains actual title of the asset, he or she may provide most or all of the funds a company needs to secure the use of the asset. Commonly leased assets include computer systems; laboratory, manufacturing, and office equipment; and real estate.

Leasing is generally more expensive than general debt, but for small or growing businesses, the cost of leasing may be offset by several benefits:

- Leasing requires little or no cash up front.
- Credit approval is frequently less stringent.
- The payments may be less than the amount needed to fully amortize the debt, so periodic payments may be lower.

Leasing is available for companies at all stages of development, although the maturity of the company may affect the terms of the lease. Personal guarantees may be required for small or "immature" businesses.

There are two classes of leases, depending on the lessee's option at the end of the term of the lease: the financial lease and the tax-oriented operating lease. In a finance lease, the lessee has the option to purchase the equipment for a nominal fee (e.g., $1 or $100) at the end of the lease. The tax-oriented lease, or fair market purchase option, provides for lower monthly payments over the lease term. This lease is commonly used when the lessee expects to replace the equipment (e.g., with a newer model) at the end of the lease term. Because finance and tax-oriented leases are handled differently for accounting purposes, an accountant or financial advisor is the best source of information to help determine which type of lease is best for any given situation.

STATE-SUPPORTED VENTURE CAPITAL PROGRAMS

Until 1980 only a few states had adopted programs providing assistance for start-up ventures. Since then, encouraged by the obvious advantages that can be brought to their states through an active program, many states followed the pioneering examples of California and Massachusetts and created their own programs. By 1996 over 25 states had established or were considering the adoption of some form of state-sponsored venture. Today more than half of the states have established or are considering the adoption of some form of state-sponsored venture.

State agencies may seek a variety of structures in pursuing investments in early-stage technology companies. Although the state's objective is typically the assistance of business development within that state, the state program must include an element of self-funding. In other words, administrators still expect investments that will create a return so that they can continue to make additional investments.

These programs employ a multitude of vehicles, depending on the creativity of the venture capitalists who are administering the programs and the complexity of the companies in which the programs will be investing. Typically, a company seeking investment from the state will be presented with several agreements: a security purchase agreement, a registration rights agreement, a warrant agreement (to the extent that warrants may accompany the investment), and/or a note or loan agreement. In addition, the company may have to file a certificate of designation with the secretary of the state of incorporation, which sets forth rights and preferences of any preferred stock that is being used.

A state that invests in preferred stock would use this method to establish an instrument that provides it with influence through voting control over many of the corporate activities of the investee company, including restrictions on the sale of assets, issuance of additional securities, and incurrence of debt. As with involving venture capitalists, these restrictions can impact substantially more activities than a company may wish others to have control over.

The shareholders' agreement establishes methods by which the agency as well as current management and other investors may dispose of their securities in the future. This agreement may involve rights of first refusal for sales by management, by employees, or by other investors, and it might provide the state agency with the right to make any such acquisitions or to control such dispositions. In addition, the shareholders' agreement could be used to protect the company's founders and management from activities by other stockholders and by state agencies that might jeopardize their position in the company.

State fund managers, because of their declared intention of maximizing the development of local, regional, and state companies, would appear to be less restrictive in connection with their approach to documentation for an investment than venture capitalists might be. Whereas venture capitalists often might seek to take active positions on the board of directors and actively participate in much of the management of the company, state venture capital corporations have not shown as much of a desire for control. However, they usually contribute much less money than private venture capital funds.

Like venture capital funds, these state funds also must justify their existence and will be seeking a quality return. In preparing to meet with state authorities, it is important for entrepreneurs to remember the particular goals of the state authorities and to shape their presentations accordingly. The Massachusetts Technology Development Corporation, for example, receives close to 200 business plans each year. Out of those 200 plans, only 6 or 8 companies will receive funding. Therefore, it makes sense to spend a lot of time adjusting the company's business plan to address the issues that are important to the particular state program. In this example, a Massachusetts-based company's business plan should clearly establish that, besides having significant growth prospects for employment, the company has been unable to finance expansion from conventional sources.

In addition, it is prudent to pay attention to corporate housekeeping. When it comes time to set up an investment, even a state authority often pays a great deal of attention to the details of corporate structure. Before approaching a state agency, a company should consider:

- The structure of the corporation
- Its corporate minute books and stock records
- The composition of the board of directors
- Stockholder agreements that may be in place with other founders
- Employment agreements with management; any combinations with affiliated companies
- Stock option plans, debt and lease agreements
- Confidentiality agreements with scientists and with other venture partners

State venture capital funds present an opportunity for states to facilitate the growth of high-technology companies within their borders. Over half the states in the country have adopted some form of program with varying degrees of success. A well-structured venture capital program, when coordinated with other state efforts, can be a very effective source of capital for a fledgling company. More important, many private venture capital investment sources seek advice and leads from these state agencies and often follow on with more substantial investments.

STATE VENTURE CAPITAL PROGRAMS

Massachusetts Technology Development Corporation

Massachusetts was one of the first states to actively encourage the growth and finance of technology companies. The state created the Massachusetts Technology Development Company (MTDC) in 1978 to facilitate venture capital investments in its state. As a leading-edge venture capital firm that fills the financing gap for start-up and expansion-stage technology companies, MTDC has functioned as a model for other states over the years in the creation of technology development programs.

The development corporation was created with $3 million from the state economic development administration and $1 million from state contributions, and additional state grants were made through 1988. Since then the MTDC has been completely self-funding, covering its operating costs and the cost for investing in additional companies from its internal return.

The stated goal of the development corporation is to act as a catalyst for funding, rather than to focus on maximizing total returns. This is a welcome relief from venture capital investors and investment bankers who seem to put a lot of pressure on the boards of directors of companies that accept funding.

The established criteria for investments seem to be paralleled by other states in the union. To qualify for funding, a company must:

- Be technology based
- Be located in the state
- Present significant growth prospects for employment
- Demonstrate that it has been unable to finance its expansion from conventional sources
- Be able to show a high rate of return on the funds invested in the enterprise to date

Initial investments in Massachusetts are typically between $250,000 and $500,000, determined by the capital needs of the firm and the investment of its co-investors. While investments are made primarily as equity (where MTDC purchases preferred or common stock in the company), investments have taken several forms, including debt, promissory notes, warrants, or combinations of all of these. Debt, when included as part of the financing package, is often unsecured.

The MTDC has reported throughout its entire history that its internal rate of return, at least through 1995, has been in excess of 15 percent per year. On a very interesting note, unlike private venture capital firms that distribute their profit to investors, the development corporation reinvests its profits into more companies. From 1980 through June 2001, the MTDC's cumulative investments from all of its programs totaled more than $57 million in 109 companies, creating 11,200 jobs and adding more than $620 million to the annual payroll.

While the MTDC receives over 200 business plans for companies every year, the corporation's administrators project that many more companies are eligible to receive venture capital investments from the state. For more information about the MTDC, visit the Web site www.mtdc.com.

Connecticut Innovations

Created by the state legislature in 1989, Connecticut Innovations (CI) has a mission to grow the state's entrepreneurial technology economy by making venture and other investments. CI believes that by building a vibrant technology community, it can create substantial, long-term economic opportunities for the citizens of the state.

Connecticut Innovations was originally funded by state bonding, but since 1995 has financed its equity investment solely through its own investment returns. For more than seven years, CI has become the state's leading investor in high-technology companies, with total investments of more than $56 million in 51 Connecticut firms.

To be eligible for CI support, companies must be able to:

- Demonstrate that they can build a rapid-growth emerging company with a sustainable competitive advantage founded in technology or technological expertise
- Show that the venture has the potential to capture a sizable share of a growing market
- Demonstrate the strength and appropriateness of the management team
- Have headquarters, key technology foundations, and a majority of operations in the state
- Have a growing employee presence in the state
- Have the ability to obtain funds from other investors

CI's support goes beyond dollars and cents. Companies that receive funding from CI can expect to receive ongoing help in various ways, from board attendance, to advice on business and financial strategies and introductions to potential investors and partners. For more information about Connecticut Innovations, visit the Web site at www.citinnovations.com.

New Jersey Economic Development Authority

The New Jersey Economic Development Authority (NJEDA) has a mission to make it easier and cheaper for companies and nonprofits to get the capital they need to invest and expand in New Jersey. Building on the relationships that companies—from start-ups to Fortune 500 corporations—have with their banks or other lenders, the NJEDA has over 20 different programs to choose from.

The NJEDA is a self-supporting, independent state financing and development agency. Since 1974 it has provided more than $15 billion to eligible businesses and nonprofit groups. The agency works with companies of all sizes and types and has assisted more than 7,500 manufacturers, distributors, service providers, retailers, high-tech companies, and not-for-profit groups.

Help is extended in a number of ways. The NJEDA will arrange low-interest financing, loan guarantees, tax incentives, and creative financing packages to increase access to capital for small to-midsize businesses and not-for-profit agencies. In addition, it offers a full range of real estate development services and technical support to strengthen the targeted business sectors that are important to the state's economy. For more information about NJEDA, visit the Web site at www.njeda.com.

New Jersey has a range of funding resources that are of interest to high-tech and biotechnology companies. The following examples are representative.

Edison Venture Finance Fund   This fund makes investments in emerging technology businesses in the mid-Atlantic states, including New Jersey. The fund has committed to target one-third of its venture capital to New Jersey-based businesses. The NJEDA has invested in the fund and often refers quality high-tech companies to it for financing. For more information, visit www.njbrc.org.

New Jersey Seed Capital Program   This loan program, offered by the NJEDA, recognizes that many cash-poor R&D and emerging-technology companies cannot obtain capital from traditional sources. The New Jersey Seed Capital Program offers loans from $25,000 to $500,000 to technology enterprises in New Jersey that have established an emerging technology and need capital to bring their product to market. Loans are offered at a market rate and can be used for both working capital to meet day-to-day expenses and for fixed assets, such as buildings and equipment. For more information, visit the NJEDA Web site at www.njeda.com.

New Jersey Technology Funding Program   A partnership between the NJEDA and area banks, this program is designed to bridge the financing gaps in the availability of expansion capital for growing, second-stage technology-based companies in the state of New Jersey. The NJEDA leverages its funds with bank financing to make term loans available in the range of $100,000 to $5 million. Eligible companies are those that:

- Have received venture capital, other investor financing and/or are raising funds through an initial public offering or private placement

- Received or are close to receiving regulatory approval, if applicable
- Have licensing arrangements with or are selling to established companies
- Have historic financial statements showing limited cash flow or profitability
- Have reasonable forecasts of profits/cash flow to reach key milestones
- Have a detailed business plan

For more information, visit the NJEDA Web site at www.njeda.com.

New Jersey Technology Council Venture Fund   The New Jersey Technology Council (NJTC)Venture Fund addresses the critical need of the state's emerging high-tech companies for financial support. The fund typically invests between $300,000 and $3 million in private high-tech growth companies in the seed, start-up, and early stages. It funds focused businesses with the potential to dominate a promising market niche.

NJTC capital is raised from corporations, public and private funds, partnerships, and individuals. It currently has commitments of nearly $30 million, which is leveraged with a $10 million NJEDA loan. The fund also has a network of strong relationships with other venture capitalists, bankers, lenders, and institutional and foreign investors. To learn more about the fund, visit the Web site at www.njtcvc.com/.

New York Venture Capital Investment Program

The New York Capital Investment Program (NYCIP) was established in November 1999 in conjunction with the state's Job 2000 Act. The program's primary objective is to provide significant investment returns for the fund while providing a source of capital for privately owned businesses that wish to expand within New York State. The NYCIP is part of the New York State Common Retirement Fund (CRF), the second largest pension fund in the country, and has selected three firms to manage the program:

1. FA Technology Ventures, part of First Albany Companies, which brings a $50 million commitment from the CRF, with the partnership expecting to total $125 million
2. Exponential Business Development Corporation, which brings a $20 million commitment from the CRF, with the partnership expecting to total $50 million
3. Summer Street Capital partners, which brings a $30 million commitment from the CRF, with the partnership expecting to total $105 million

This venture capital commitment is part of the $250 million Venture Capital Program initiated by then New York State comptroller H. Carl McCall to increase venture capital and business development funding for high-growth and high-technology companies in the state. The NYCIP will invest in a variety of industries through its managers, including manufacturing, software,

---

WHY NYCIP?

- In 1999 venture capital investments totaled $35.6 billion in the United States.

- Companies in New York State received only 5 percent ($1.8 billion) of this pool, while California's Silicon Valley received 37.7 percent ($13.4 billion).

- Companies located in New York City received $1.5 billion in venture investments—80 percent of the total for the state.

- Upstate New York investments in 1999 totaled a little more than $200 million—less than 1 percent of the national total.

Source: New York State Comptroller's Office press release, August 2000.

---

networked communications, information technology, telecommunications, and more. While New York City's "Silicon Alley" received a significant amount of venture capital attention and funding in the mid to late 1990s, New York State overall—especially upstate New York—has not received the attention it needs or deserves. The NYCIP intends to remedy that situation.

Investments will be made to allow businesses to conduct their operations within the borders of New York State. Businesses that have their headquarters in New York are eligible for investments to expand their operations. Businesses located outside of the state are eligible if the investment will be used to establish a presence in the state. For more information about the NYCIP, visit the Web site at www.osc.state.ny/us.

NOTES

[1] Terry Bibbens, Fred A. Tarpley, Jr., Ph.D., and Gregory J. Dean, Esq., "The Process and Analysis Behind Ace-Net," published October 1996 on the Small Business Administration Office of Advocacy Web site: www.sbaonline.sba.gov/ADVO/acenet/.

[2] Freear, Sohl, and Wetzel, "Creating New Capital Markets for Emerging Ventures," June 1996, Center for Venture Research, Whittemore School of Business and Economics, University of New Hampshire, Durham, NH. SBA Office of Advocacy contract SBAHQ-95-M-1062.

[3] Bibbens, Tarpley, and Dean, "The Process and Analysis Behind Ace-Net."

[4] "Next Wave 100: Emerging Leaders of the New Economy," published on the Next Wave Stocks, Web site: www.nextwavestocks.com/angeldirectory.html.

[5] Ibid.

[6] "What Is ACE-Net?" published on the ACE-Net Web site, http://ace-net.sr.unh.edu/pub/wel/whatis.htm.

[7] "The SBIR Program," published by the U.S. Small Business Administration on its Web site: www.sabonline.sba.gov/SBIR.

CHAPTER **6**

Strategic Alliances and Corporate Partnerships

Any high-tech company, in order to be successful, must partner with the powerful giants in the industry.

—Jack Nelson, Chairman of the Board and CEO,
Advanced NMR Systems, Inc. (now Caprius, Inc.)

There is a desert that biotech companies have to cross over in drug discovery and development, and they need lots of camels and water sacks to get across. Partnership provides that.

—Charles M. Hartman, General Partner, CW Group, Inc.

NEED FOR CORPORATE PARTNERING

Intensified competition for capital from traditional financing sources such as venture capitalists and lending institutions has led entrepreneurial companies in recent years to seek creative strategies to satisfy their financing requirements. One highly effective capital-raising strategy for young technology companies is to form collaborative relationships with other companies. With the right partner and careful planning from the outset, emerging technology companies can gain access to the capital, markets, and relationships needed to grow their businesses.

The evolution of the global economy and downsizing by larger, more prominent corporations have greatly expanded the opportunities available for strategic relationships between businesses in need of technology and innovative ideas and businesses with the technology and ideas. Indeed, many large corporations are increasingly looking to a portfolio of independent companies to replace the technical and innovative resources lost in cutbacks in research and development (R&D). The larger corporate partner benefits from the R&D efforts of the company, as well as from eventual licensing or production rights when the technology is commercialized.

Although commonly referred to as corporate "partnerships," these arrangements are not partnerships in the legal sense. *Business partnerships*, *strategic alliances*, and *corporate partnering relationships* are terms used to refer to a wide variety of collaborative business relationships between companies. They are usually contractual working relationships with specific rights granted to both parties (see Exhibit 6.1).

Their popularity is driven by the flexibility they offer in defining the scope, terms, and duration of the alliance. Thus the forms of intercompany relationships vary widely. Partnering relationships must be determined based on the technology involved and each company's needs. Generally, these relationships can be broken into three categories:

1. At one end of the spectrum is the *simple contractual agreement*. Such relationships tend to have a relatively short-term focus and usually are designed to achieve a single purpose of task. The typical licensing arrangement, in which an owner of existing technology permits another to exploit such technology for a given purpose in exchange for royalty payments, is an example of such a relationship.

2. In the middle of this spectrum are *cooperative contractual relationships*, such as R&D contracts, technology transfer agreements, and contract manufacturing agreements. A biotech company's collaboration with a pharmaceutical company partner often entails research funding for drug

EXHIBIT 6.1   Growth of New Biotech/Large Pharmaceutical Collaborations

Year	Number of Collaborations
1993	69
1994	117
1995	165
1996	180
1997	228
1998	224
1999	229
2000	373
2001	425

Source: BioWorld Financial Watch, American Health Consultants, BioCentury.

discovery and grants the partner specific product development rights for discoveries with commercial potential. In a distribution/delivery agreement, a high-tech company with a new Internet service, for example, may partner with a telecommunications company that has expertise in delivering information or with a computer manufacturer that can create access devices.

3. At the other end of the spectrum lies the intimate relationship in which companies agree to join forces through the formation of a *joint venture*. Joint ventures are typically long-term commitments. The participants seek to capitalize on the respective strengths and competitive advantages of each other, in the hope of achieving synergies and growth not otherwise attainable independently. The most complex joint venture involves an arrangement whereby two or more companies form a separate entity into which they pool their expertise and resources to develop and market a particular technology.

As varied as corporate partnering arrangements may be, they all involve common issues that, with careful planning at the beginning of the relationship, must be resolved if the goals originally envisioned are to be attained. These issues include:

- Defining the scope of the relationship
- Exit strategies
- Technology ownership
- Depending on the comprehensiveness of the relationship, ownership and control, management, and governance

How these issues are resolved is largely a function of negotiation. Each party needs to understand clearly its own, as well as the other party's, motivations for the collaboration. When the parties' respective bargaining positions are roughly equal, an understanding of these motivations prior to forming the relationship is of paramount importance in identifying potential areas of conflict. Early identification of such conflicts provides the future partners with an opportunity for resolution before an irreconcilable division cripples—and ultimately causes the failure of—the collaborative effort. Of course, all of this requires open and honest communications between the parties and the absence of hidden agendas.

THE RIGHT PARTNER PROVIDES MORE THAN JUST MONEY

Companies pursue corporate collaborations for a variety of reasons, including to:

- Obtain access to other technologies
- Finance activities

- Enter into new markets
- Spread the risks involved with research and product development

Whatever the specific reason, companies enter into partnering relationships because they believe that the combination of their strengths and the synergies to be achieved by the collaboration are greater than the sum of their respective parts.

Indeed, the more complex partnering arrangements require a long-term commitment by each party to the venture and to each other, because they require far greater resources to establish, nurture, and maintain it. If well conceived, properly structured, and documented from the outset, a corporate partnership can provide greater opportunities not attainable by either of the companies independently.

In addition to providing capital and resources, corporate partnerships provide a means of continuous learning for each company, which is often why they were attracted to each other originally. Each can learn from and apply the strengths of the other in the operation of its own business. Moreover, through the joint venture and other partner, each can establish valuable business relationships with other potential customers and suppliers, as well as with the associations and governmental and regulatory institutions that affect their markets. Relationships, as much as capital and resources, serve as catalysts for growth. The ability of the potential partner to initiate and foster such relationships is a key factor in the overall partner selection process.

SELECTING THE RIGHT PARTNER

No matter how carefully the parties structure the relationship, however, the venture is doomed to failure if the wrong partner is selected. Each prospective partner needs to have assessed its company's economic objectives and analyzed the capability of the other party to satisfy those objectives. An emerging company in need of financing will want to be sure that its partner possesses not only the financial wherewithal, but also the commitment, to fill that need. Evaluating the relationship from the perspective of the other party, as well as the economic objectives that it seeks to accomplish, can be very helpful in making the venture work when the inevitable dispute arises between the partners.

Each party also needs to understand its philosophy toward business relative to the other's. The extent to which each party's company culture, values, risk-tolerance, management, and decision-making processes are compatible is a good indicator of the likelihood of the success of the collaborative effort. The operational and cultural differences between a small company and its larger counterpart can be as wide as those between a company based in the United States and its foreign counterpart. Each has its own language, customs, and political structures. Parties committed to a successful relationship strive to learn these differences and incorporate the best of them into the partnership, both at the formation stage and throughout its evolution.

Most important, perhaps, are the human dynamics underlying all of the issues discussed. The ability of the people involved in the effort to get along is critical to success. To promote a willingness to work together, each of the parties must continually strive to foster an environment of trust and mutual respect.

CORPORATE PARTNERSHIPS AND FINANCING STRATEGY

Start-up technology companies tend to follow one of two basic financing strategies. Each strategy incorporates corporate partnerships as a means both to raise capital and to assure potential investors that its technology is commercially viable. In the first model, the company's financing strategy leads to an initial public offering (IPO). The company starts with venture seed financing, followed by several venture capital rounds, an infusion of capital from one or more corporate partnerships, and then may include a mezzanine or bridge financing before approaching the public market through an IPO (see Exhibit 6.2).

An alternative financing strategy, which offers a different exit strategy for investors, bypasses venture capital. The company obtains its seed money through a private line (an increasing number of large corporations are providing venture financing to promising technology start-ups), then moves on to multiple corporate partnerships. Under this financing strategy, a company receives small, early-stage funding, confirms the commercial value of its technology, receives capital infusions through one or more corporate partnerships, and then approaches the public market or is sold (see Exhibit 6.3).

Under either strategy, obtaining at least one equity infusion from a major, established corporation is the last, crucial step before the public offering or sale that provides a return on investment for the company's founders and early investors.

During financing droughts when the public market shies away from

EXHIBIT 6.2   Typical Emerging Company Financing Strategy

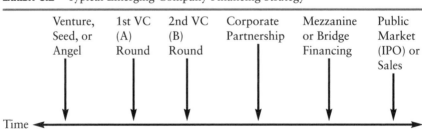

EXHIBIT 6.3 Alternate Emerging Company Financing Strategy

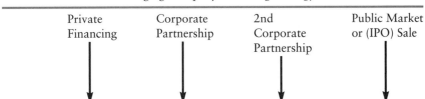

highly volatile industries such as high-tech or biotech, partnering becomes especially important—the very survival of the company may depend on cash infusions through one or more successful partnering arrangements. When large amounts of capital are available, partnering becomes more of a strategic or operational issue. Under either circumstance, in today's world many investors see a well-articulated partnering strategy as an absolute necessity for emerging high-tech and biotech companies.

PARTNERING: THE TECHNOLOGY COMPANY'S VIEWPOINT

Corporate partnering offers many advantages for the emerging company. First and foremost, a corporate partner can be a key source of the capital needed to fund the process of discovering new technologies and developing them into viable consumer products. Second, and equally important, is that corporate partners provide a kind of endorsement, or validation, for the breakthrough technology or service under development. In most cases, both venture capital investors and investment bankers look to corporate partnerships as confirmation of the commercial potential for the company it is supporting. For these reasons, a clearly defined partnering strategy is virtually required for companies working on the frontiers of science and technology.

> *Our company is developing a product that will help link business-application software from different vendors. Our investors include 15 top executives from these vendors.*
>
> *Their insights about the market, what works and what doesn't work, and their daily contacts with customers are priceless. No other set of investors or venture capitalists would match this knowledge base.*

—Katrina Garnett, Founder and CEO, CrossRoads Software, Inc.[1]

Corporate partners bring more to the table than a large sum of money. The larger company can give the start-up or emerging technology company a competitive advantage over unpartnered competitors. As previously mentioned, in addition to a knowledge base, a corporate partner also may provide:

■ *Validation.* A partnership arrangement helps validate the company, particularly in the eyes of the financial community. A "no-name" start-up that is linked to the name of an industry leader wraps the start-up in the leader's cloak of credibility.

■ *Access to infrastructure, expertise, and information.* Large, established companies have organizational resources, market knowledge, and an established customer base and distribution system. The high-tech or biotech company able to tap into those resources can advance its product development programs in substantial ways.

■ *Access to markets.* Eventually, once there is a product to sell, the larger company has the organization in place to market, distribute, and sell it.

■ *A boon to investors.* The investment community responds positively when an emerging company announces partnering arrangements, because the corporate partner will have performed due diligence on the company's technology.

■ *A competitive advantage.* Forming an alliance with one company can preclude the larger corporation from forming an alliance with other. When a corporate partner with an equity investment stands to gain financially from its stake in one emerging technology, it will not invest in a competing technology. A strong corporate partnership raises a barrier to entry for any other start-up wishing to explore the same or similar technologies.

Corporate partnerships often increase the value of the emerging company and the money that can be raised in the IPO by establishing validation in the eyes of the market as well as establishing a valuation measuring point.

But entering into a corporate partnership also has its disadvantages. In order to receive the capital and other benefits that accrue from a corporate partner, the smaller company must make certain concessions, which often include:

■ *Loss of future profits.* In order to secure short-term financing, the technology company may have to share future profits with its corporate partner.

■ *Loss of autonomy.* A technology company that agrees to a corporate partnership should expect to relinquish some of its independence. Depending on the size of the larger partner's investment, the company may find its operations and budget now come under the watchful eye of its larger partner, which sees itself as having an ownership position in the company. This means the partner will want to know a great deal about the smaller company's operations and may try to influence or participate in management decisions.

■ *The complexity of balancing multiple partner arrangements.* Partnership arrangements can be difficult and complex to negotiate and subsequently manage. Senior management may find it necessary to assign a full-time business development person to manage these relationships and the sometimes-competing interests of multiple corporate partners.

If the interests of the company subsequently diverge from the interests of any of its corporate partners, the dissolution of the partnership can be just as difficult and complex as its creation. When considering the benefits of forming a corporate partnership, management needs to consider what will happen when its partner leaves. How will issues of intellectual property and ownership be addressed? The agreement should specify exactly who will hold exclusive rights to use all of the data and information generated by either partner, and what events (e.g., if program funding stops) will trigger the return of all material from the corporate partner. Consideration also should be given to the fact that the corporate partner that walks away will become a disinterested investor holding significant ownership in the technology company.

PARTNERING STRATEGIES

The high-tech or biotech company considering a corporate partnership must consider an overall partnering strategy. In fact, some corporate partners will not even consider partnering arrangements unless the smaller company has a clearly defined partnering strategy.

Corporate partnering can be incorporated into a company's business strategy in various ways. The two most common are: (1) commercializing totally through partnering, i.e., a royalty approach, and (2) a hybrid strategy that combines partnering with internally commercializing proprietary products through one or more partnering agreements. Any partnering arrangement, including these approaches, must be tailored to a company's needs and objectives, and the structure of the partnering agreement must be compatible with the company's management and decision-making style.

Commercializing through Partnering

Companies with a broad technology platform or drug discovery platform have the opportunity to develop a path to commercialization through multiple partnering deals. Under this strategy, the company licenses out its technology across diverse large-market products, which will be produced and marketed by their partners. Until the royalty stream begins to flow, the corporate partner's cash infusions help the development company fund its R&D costs and build its technology discovery infrastructure.

Hybrid Strategy

A company that adopts a hybrid strategy combines partnering with developing its own products. Development agreements with partners, or outlicensing to them, are important sources of funding for a company that has not yet commercialized its own products. A partner that dominates its market also can help the smaller company partner gain entry into that market.

Commercialization through multiple partnering has advantages during the early stages of a company's growth, but has significant disadvantages once the company has reached a certain size. A company that relies solely on partnering and royalties for its income stream ultimately have not been rewarded on a price-equity basis.

Companies that use a hybrid strategy seek to alleviate this shortcoming by developing their own products and selectively retaining rights to market niche areas. For example, in the biotech industry, Genentech used this strategy early on, partnering insulin, growth hormone, and other products on a global basis, while simultaneously building its own marketing organization in critical care and medicine.

PARTNERING: THE CORPORATE PARTNER'S VIEWPOINT

To structure and negotiate a partnership arrangement successfully, it is important for the emerging company to understand what corporate partners look for in a partnering arrangement and why these arrangements are almost as important to the corporate partner as they are to the emerging company.

For large companies, partnering with a discovery company has become a price of entry into advanced technological fields. As consolidation occurs within the high-tech and biotech fields, the pressure to do more partnering will only intensify. There are many reasons why large companies need these partnering arrangements, including:

- *Access to technology.* A large company may have a thin product pipeline, which means it needs access to emerging technologies. For example, in the pharmaceutical industry, the current thinking is that large drug companies must drive at least three new chemical entities through their pipeline each year. Large companies are always looking for "blockbusters," which typically come from the research laboratories of smaller, innovative companies.

- *Access to talent.* Although they might not admit it, big corporations want access to the type of talent that typically gravitates toward smaller, entrepreneurial companies. It is difficult for large companies to recruit—and retain—people with an entrepreneurial bent, including those from academic environments, that small companies can attract. Large companies usually cannot offer the motivators that many of the most talented, creative people seek—namely, a flatter organizational structure that allows greater independence and the promise of large financial rewards through an eventual IPO. A research partnership with a smaller company is a direct route to tapping the intellectual assets of these people.

■ *Stronger balance sheet.* Partnering can be a way for the corporate partner to strengthen its balance sheet. Research and development costs funded internally must be expensed, whereas an equity investment in a discovery company can, subject to impairment rules under generally accepted accounting principles (GAAP), be capitalized. For the corporate partner, this is a very significant distinction.

One factor that should influence the partnering process is the success of some existing older partnerships. Corporations are beginning to see significant returns on their investments, which senior executives at large corporations are now using as a motivator for getting equity in a partnering arrangement.

Equity versus Nonequity

Partnership profiles differ. It is important to understand where the large partner is coming from—or, more specifically, where its money is coming from. As mentioned previously, the corporate partner either can make an equity investment in the smaller company—which is capitalized as an asset—or it can divert some of its R&D money to the company—which is recorded as an expense on the corporate partner's books. Thesource of the money within the corporate partner is important, because it shapes the negotiating process.

PARTNERING ARRANGEMENTS: A CAVEAT

Although large companies are strongly motivated to enter into partnering arrangements, the number of these alliances may decrease in the future. Two factors can push alliances aside.

1. Large corporations are rapidly internalizing many of the new technologies that are the lifeblood of discovery of development companies, particularly in the pharmaceutical/biotech industry. This poses a significant problem for smaller organizations: How are they going to compete not only against companies their size, but also against the potential corporate partner?

2. Large companies' partnering strategies must consider the ideal number of partnerships that can be managed at any given time. Unless the decision is made to allocate the additional capital, as well as personnel, needed to manage more partnerships, there will be increasing competition among early-stage companies for their share of the partnership deals available in the future.

In the case where the corporate partner will record the transaction as an expense, the emerging company needs to identify a corporate champion, someone who will stand up for the technology company in front of senior management, explaining why the large corporation should cut into its own research budget and give another company that cash. The champion must explain why he or she believes this outsourcing approach to R&D is worthwhile. Additionally, the champion must continue to work behind the scenes within the corporation, helping to keep negotiations moving forward through the successive layers of management involved in the approval process.

Conversely, if a company makes an equity investment, it becomes a part owner of the emerging company and expects to receive a return on its investment. Furthermore, the company probably will take the initial investment out of future funding or arrange for some other trade-off downstream. So, while the early-stage company might receive significant equity up front, it will get less and less R&D expenditures in the future.

One thing to consider in this profit and loss versus balance sheet trade-off is the relative money supply. While even a large corporation's research budget has its limits, the corporate side—that is, the possibility for equity investments—potentially is much less restrained. A huge amount of money is sitting in the balance sheets of major companies around the world, and small technology companies need to focus on tapping into that pool of funds.

Senior management of the small technology company, their accountants, and their advisors can serve a valuable function in helping larger corporations understand how to tap their balance sheets more effectively to do deals. Many deals are never completed because the money has to come out of the corporate partner's R&D budget. Shifting R&D money away from the corporation's own researchers can create tension within the large organization. Another barrier to entering into partnering arrangements occurs when the corporation's management suffers from the "not invented here" syndrome, in which they devalue the work of outside (or competing) researchers or innovators.

Other Considerations

Let's say a venture capitalist finances three guys out of Stanford in some area of research. The other venture capitalists find out about it and go up to the University of California at San Francisco and find different guys in the same area. The venture capitalists in Boston run down to Harvard and find the guys there. Someone else does it at Johns Hopkins. Then San Diego. Pretty soon you've got five biotech companies attacking the same area.

—Sanford Robertson, Chairman, Robertson Stephens & Co.[2]

One other important point the development-stage company must consider is whether the corporate partner is genuinely interested in obtaining a competitive advantage or has merely fallen victim to the me-too syndrome, as described by Sanford Robertson.

The corporate partner should be playing, first and foremost, to build or strengthen its competitive advantage. The need to achieve competitive advantage is a primary motivator for the large corporate partner, and that competitive pressure is behind the me-too syndrome. Once a major deal has been struck in the industry, very frequently other players want to get on the bandwagon. Suddenly there is high-level corporate interest in doing a deal, sometimes with little understanding of why they are seeking one, except that a deal must be done to keep up with the competitors.

When a discovery company negotiates its equity investment, management should think about what is really driving the corporate partner. Is it truly the competitive advantage they are looking for? Or is senior management mainly interested in demonstrating to their own organization that they are dealmakers? If the latter is the case, the smaller company could find itself in a pretty flimsy partnership that its corporate partner's management will not be sufficiently committed to.

LICENSING—REALIZING THE TECHNOLOGY'S VALUE

Licensing involves the grant to another of the right to exploit technology in exchange for royalty payments. A licensing strategy may prove to be very beneficial to both early-stage and well-established companies—but there are pitfalls to watch out for, as well.

Advantages of Licensing

- Licensing is relatively inexpensive to the licensor and is of comparatively low risk to the licensee. This is because the licensor has already made the initial investment in developing the technology and will not need to invest capital in manufacturing or distributing capacity for products.
- For the licensee, royalty payments spread the cost over the life of the product and reduce the requirement of significant up-front investment with reasonable assurance of a favorable outcome. In addition, an established company can select among various potential partners' technologies at various stages of development and commercialization and avoid being locked into its own, perhaps less advantageous, technology.
- Licensing provides the licensor with an immediate cash flow, depending on how the royalty payments are structured.
- A properly structured license from the licensor's perspective also permits the licensor to retain ownership and control of the technology and any improvements that may be made by either the licensor or the

licensee while, at the sane time, providing the licensee what it needs to commercialize the product.

■ A licensing strategy permits a relationship that provides the necessary capital and resources of others with minimum involvement of the parties in each other's corporate affairs.

Disadvantages of Licensing

■ Because a licensor typically is not manufacturing or distributing the products sold, it has little practical day-to-day control over either the amount of effort made by the licensee in selling products or the quality of the products sold. Thus the licensor is well advised to incorporate performance standards, minimum royalties, and complete quality control requirements in the licensing agreement. Doing so will allow the licensor to terminate the agreement, should the licensee fail to achieve the intended performance.

■ Licensees also generally require the licensor's grant of exclusive rights to exploit the technology in defined geographic territories or product markets. Licensing agreements, therefore, have the potential to keep the licensor out of a potential market. To reduce the risk, the licensor should seek to define both the geographic reach and scope of products covered by the license as narrowly as necessary to achieve its business objectives.

An emerging company with valuable technology but insufficient manufacturing or distribution resources to exploit it efficiently can use licensing to raise needed financing for continued development of the technology and to expand its resources. Under this arrangement, the emerging technology company enters into a licensing agreement with one or more companies that have the product development, manufacturing, or distribution capabilities necessary to exploit the technology efficiently. A licensing strategy can be based on product markets, geographic markets, or both.

Technology does not need to rise to the level of a patentable invention to be the subject of a license. Many small companies that have developed proprietary expertise, methods, processes, or technical knowledge have been able to leverage these developments and obtain valuable benefits through the licensing of their technology.

Royalty Structuring

Although the value placed on the technology is subject to negotiation, it ultimately depends on the value that potential licensees place on it. For this reason, royalties usually are based on a percentage of revenues derived from the sale of products or set at a fixed rate per unit of product sold. If it is known that it will be relatively difficult to monitor and audit dollar sales volume, it may be appropriate to establish a fixed royalty per unit sold. More typical, however, is the percentage of revenues approach.

Because the amount of royalty payments is based on products sold by the licensee, a properly structured license agreement must define carefully the scope of the products on which such amounts are based. Thus the parties need to consider these potential collateral uses of the technology:

- The combination of products, each of which incorporates the technology
- Improved products, whether improved or not as a result of an improvement in the technology
- New products incorporating the technology

Confidentiality

A license must impose an obligation on the licensee (and perhaps on the licensor) to maintain the confidentiality of the technology and any other trade secrets that may be disclosed to the licensee incident to the licensee grant. In the absence of such an obligation, the trade secrets may fall into the public domain and become available for use by the licensor's competitors. The license also should impose a restriction on the use of the licensed technology or trade secrets for a defined purpose, and then only as necessary to implement the license.

Obligation to Exploit

The licensor, especially an emerging company, usually wants to establish its name and products in the commercial marketplace and maximize its royalties quickly. It is in the company's best interests, therefore, to ensure that the licensee exploits the technology to the fullest extent possible. Accordingly, the licensor should impose on the licensee an obligation to use its *best efforts* to exploit the technology.

Defined more precisely, "best efforts" means that the parties agree to set minimum levels of sales and provide that the licensee's failure to achieve those levels shall be deemed to be a breach of the best efforts standard—and grounds for the licensor to terminate the license or convert an exclusive license into a nonexclusive one.

NEGOTIATING THE ARRANGEMENT

There is no reason to be timid in negotiating with an industry giant. In our industry it was General Electric, which owned 56 percent of the MRI [magnetic resonance imaging] industry. I remember in our very last negotiations with GE, it got very heated and the head of GE Medical Systems turned to me and asked how a little company that does a few million dollars in revenues and keeps losing money every quarter dared tell him what is the best product for our marketplace. And the answer is honest, and that is that sometimes the tiniest flea that sits on the back of the elephant can see the landscape a lot better than the beast beneath. If they are aware of that, and on some level they do have that awareness, there are great inroads you can make, there's great advice you can give, and there's great benefits that you can obtain for your shareholders.

—Jack Nelson, Chairman of the Board and CEO, Advanced NMR
Systems, Inc. (now Caprius, Inc.)

Every marriage needs a prenuptial agreement.

—Raymond S. Fersko, Managing Member, Fersko LLC

Negotiating a partnering arrangement is time consuming, and it is not unusual for the negotiations to extend over a year or even longer. A substantial amount of that time—nearly one-third, typically—is used in the corporate partner's due diligence investigations, technology review, and equity valuation.

Each partnering arrangement is unique, and for that reason it is important to suggest a model for the typical deal. In general, the basic issues that arise in every partnering arrangement revolve around the questions of how much money and in what form.

How Much Money?

When deciding how much money to ask for, it is important to remind large companies that when they enter into a partnering arrangement, they should seek to fund them fully. It is not in their best interests to provide stingy resources to the technology company because, over the long term, neither partner will achieve what it wanted from the deal. The scale of some of these deals does seem large when first put on paper. However, when the companies actually begin using that money, they tend to spend it pretty quickly. To ensure long-term viability, the technology company must seek committed funding over a period of several years.

When the technology company has a success—whether it is strong clinical trial results for a biotech company or a significant increase in market share for a high-tech company's product or service—that proves the value of the equity investment to the corporate partner, then corporate investors have shown they are willing to up the ante considerably for a stake in a strong high-tech or biotech company. Often the corporate partner will invest at a substantial multiple over previous equity rounds.

Companies looking for an equity investment also should consider how much equity they are willing to give up and should seek to stay within the "comfort zone" indicated in Exhibit 6.4.

Equity versus Nonequity

Equity investment is a component in a large number of the partnering deals completed in the past dozen years or so and is steadily increasing.

An equity investment is a mixed blessing. When a technology company accepts an equity investment, or considers an equity component in its deal structure, management needs to answer a series of questions.

- What does the company give up?
- What does the company gain?
- How does equity affect its valuation?

There is a relationship between a company's valuation and how long it has been in business—its track record. The more mature a company is (i.e., the closer it is to commercialization, an IPO, or a sale), generally the less inclined management is to give away equity and thus give up a portion of the company. The need for capital and the desire to maintain control must be balanced. In addition, the company's other investors may not appreciate any dilution of their position.

> *Typically, the most common mistake is that entrepreneurs get hung up about what percent of the company they own at each stage of financing. What I try to get people to focus on is the last stage, and that you don't necessarily get the best last position by maximizing your position at each point along the path.*
>
> *People always want to get a high price. You can raise money at a better price—give up less of the company for the same amount of capital—but it takes longer. If it takes three to six months to raise capital, it might take nine months to raise capital at a better price. If the opportunity is dynamic at all and you've just spent three months trying to increase your percentage owned on day one, you might have shot yourself in the foot. So winning the first battle may not be winning the war.[3]*
>
> —William Sahlman, businessman, professor, Harvard Business School

EXHIBIT 6.4 The Comfort Zone—Pharma Investment in Biotech

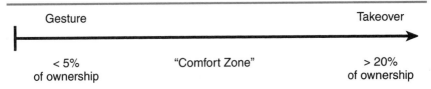

Gesture		Takeover
< 5% of ownership	"Comfort Zone"	> 20% of ownership

In a well-structured deal, the capabilities a technology company builds for its corporate partner also provide its own internal research programs with significant leverage.

Selling the Deal

At all stages of the negotiating process, the main hurdle for the high-tech or biotech company is to convince the corporate partner that what its paying for is worthwhile. Doing this can be difficult, because often there is no clear means of valuing equity in a private company. Companies that are successful in obtaining corporate partnerships typically put a great deal of time and effort (e.g., by presenting information on comparable deals) into convincing others that the equity is worth what they say it is worth.

The technology company must do its homework to prepare a convincing case. Management at large companies is becoming more conversant with the tools of investment and venture capital. Increasingly, sophisticated concepts and negotiation possibilities once limited to venture capital funding are appearing in corporate partnerships' negotiations.

Chief executive officers (CEOs) who have been trained in going through venture capital fund-raising will be well prepared to have these discussions. They may even be better prepared than their corporate partners. But CEOs who are unfamiliar with the negotiating strategies and concerns of venture capitalists would be well advised to prepare themselves before beginning negotiations with a prospective partner.

Finally, negotiating a corporate partnership agreement is a people business. No matter how good the tools and technologies are, it is talent, drive, and creativity that make things work. Partnering deals are really agreements between equals: for example, between CEOs and presidents of divisions, or between CEOs and CEOs. In other words, partnering deals get done between the people who really are the thought and opinion leaders, the high-powered executives. If a small company lacks these people, it will not be as successful in partnering. Business development people serve an enormously important function in making sure that the collaborative agreements are put together properly—but they are not the people, ultimately, who will commit each side to the arrangement.

Of course, even in the best of situations, disputes may arise. When and how to terminate the arrangement is often a stumbling block. Other issues that may arise include funding, intellectual property ownership rights, product development, and conflicts of interest. Reasons for terminating a joint R&D agreement, for example, might include:

- Failure to obtain results
- Slower than anticipated rate of progress
- Differences in corporate cultures between the parties

- Failure in technology integration phase
- Changed priorities (due to merger or acquisition)
- Change in business environment

Given these possibilities, it is wise to enter into a partnering agreement with the equivalent of a prenuptial document outlining all foreseeable situations—and determining in advance the appropriate dispute resolution mechanism.[4]

MANAGING THE RELATIONSHIP

Strategic alliances. I think sometimes it's an oxymoron. Most of the times they're not strategic and most of the times they're not alliances. The large company generally doesn't do what it says it's going to. Not because it doesn't want to. It just doesn't know how. And then the resulting model can be something very different from what both companies had thought.

—Frederic D. Price,
Former President and CEO,
AMBI, Inc. (now Nutrition 21, Inc.)

Negotiating a partnering arrangement and putting it in place does not necessarily guarantee success. In order for both parties to the agreement to realize what they hope to, the relationship between them must be actively managed.

Partnering relationships can significantly affect the operations of the smaller company. A company that makes multiple deals with multiple equity partners ends up having a number of people who feel they have an ownership position in the company. These partners will want to know a lot about the company, and they are going to know a lot about what the company is doing.

Left unmanaged, this corporate partner involvement can present problems. However, if the smaller company properly manages and controls the relationship, it can use the corporate partner's need for participation to its advantage. It is an opportunity to get a corporate partner that truly is a collaborator, not just simply a partner. The emerging technology company wants a corporate partner that is going to take its ownership seriously and look for ways to add value to the company, not just to the partnering arrangement. For example, in an operating committee meeting where a decision about R&D expenditures is being discussed, the corporate partner might advance ideas about what will give the best return on investment *to the company*, not necessarily to the corporate partner.

The technology company's management should focus on having a manager of the partner relationship. These relationship managers concern themselves not only with the product that will result from the venture, but, more important, with how the product will benefit the corporate partner's equity position. For example, Human Genome Sciences, Inc. (HGS) is a biotech company that, among other pursuits, discovers and characterizes human and microbial genes. It has several rather broad corporate alliances with large pharmaceuticals companies. According to Dr. William Haseltine, chairman and CEO, the partners in these alliances wanted a great deal of control—not just over the operations of HGS, but also over the partnering relationship.

To make this arrangement work, HGS hired people from the pharmaceutical industry, people who "looked and talked like them," and appointed them as ambassadors to the pharmaceutical partners. These ambassadors spent most of their time talking to the pharmacologists and eventually setting up working groups, establishing a dialogue to fund out their true needs, and bypassing the partner's control mechanisms. In this way, HGS was able to make sure that its technology was successfully incorporated into its partner and that the partnership worked.

According to Haseltine, "One of the things corporate entities do is exert control, not only of their own operations as they ought to, but also control of relationships—especially a relationship that was as broad as the one we had structured. [Our partner] put a cap on it, and if that control mechanism had worked, nothing would have happened. Relationship management is a very, very important part of partnering."

Information and Communications

A key consideration in managing a partnership alliance is control over information. The partnership generates a huge amount of data, and when the relationship ends, the high-tech or biotech company may find itself locked out of its own database with a lawsuit as its only option for recovery.

For that reason, unless transfer of data at the end of a relationship is clearly defined in the partnering agreement, it is important to make sure there is an ingoing process that gives the smaller company as much information as possible on a continuing basis. That process should be built on the assumption that the smaller company will get no more when the agreement comes to an end. Many companies periodically perform a complete review of all the program data (e.g., every two weeks). Doing this is absolutely necessary if these companies are to get value out of a relationship.

Often, however, there is a mismatch of expectations, and a huge amount of work has to go into establishing good communications between the two organizations. Be prepared for competing issues: for example, the large companies may not want to share information with the smaller companies. It is up to the smaller company to manage the relationship with the people who have made a commitment to keep the lines of communication open.

The smaller company also should be prepared to deal with a change in personnel at the corporate partner. Surprisingly, there usually is more turnover in large companies than in smaller ones. So the small company should consider that, in the future, it might be dealing with different people from those with whom it started out—and that may extend all the way from the program manager to the CEO.

EXIT STRATEGIES

It's very important to consider the end [of the partnership] and what assets you'll have. What we think we've tried to do is get substantial help from our partners in building an appreciating asset, which we will own after we've leased it to them for some time.

—William Haseltine, Ph.D., Chairman and CEO, Human Genome Sciences, Inc.

All corporate alliances will end. When that happens, the corporate partner is either going to acquire the smaller company, or it is going to leave. In the beginning of the corporate partnership, as smaller companies think about structuring a deal, they should not think only of the joys of getting in. They also need to think about what happens when the partner leaves.

Human Genome Sciences spells out the ending right at the beginning. Its partnering agreement specifies a finite term of five years. At the end, HGS has exclusive rights to use all of the data materials and information generated by the firm or its partners. The details are explicitly written out, including an early escape clause. If the corporate partner does not have an active funded program, or if it stops funding the program at any time during the life of the partnership agreement, all rights and information return to HGS for its exclusive use.

The end of a corporate alliance is not a bad thing. The end of a partnership allows the smaller firm to change and develop. If an emerging high-tech or biotech company structures a deal early in its development, it will go through fundamental changes over the term of the agreement. That means the partnering arrangement that was a good fit when it was negotiated may not be the arrangement that should be in place three years hence. It does not mean that the parties walk away unhappily; it just means the time may be ripe for a new deal (see Exhibit 6.5).

Through careful planning, the selection of the right partners, and an honest evaluation of the nature of the contemplated collaboration by both partners, an emerging company can gain access to the capital, resources, and further relationships that will enable it to build a successful partnership and prosper.

EXHIBIT 6.5 Termination Issues for the Joint Venture R&D Prenup

Triggers for Termination	Key Issues to Be Addressed
■ Expiration of agreement	■ Length of time in which exit opportunity is available
■ Third party offer for the business	■ Length of time offers to sell must remain open
■ Breach or other default by one party	■ Pricing mechanism for the selling interest
■ Force majeure	■ Who may buy and the other party's consent to such buyer
■ Deadlock	■ Transfers to affiliates automatically permitted
■ Bankruptcy	■ Provide that all transfers are subject to initial joint venture agreement
■ Change of control	■ What must remain for the remaining party to continue the venture (intellectual property, personnel, assets, raw materials, etc.)
■ Failure to meet targets/milestones	■ Indemnification, releases, and representations between exiting and remaining party
■ Mutual agreement	■ Security law issues of transferring interest
■ Fulfillment of business purpose	■ Return of confidential information and continuing confidentiality obligations
■ Open-ended (exit at any time after a stated period)	
■ Alliance success	
■ Going public	

Source: Raymond S. Fersko and Sedi Doohay, "Prenuptials for the R&D Agreement," Mintz, Levin, Cohn, Ferris, Glovsky, and Popeo, P.C., June 2001.

Postscript

There is no doubt that the face of corporate partnerships has been evolving since the 1990s. While more and more partnerships are being negotiated—particularly in the life sciences arena—they are not always of the "big pharmaceutical company buys small emerging company" type. According to life sciences guru Steven Burrill, the large pharmaceutical companies are experiencing an "integration/disintegration" phase, as evidenced by recent activity that includes:

- Big pharma combinations (mergers)
- Big pharma split-ups
- Pharma/biotech acquisitions
- Pharma/biotech strategic alliances
- Biotech/biotech combinations
- Spinouts from pharma/biotech partnerships

Burrill reports that, in 1999, there were six or seven major players in the traditional "big pharma" arena and a handful of large companies looking toward the "life sciences" opportunities, including human healthcare, agriculture, animal health, nutrition, and specialty chemicals. But today, he says, the market is changing. Life sciences companies are growing up, and big traditional companies are redefining themselves for strategic reasons: acquiring companies for innovation, acquiring companies for size and clout; acquiring companies that will provide more focus; and so on.[5]

The evolution of the biotech industry will be an exciting one to be part of, as new disease-predicting and fighting technologies continue to emerge, as new drugs replace expensive hospital stays, and as an aging population looks to prevention, healthful foods, and total wellness to help take control of their well-being.

CASE STUDY: A CORPORATE COLLABORATION MODEL

Few companies have greater depth and breadth of experience in setting up corporate partnerships and alliances than Genencor International, Inc., a 20-plus-year-old company based in Palo Alto, California. Genencor is a global leader in the discovery and development of powerful, integrated molecular technologies that have resulted in a range of novel products to address the needs of the healthcare, agricultural, and industrial chemical markets. Dealing with matter at the molecular level, Genencor specializes in developing and commercializing enzymes using proteomics (protein engineering technologies).

The company began in 1982 as a joint venture between Genentech, Inc., and Corning Glass Works, Inc., dedicating itself to the development of pro-

Product	Application
Protease, amylases, and cellulase enzymes	Detergents and textiles
Glucoamylase and protease enzymes	Corn ethanol
Isomerase enzymes	High-fructose corn syrup
Continuous biocatalytical systems	Ascorbic acid (vitamin C)
Biologically produced 1,3 propanediol	Wearing apparel, upholstery, carpeting
Sensory devices	Air, food, and water monitors

tein engineering and protein expression technologies as tools to dramatically improve naturally occurring enzymes. These technologies enable the synthesis of new molecules, resulting in innovative enzyme products for a variety of consumer applications.

In addition, the company is working on the development of molecules that will have applications in therapeutic cancer vaccines and treatment.

Since its beginnings, Genencor has built a profitable, global business—with over 15 biological production systems in manufacturing plants worldwide—driven by blue-chip customer relationships that generate both profits and cash flow for the continued development of its technology. Those customer relationships include Procter and Gamble (P&G), DuPont, Eastman Chemical, Danisco A/S, Dow Chemical, and ADM. The ability to build strong and lasting partnerships is one of Genencor's greatest strengths and most critical success factors. Very different from a contract research company, Genencor marries its customer's needs with its proprietary technology platforms to create customized solutions for its customer's end users while successfully maintaining ownership of the technology and manufacturing rights.

Genencor has perfected this strategic approach and built its business around it. Its long-standing partnership with P&G is the longest running research alliance in the biotech industry and was celebrated in 1999 with the American Chemical Society Award for teamwork. The two companies have been working together since 1984, when a representative from P&G heard a scientist from Genencor present the company's technology at an industry conference. The first partnership was created to develop an enzyme technology for use in P&G's laundry and cleaning products. The alliance had Genencor re-create the conditions of a washing machine in a test tube and, using biological systems, engineer novel proteins with enhanced cleaning capabilities. The P&G scientists set the performance criteria, developed optimum detergent formulations, and provided feedback on how Genencor's variant proteins performed under specific conditions. And a relationship model was formed.

Genesis of Genencor

*Our pedigree is in alliances, deal-making, and convoluted owner-
ship, if you will.*

—Margaret Horn,
Vice President, Assistant General Counsel,
Genencor International, Inc.

In the early 1980s, the entire U.S. biotech industry consisted of two companies: Amgen and Genentech, which was working on a disruptive technology using recombinant DNA, with the hopes of creating proteins for
therapeutic use. No one was thinking about industrial use at the time. In 1982
Genentech and Corning Glass Works contributed their respective intellectual
assets pertaining to industrial applications of recombinant technologies to
form Genencor, Inc., which would focus on industrial applications.

Between 1982 and 1990 Genencor, Inc., was financed through a
combination of existing partner capital infusions and new partner capital
infusions—including A.E. Staley and Eastman Kodak. In 1990 Cultor,
Ltd., a Finnish biotech company, and Eastman Kodak formed a new company by contributing their biotechnology businesses and some cash. This
new company acquired Genencor, Inc., the original research company
spun out by Genentech, and renamed the combined businesses Genencor
International, Inc. By 1992 the partners had lent $70 million to the entity,
which was converted into preferred shares and guaranteed senior debt of
$55 million. In 1996 the company's owners guaranteed additional senior
debt of $85 million, which financed the two acquisitions the company had
made in 1995 and 1996. In July 2000 Genencor International went public, raising $126 million. The company currently trades on the Nasdaq
exchange under the symbol GCOR.

Partnership Model

*We sought out the market leaders for our industries and partnered
with them—in the belief that they would have perfect market
intelligence—to develop products or enzymes specifically for their
needs. And the first one we did was Procter & Gamble.*

—Raymond J. Land, Senior Vice President,
Chief Financial Officer, Genencor International, Inc.

From the beginning, the company's strategy was to use its limited
resources to invest in technology and to partner with market leaders. It was
an intentional strategy, based on a belief that the emerging technology was
the best use of resources. It worked. Today Genencor considers its blue-chip

technology development partnerships one of its greatest assets. Among its clients, in addition to P&G, are firms like Eastman Chemical and DuPont. A key component of Genencor's corporate strategy has been, and will continue to be, forming strategic alliances with industry leaders in its defined target markets. But how does a company—especially a young company— begin to identify potential partners? And what does it take to make a partnership successful?

In the case of Genencor, it researched potential markets that could develop products based on its technologies. However, Genencor's initial research identified 80 different industries that could use molecular-based biotechnologies. Further market research narrowed the search down to those industries that Genencor believed would benefit the most. Today the company is marketing its technologies to the healthcare, personal care, agricultural, chemical, and other industrial markets that use enzymes, such as ethanol and detergent. Genencor then looks for opportunities, such as trade or investor conferences and forums, in which to present its capabilities. People invariably come up and want to know more about its technology and track record. In addition, the company meets on a frequent basis with members of governments to discuss the benefits of molecular biotechnology and educate them on the benefits of a bio-based economy.

The partnership negotiation begins when the technical people from both organizations get together to determine if a biotech solution is possible for the company's problem. Genencor's management team cannot emphasize enough how critical it is to be very specific about what the solution might be and what the criteria for success would be before any relationship begins. Since Genencor is in the business of solving its customers' problems, the teams work very hard to define responsibilities, be clear about potential financial ramifications, clarify the value of the technology, and know ahead of time what will happen if one partner wants or needs to pull out early. Genencor looks for alliances that have the potential to be long term and multiproject; it is not in the business of doing contract research, nor is it in the business of turning over its molecules outright to a customer. In fact, it maintains ownership of every one of its enzymes. It is important to recognize that a project may not continue to be a vital aspect of a partner's strategic direction. This is particularly true today, when the tenure of a CEO continues to grow shorter. Therefore, a key aspect of a successful negotiation is for both parties, up front, to agree on the ownership of intellectual property and any other assets, in the event that the project is terminated (see Exhibit 6.6).

Experience shows that the best kind of deal is one in which the partner supplies the definition of the need (i.e., a customer problem that needs solving) and in which Genencor is called on to provide the technical expertise: knowing enzymes, knowing how to develop the right enzymes for the particular problem, and knowing how to produce that enzyme effectively and

EXHIBIT 6.6 Keys to a Successful Corporate "Marriage"

KEY FACTOR	EXPLANATION
Understanding each other's needs	The needs of the biotech company may differ from the needs of the partner company. The biotech company will most likely want up-front funding; clear milestones for technical achievement; publicity; participation in the commercialization efforts; to build the technology and intellectual property base; to retain commercialization rights for other product opportunities that result from the collaboration; and a reasonable exit strategy.
Long-term commitment from both parties	Chemical companies, for instance, are used to 10+ year commercialization time lines. In the biotech arena, a reasonable time line for commercialization is 3 to 5 years. Creating clear go/no go decision points is a must.
Creating a win-win partnership	Avoid forcing a "control" versus "collaborative" relationship. Is there a proper risk/reward balance? What is the resource commitment of both partners? Is there recognition of the value of the contributions of each partner? Is there a common goal driven by market needs and the strengths of the partners? Is there a cultural fit? A clear path to commercialization? A desire for open communication by both parties?
Prenuptial considerations	A partnership is like a marriage. Think about the "divorce" scenario at the beginning. Deal with financial issues up front: funding/milestones/commercial share. Arrange for the disposition of preexisting property/assets as well as property/assets acquired during the collaboration: Who has access to which assets and for what purpose? Clearly define the rights and obligations of both parties during the collaboration as well as upon dissolution.

efficiently. Once the value of each partner's contribution is established, open communications and information sharing are critical to making the alliance a success.

In a nutshell, Genencor's partnership model is to:

- Choose partners that are leaders in a market, a region, or a product line.
- Build an open partnership that leverages the strengths of each partner.
- Develop new products in a defined field for an agreed-on time.

The company's mantra is to choose a partner that has a strategy for *growth*, a sense of *urgency*, a belief in *innovation* as a source of growth, and a key *need* that Genencor's biotechnology can satisfy. In terms of risk-sharing devices, it is important to define which are appropriate with each customer. These could include R&D payments, technology access fees, milestone payments, exclusivity fees, and royalties. Risk sharing ensures that only the "true needs" are developed and directs the scrutiny of each partner during the process. It also recognizes the value of the exclusive partnership for the duration of the project.

It is clear that significant technological innovations are driving the growth of many industries, and biotech is high up on the list. It is also clear that collaborations between the chemical companies and the biotech companies will drive new opportunities. New approaches, like these collaborations, will help to commercialize innovative products faster and more efficiently than ever—the whole is greater than the sum of its parts. Genencor believes that sustainable development in the chemical/biotech arena will require a focus on technical, environmental, and business issues, leading to a big win for those companies that can collaborate successfully.

NOTES

[1] Stephanie N. Mehta, "Top-Notch Start-Ups Get Picky About Their Partners," *Wall Street Journal*, May 7, 1997.

[2] Norm Alster, "Natural Partners," *Forbes*, April 11, 1994.

[3] "Sahlman Says," *Wall Street Journal*, October 15, 1993.

[4] Raymond S. Fersko and Sedi Doohay, "Prenuptials for the R&D Agreement," Presentation at New York Biotechnology Practice, June 2001; also, internal memo from Fersko and Doohay to their partners in Mintz Levin Cohn Ferris Glovsky and Popeo PC, the same month.

[5] G. Steven Burrill, "Life Sciences: State of the Industry," presentation to BIO2002 conference, June 2002.

CHAPTER 7

Mergers and Acquisitions

Speculation that there may be several megamergers among the large pharmaceutical companies may be premature. But there is no doubt that all of the big pharma companies have an insatiable appetite for growth that cannot be completely satisfied through organic evolution and new-product development. They will be trolling in the M&A market for deals in 2002 and beyond.

—Ken Weixel, National Director of Healthcare,
M&A Services, Deloitte & Touche LLP[1]

CHANGING FACE OF MERGERS AND ACQUISITIONS

Just as strategic alliances and corporate partnerships provide a way for emerging companies to achieve their strategic goals through creative financing and licensing programs, so, too, do mergers and acquisitions (M&As). They also provide a way for large corporations to keep their pipelines full of new products and even can act as a defensive weapon against burgeoning competition (see Exhibit 7.1).

Traditionally, M&As are thought of as transactions between established companies—agreements (friendly or hostile) among peers. But as the capital markets have all but disappeared in some sectors since the bubble of the late 1990s—most notably in technology—M&A activity is redefining itself, especially in the life sciences arena. Based on early indications from the private equity, venture capital, and initial public offering (IPO) markets, the pace of M&A activity in the pharmaceutical, biotech, and medical-device areas is accelerating.

According to John Rhodes, managing partner of Deloitte & Touche's Pharmaceuticals and Life Sciences area, "Many of the larger pharmaceutical

EXHIBIT 7.1   Life Sciences M&A Activity on the Rise

YEAR	# of Deals
1998	254
1999	135
2000	93
2001	379
2002	444

Source: Deloitte & Touche LLP, The 2002 HealthCare College, Orlando FL, September 2002.

companies have great needs to fill their short-term product pipelines to continue to deliver double-digit earnings growth to their investors. That, as well as the technological advances in the scientific area, has resulted in many alliances between pharmaceutical and biotechnology companies."[2]

Elements of the Deal

According to the experts, most companies approach a merger or acquisition transaction in one of two ways, both of which can be extreme. The first method entails little or no due diligence and usually happens quickly. The other method entails what one pundit calls "paralysis by analysis," where so much due diligence is done that, in the quest for the perfect deal, no deal ever gets done. The successful transaction is a blend of the two, and is more of an art than a science. According to Deloitte's Ken Weixel, "Doing deals has more to do with gut intuitive feel when it's time to pull the trigger than it does in saying 'Well, this analysis proves that we have a 97 percent probability that this is going to be a successful acquisition.'"

Four elements are involved in making a go-no go decision regarding M&As.

Element #1: Due Diligence   A company performs due diligence to learn, to avoid surprises, and to create a basis for concluding whether a transaction should go forward or not. Numbers are dissected, backgrounds are checked, markets are studied, and technologies are put to the test. This homework is critical. Unfortunately, there is no magical point at which people can know they have done enough; no information that provides an "aha!" moment so that it is obvious that the deal should go through. Due diligence is both an art and a science, and must be done in combination with consensus and a long view of the market to be most valuable.

Element #2: Chief Executive Officer Champion   The CEO champion is the person who is willing to stake his or her reputation—and the reputation of the company—on the fact that the deal is the right thing to do. He or she will say to the board, "I want to do this deal, and I think it's good for our company for the following reasons." Even after all the due diligence in the world, there needs to be an individual or—from a governance standpoint, a board—who says "This is the right thing to do."

Element #3: Intuition   Looking for the right deal is often more a qualitative process than a quantitative one. Without diminishing the importance of the quantitative (due diligence, numbers) side of the equation, most seasoned M&A professionals agree that it is ultimately the qualitative piece—personalities, vision, shared goals, and culture—that wins out at the end of the day. If these pieces do not fit well together, the deal probably will not succeed in the long run.

Element #4: Integration   In simplistic terms, integration means finding a way to prove that the deal makes sense for all parties, that is, that one plus one equals more than two. Integration consists of developing a plan to deliver on all the promises that were made during the selling process to the institutional investors and the companies' respective boards. In many cases, M&A deals create a "Noah's Ark" problem, where the resulting company is left with two of everything. How to manage and merge these, how to deliver on the synergies and on the financial models, and how to say with some assurance that the transaction will work—and maximize the company—are all a part of the integration process.

WHY MERGERS AND ACQUISITIONS? WHY NOW?

Since the bubble of the 1990s burst, and with a 3-year bear market, the capital markets for healthcare and life sciences have been difficult. And when capital markets are not user-friendly, acquiring companies have a few different options.

One natural response is to do nothing. Referred to by one leading M&A maven as the "Woody Hayes syndrome," this response basically says that the best thing to do if the capital markets are going to punish the company for acting is to do nothing. Named for famed Ohio State Buckeyes football coach, Hayes believed that the pass (action) should be used only as an element of surprise. "There are three things that can happen when you pass, and two of them ain't good," he said. So a CEO looking for a possible big deal in the current market environment might not get too far down the road, it can be surmised, because there are a few things that could happen and most of them "ain't good."

The other thing companies can do is to look for smaller deals, which tend to be less objectionable. So instead of a merger of equals, they can do small deals, which are less noticeable and more quickly accretive to earnings. Of course, these smaller deals will not make as big an impact on the earnings of the merged companies. But this route might be safer.

Most successful companies, however, have grown at a substantial rate over a long period of time. They did not achieve all their growth from internal year-over-year growth; rather, a significant portion came through acquisitions. When companies go through periods of time when no deals are done, or no big deals, they tend not to get rewarded in the same way. They do not realize significant price-to-earnings (P/E) multiples in their stock price over their growth rate. It could mean expanding at 5 percent and having a P/E of 10 as opposed to 20 percent and having a P/E of 30 or 35. So dropping back from an acquisitive mode has its consequences.

Scope of "M&A"

In the life sciences arena, there are a few different categories of deals that fall under the general umbrella of M&A.

First there are contractual relationships or alliances, also called in-licensing. (See Chapter 6 for additional discussion.) Under this scenario, Company A says, "I like what Company B has. I'm not going to buy Company B and will not directly invest in it, but I will give it money today to secure revenue tomorrow." Usually this occurs when Company B has already completed the R&D and has gotten a drug to a certain stage. Essentially, Company A advances Company B money against a future revenue stream. This is good for Company B because it does not have to bother about getting into manufacturing or distributing or selling the drug; it can concentrate on R&D. So Company B is going to take that money and reinvest it back into the R&D process to generate the next discovery. And the next. This been a common way for the big pharmaceutical companies to fill their pipeline over the past 5 to 10 years and will likely continue.

Another way to do this is to say, "I like what Company B is doing, but I'm not ready to buy the whole company yet. Or maybe I don't want the whole company, just a piece of it—the piece that aligns with my core strategy." In this scenario, Company A becomes a minority owner of Company B, buying 10 to 20 percent of the company, and negotiates a revenue agreement as a result of its investment.

An outright acquisition has come to mean, by inference, a larger company buying a smaller company. Occasionally a smaller company buys a bigger company, but not very often. When Company A buys Company B, it can allow Company B to operate independently, so it is more like a 100 percent investment. Or Company A could fold Company B into its existing infrastructure and then have to deal with the integration issues that were mentioned earlier in this chapter.

As for mergers, most experts believe that there is no such thing as a merger of equals. But often there are companies that are similar in size where one is acquiring the other (for accounting or tax purposes) and these deals get pitched to the Street as mergers: "With this deal, one plus one is going to equal four, because we're merging the best of each of us." Ultimately, of course, there can only be one head to the monster, although sometimes companies will announce that they are going to have co-CEOs or co-chairs. In today's market, some big mergers are happening, despite the nomenclature. The $60 billion Pfizer-Pharmacia deal, announced in 2002 and completed in 2003, which has been billed as an acquisition, is really a merger of two very substantial companies. And the likelihood is that we will see more of this kind of transaction in the future (see Exhibit 7.2).

Why Consider an M&A Strategy?

One company simply cannot be the best at everything. Smart managers know that there is eventually going to be another company that might do something better and—rather than compete against that company—will seek them out. To be the dominant player in an industry usually takes more than growing from the inside. It usually entails taking out some of the competition.

A merger or acquisition makes sense for many reasons: synergies of strategy, of focus, of direction, of science, of vision. It also makes sense as a pipeline strategy. And from a pure growth point of view, it makes a great deal of sense. For example, if a company decides it needs to double in size in three years to achieve or maintain its lead position in the market, it most likely will not be able to do that with "same store growth" or internally generated revenues. So some portion of that growth has to come from acquisitions.

If half of the doubling can be realized from internal growth, it follows that the other half must come from acquisition growth. So today's $2 billion

EXHIBIT 7.2   Recent Noteworthy Healthcare Transactions

- Guidant's acquisition of the Cook Group ($3 billion)

- Quest's acquisition of Unilab ($1.2 billion)

- Medtronic's purchase of MiniMed ($3.7 billion)

- Cardinal Health's purchase of Syncor International ($1.1 billion)

- Amerisource and Bergen Brunswig merger ($2.42 billion in stock + $2 billion in debt)

- Anthem's purchase of Trigon ($3.8 billion)

- Amgen's purchase of Imedex ($18 billion)

Source: Deloitte & Touche, The 2002 Health Care College.

revenue company—which is striving to be a $4 billion revenue company in three years—must acquire $1 billion worth of revenue in one or more deals (half of its present size). Most companies approach purchases in this way— first from the macrolevel and then from a very tactical level: How do we approach this? How do we do that? And that brings them into the target identification phase. A company like Genentech has looked at more than 300 deals—doing due diligence to one degree or another on each of them— and has signed deals with perhaps 30 companies. It is a grueling but necessary process for growth.

Of course, from the point of view of the emerging company, being acquired also has its pluses and minuses. On the plus side, the emerging company—at least in theory—gets access to the financial, technological, and scientific resources of the acquiring company. In practice, this has not always proved to be the case. Instead of the acquired company's technology being at the center of an entire company, it may now be only one of many projects and it may not be considered to be central to the parent's strategy.

In addition, profitable companies are generally valued at a multiple of earnings, while companies in a research stage are all losing money and are valued in less quantitative terms. This more qualitative approach can work to the benefit of the emerging company. Once it is part of a larger, profitable company, R&D expenditures are scrutinized differently, since they reduce the company's bottom line and often the selling price of the stock.

Control is another issue. Once subsumed into a larger company, C-level executives of the acquired company are no longer in the same position of control as they enjoyed as heads of a free-standing company.

CASE STUDY: ONLINK AND SIEBEL SYSTEMS

The key to acquisitions is that senior management has to stay around and help their people get integrated. Too often it's a cashout mechanism. We didn't do that. We went in without a contractual commitment. We had a moral commitment.

—Buck French, General Partner, JPMorgan Partners
(Former Vice President/General Manager,
Siebel Systems, Inc.)

In 1995 Buck French and two partners founded a company called OnLink Technologies, Inc., with the goal of creating a software system that would lead a customer through the entire buying process. The team's vision was to engage customers or prospects online, qualify them, do a needs analysis, recommend a product, take customers through production configuration and pricing and, finally, generate and place an order, transact the order, and manage the order. It was a three-part strategy, and the team began at the beginning.

Working on the needs analysis, product cataloging, configuration, and pricing end of the system, French shopped the deal around in search of venture capital financing. In 1997 they were still an inexperienced team and had no luck. "We were in a great market," says French. "But we couldn't deliver the message effectively. We stuck with it because we believed in what we were doing."

French and his team did everything entrepreneurs do: worked hard on the business, bootstrapped the company, maxed out their credit cards, slept on each other's floors. All the classic things. But by 1998, French says, they had learned from their previous fund-raising mistakes. They were able to raise $6 million from Sierra Ventures, a Menlo Park–based venture firm specializing in early and prepublic communications, software, and Internet-related content and infrastructure companies.

Within two years, OnLink had grown to support 220 employees and was selling its front-end system to such major corporations as General Electric, Sony, Lucent, Snap-On Tools, and Amdahl. The company had raised $37 million through three rounds of venture capital and by early in 2000 had an annual revenue run rate of $20 million.

In April 2000 the company's bankers were working on filing an S-1 registration statement to go public. "The reason we were going public was to help us win in the marketplace," says French. "When we started the company, it was not about going public or getting rich. We just wanted to achieve a greater than 50 percent share of the market. That was winning for us." With only the first third of the system in place, French and his team were looking to raise money to buy the other components—the transaction and management portions of their vision—because they felt the opportunity was there but they could not build the pieces themselves fast enough. And then the market dynamics changed.

That month, the bankers informed OnLink's management that they would not be able to achieve the IPO in June, as originally planned. In fact, they said, it probably could not be done until the September–October time period—far too late, given the state of the market at that time. OnLink's team was devastated, fearing that they might never get to achieve their vision. Enter Siebel Systems, Inc., a San Mateo company that excels in ebusiness application software.

Siebel had approached OnLink in the past but had never made a serious offer. In June both companies got serious. Siebel purchased OnLink in August 2000 for $600 million and provided the team members with the opportunity they had always wanted: to finish what they had started five years earlier. The deal closed in October 2000, with French being named vice president/general manager of a business unit called Interactive Selling.

"I didn't have to stay, given the parameters of the deal," explains French. "It was a pooling transaction, and my equity status wouldn't have changed if I had just walked out the door. In fact, I probably would have made more money if I had left right away because I wouldn't have been locked up." But French and his team wanted to finish what they had begun. They remained with Siebel for 18 months and built their unit up to become the third largest business unit at the company—over $100 million.

When French left Siebel in February 2002, the team had achieved a 58 percent market share. They had won. His is a Cinderella story, of sorts. He cites luck, great people, a shared vision, and the right perspective as the keys to his acquisition success. "We checked our egos at the door," he says. "We weren't getting me on the cover of magazines or any of the other stuff. Our mantra was 'Go build great software, get customers, make customers successful. Repeat.' It worked out well." For everyone.

NOTES

[1] Ken Weixel, "Vital Signs," The Deal.com, January 28, 2002.
[2] John Rhodes, "The Global Biotechnology Opportunity," *Wall Street Transcript,* June 2001.

CHAPTER 8

Profiles of Corporate Partnerships

An emerging company pursuing a corporate partnership of any kind not only will want to have a clear understanding of the perspective from the other side of the relationship, but will have examined its own objectives carefully, as well. If management does not perform this kind of internal due diligence, the resulting relationships can be far different from what was intended.

Three of the companies that shared their experiences with us took different partnering approaches based on the business objectives of their respective companies. The profiles in this chapter highlight this interconnection between business and partnering strategy.

COMPANY PROFILE: HUMAN GENOME SCIENCES, INC. (NASDAQ: HGSI)

Date of incorporation:	June 1992
Date of IPO:	December 1993 @ $12.00 per share
Corporate headquarters:	Rockville, MD
Collaborative partners:	*Human Therapeutic Consortium:* SmithKline Beecham, Inc. Schering-Plough Corporation Takeda Chemical Industries, Ltd. Synthelabo, S.A. Merck KGaA
	Antimicrobial Consortium: F. Hoffmann-LaRoche, Ltd. Pharmacia & Upjohn Company Pasteur Merieux Connaught/OraVax MedImmune, Inc.
	Other Collaborations: Genetic Therapy, Inc. Isis Pharmaceuticals, Inc. Pioneer Hi-Bred International, Inc. (corn genomics)

Revolution in Drug Discovery

Human Genome Sciences (HGS) has pioneered a revolution in drug discovery since its inception in June 1992. The company was formed to pursue the emerging opportunities resulting from the development of high-speed gene sequencers and bioinformatics methods. Human genes lie at the root of medical discovery. HGS's mission is to use its leadership in the discovery and understanding of human and microbial genes to develop new means to detect, prevent, and cure disease. To that end, HGS has established the world's largest gene discovery laboratory and assembled a network of collaborative relationships to provide additional scientific, clinical, and marketing expertise—and financial support.

The drug discovery activity of HGS begins with the company's Human Gene Anatomy project, the goals of which are to:

- Identify virtually all human genes
- Catalog the relative abundance of expressed genes by organ, tissue, and cell of origin
- Identify changes in gene expression associated with the normal processes of development, differentiation, and activation, as well as abnormal changes in gene expression associated with the development of disease

HGS also created a proprietary bioinformatics system to process, analyze, store, and retrieve biological information. Using modern biology and computers, the company's drug discovery begins with a comprehensive knowledge of the human genome. An assembly line of computer-controlled laboratory robots is employed to isolate, characterize, and catalog genes. A database of the resulting information now describes approximately 95 percent of all human genes.

This system facilitates the selection of genes with potential medical utility. During the first five years of the company's existence, its primary focus progressed from the identification of genes having potential medical utility to the creation of proprietary products.

The company has a strong patent portfolio. As of March 1, 2002, the Patent and Trademark Office had issued 205 patents to HGS on human gene-based inventions. Many patents describing the company's gene-based inventions are pending in both the United States and abroad.[1]

Corporate Partnering Strategy

HGS's commercial strategy from the start has been twofold:

1. To discover, develop, and market therapeutic products
2. To obtain substantial revenue to support its drug discovery efforts by licensing the use of HGS drug discovery technologies to others

The company's first relationship was formalized in October 1992, when HGS announced a 10-year research and intellectual property agreement with The Institute for Genomic Research (TIGR), a not-for-profit research organization founded by Dr. J. Craig Ventner that same year. Dr. William A. Haseltine, chairman and chief executive officer (CEO) of HGS, described the original 10-year agreement with TIGR as "the biggest agreement ever signed between a biotechnology company and a research institute . . . [It] immediately propelled HGS into world leadership in the field of genomic research."[2]

The HGS/TIGR relationship was critical to the biotech company's early success. Together, HGS and TIGR were the first to isolate and characterize the majority of human genes. Under the terms of the agreement, HGS agreed to make a 10-year research grant of $65 million to TIGR, payable over 10 years in specified annual amounts and subject to accelerated funding of $1 million during the first nine years. In return, HGS received exclusive rights to the intellectual property resulting from TIGR's human gene sequencing and other research, as well as the benefits of TIGR's bioinformatics expertise. This relationship reached its conclusion five years ahead of schedule. In June 1997 HGS and TIGR agreed that HGS would cease future research payments to TIGR in return for relinquishing rights to future work done by the institute. The development of both organizations had outstripped expectations, and both agreed that it was in their best interests to separate future research.

Haseltine believes the HGS/TIGR relationship paved the way for his company's collaborative agreement with SmithKline Beecham (now Glaxo-SmithKline) a few months later, which offered HGS the potential of $125 million. Of this amount, $55.1 million was in equity and the remaining $70 million was paid out over a four-year period in the form of licensing fees, option rights, and milestone payments. HGS gave up approximately 7 percent ownership in its company and granted SmithKline first right to develop and market products in human and animal healthcare based on human genes identified by HGS.

The company's corporate collaborations are not simply technology licenses or technology transfer agreements. "They are real partnerships in which we establish close working relationships with the pharmaceutical companies," says Haseltine. "We transfer material and information on a daily basis. They have automated feedback mechanisms that query our databases to request work from us. The goal is to move forward from the information that we've created about a vast array of new genes to concrete product opportunities."

From the beginning of the HGS/SmithKline collaboration, both parties realized that success would bring more opportunities than any one company could use. Shortly after striking their own deal, HGS and the management of SmithKline Beecham worked to extend their collaboration and share the asset that they had created jointly. According to Haseltine, "The asset—that is, the human gene asset of Human Genome Sciences—we regard as one which, up to now, has been jointly created by both Human Genome Sciences and SmithKline Beecham working very closely together. So when we decided to expand this collaboration, we expanded it to our mutual and approximately equal benefit."

SmithKline and HGS now have major partnering agreements to share its human gene discoveries with their "new collaboration partners": Schering-Plough Corporation, Takeda Chemical Industries, Ltd., Synthelabo, S.A., and Merck KGaA. Under these agreements, HGS and SmithKline share equally in any license fees and product development milestone payments paid by their collaborative partners, and HGS will receive all royalties and research payments.

HGS also has other collaborations to share its microbial gene discoveries with F. Hoffmann-LaRoche, Ltd., Pharmacia & Upjohn Company, Pasteur Merieux Connaught/OraVax, and MedImmune, Inc. The company also signed an agreement with Pioneer Hi-Bred International, Inc., focusing on the genes of the corn plant. Partners use HGS information to develop independent products of their own. HGS receives licensing fees, R&D payments, and equity payments, and is entitled to receive milestone payments and royalties on the development and sale of products by its partners.

These partnering agreements provide HGS with tremendous resources. By 1997 the company and its corporate partners had, working on their collaborations, 13,000 scientists worldwide who were provided with daily updates of the information created. The collaborative partners had approximately $2.6 billion in available R&D research funds, approximately one-third of which was available for research and the remaining two-thirds for development. Together the partners had combined sales of $27 billion.

By 2002 the firms had identified some 460 drug targets from HGS's genetic data for their respective pipelines, and HGS will earn a percentage from the sale of any approved drug resulting from these collaborations.

HGS's CEO foresees a future in which HGS could receive an 8 to 10 percent royalty on about half of those sales. "I think we have a fair chance of doing that without subsequent expenditures in the product development area," says Haseltine. Even if the company is only partially successful in its goal, it should still have a substantial source of long-term revenue to finance its activities.

The original corporate partner, SmithKline Beecham, also has benefited substantially by extending the original partnership. First, SmithKline gained access to a new technology that otherwise would not have been available. According to J. P. Darnier, chief operating officer of SmithKline, up to 70 percent of the funded research feasibility studies and 30 percent of the company's current screening activities, come from the HGS source. Just as important,

SmithKline has gained access to this technology at a profit to its corporation, including its equity position in HGS (see Exhibit 8.1). When the licensing agreements with major drug makers expired in June 2001, HGS decided to keep the information largely for its own drug development activities. Today HGS is focused on mining this genetic data to develop its own drugs. At this writing, HGS's top candidates include

EXHIBIT 8.1 Human Genome Science Corporate Time Line

1992	1993	1994	1995	1996	1997 (→3Q)
HGS founded	IPO $31M	SmithKline — $16M for add'l rights	Public offering $61M	Pioneer Hi-Bred — $8M	Public offering $112M
HGS/TIGR agreement	Built gene sequencing facility		Takeda agreement — $5M		Pioneer Hi-Bred — $3M
SmithKline collaboration[a] $13M initial payment	SmithKline — $9M for add'l rights		F. Hoffman-LaRoche — $2M (deferred to 1996)	Pharmacia & Upjohn — $3M	F. Hoffmann-LaRoche Milestone
	SmithKline — $37M equity	SmithKline — Milestones 1 & 2: $25M		SmithKline — Milestone3: $25M	Construction begins on pilot manufacturing plant
				New collaboration partners:[b] Schering-Plough, Synthelabo, Merck KGaA — $17.5M initial payment	HGS, Cato, & St. Elizabeth Hospital form new virtual company, Vascular Genetics, Inc.
				Schering-Plough (outside new collaboration) — $1M	

[a]$125M paid to HGS as of March 12, 1997.
[b]Aggregate due to HGS is $87.5M through 2001.

EXHIBIT 8.1 *(Continued)*

1998	1999	2000	2001
Transgene, S.A. Gene therapy	Cambridge Antibody Technology Fully human monoclonal antibody therapeutics	Cambridge Antibody Technology New 10-year agreement	Medarex Human antibody therapeutics & diagnostics
	Abenix, Inc. Novel human antibody technology exchange	Dyax Corporation 10-year deal for therapeutic and diagnostic products	MDS Norton Clinical manufacture of radioiodinated drug
		Vical Inc. gene therapy	
		Praecis Pharmaceuticals metabolic disorders & infectious diseases	
		Aventis-Behring Plasma proteins	
		Dow Chemical Chelator technology	

Repifermin, an artificial protein that can speed up the healing process of slow-healing skin ulcers; Albuferon, which works against hepatitis C; and BlyS, a potential immunodeficiency treatment that has received orphan drug status. It is also working on drugs that will protect blood cells from the damaging effects of chemotherapy and work against lupus. HGS has a unique ability to bring drug candidates into human trials, causing it to be a standout in a crowded field. As a result, it began building a manufacturing plant to make commercial products in October 2001.

Financing Human Genome Sciences's Growth

Human Genome Sciences received $10 million in its first, and only, venture financing round, from HealthCare Ventures. Since then the company has financed its internal R&D with funding from the corporate collaboration with SmithKline and capital raised through several public offerings of stock. HGS realized $31 million from its IPO in 1993 and returned to the public market two more times, to raise $61 million in 1995 and $112 million in 1997. In addition to its collaborations with SmithKline, HGS's other collaborations resulted in approximately $17 million by the first quarter of 1997.

It is the HGS/SmithKline collaboration, however, that has driven HGS toward its goal of becoming a fully integrated pharmaceutical company. The original agreement with SmithKline had already resulted in payments to HGS totaling $125 million by March 1997. Approximately $55 million of that sum related to equity payments, and the balance of $70 million related to license fees, option rights, and milestone payments. As product development continues at SmithKline, HGS is entitled to product development progress payments. Once a product is on the market, HGS will receive royalties on the net sales and the option to copromote up to 20 percent of any product developed by SmithKline under the collaboration agreement (see Exhibit 8.2).

The collaboration agreement was amended in 1996 to give HGS the independent right to discover, develop, market, or outlicense therapeutic proteins and, beginning in 1999, small molecule drugs. The new agreement also enabled HGS and SmithKline to jointly collaborate with several other pharmaceutical companies in specified therapeutic areas. SmithKline and HGS share equally in the resulting license fees and product development milestone payments by the new collaboration partners, while HGS receives all royalties and research payments. Aggregate payments due to HGS/Smith Kline for license and research payments during the initial research term (which expired in June 2001) are $140 million; HGS's share will be $87.5 million. By March 1997 HGS had received $17.5 million from the new partners in license fees, research, and additional payments.

HGS has been successful so far in implementing its financial plan. Haseltine reported to shareholders in the company's 1996 annual report that corporate partners had committed more than $120 million over a five-year period through collaborative agreements. This will guarantee the company approximately $25 in annual revenues for the next four years.

A significant event occurred in 1997 that moved HGS close to its goal to become a fully integrated pharmaceutical company: The company began

EXHIBIT 8.2 HGS: Development Pathway of Therapeutic Proteins

OUTLICENSE		CLINICAL TRIALS
License, royalties, comarket income	←Preclinical Therapeutic Protein Candidates →	Sales/Revenue

EXHIBIT 8.3A Human Therapeutic Consortium—HGS and its Consortium Partners

HGS Technology					
SmithKlineBeecham Therapeutics & Diagnostics	Merck KGaA Therapeutics	HGS Therapeutic Proteins	Synthelabo Therapeutics	Schering-Plough Therapeutics Gene Therapy	Takeda Therapeutics

EXHIBIT 8.3B Antimicrobial Consortium—HGS and its Gene Technology Partners

HGS Bacterial Gene Technology				
MedImmune Vaccines	Pasteur Merieux Connaught/OraVax Vaccines	HGS Antimicrobials	F. Hoffmann-LaRoche Antibiotics	Pharmacia & Upjohn Antibiotics

construction of its own pilot drug manufacturing facility in Maryland. The new facility marks HGS's transition from a drug discovery to a drug development and testing company (see Exhibit 8.3).

COMPANY PROFILE: CAPRIUS, INC., (FORMERLY ADVANCED NMR SYSTEMS, INC.) (OTC: CAPR)

Unlike the previous case study, which described a company with successful multiple corporate partnerships, the story of Advanced NMR Systems, Inc., and Advanced Mammography Systems, Inc. (AMS)—merged into one entity, Caprius, Inc. (CAPR) as of November 12, 1997—is one of a corporate partnership that encountered its share of problems before a successful relationship was established.

Advanced NMR Systems, Inc., was founded in 1983 to develop echo planar imaging, an ultra-fast magnetic resonance imaging (MRI) technology. The company was a pioneer in this field, developing the first FDA-approved product for real-time MRI imaging. For the first nine years of its existence, the company engaged only in research and development, until the FDA approved the company's InstaScan System for real-time imaging and the company began marketing it to clinical institutions. The groundbreaking potential of this technology was impressive enough to recruit the former chief scientist—as well as the former head of sales and marketing—from General Electric (GE) to work at Advanced NMR.

Date of incorporation:	1983
Corporate headquarters:	Wilmington, MA (now Fort Lee, New Jersey)
Collaborative partner:	GE Medical Systems

In July 1992 the company formed Advanced Mammography Systems, Inc. as a subsidiary and licensed its technology to AMS for the development of the Aurora magnetic resonance (MR) breast imaging system. Several months later, in early 1993, Advanced NMR completed its initial public offering. In 1994 the company entered into an exclusive five-year agreement with General Electric Medical Systems (GEMS) for the sale of its 3T and 4T research MR systems, which guaranteed the integration of InstaScan in GEMS' systems.

Advanced NMR soon encountered problems in its relationship with GEMS. First, Jack Nelson, then chairman and CEO of both Advanced NMR and AMS, learned that GEMS was developing a competing device of its own. He grew concerned that GEMS' primary motivation in obtaining Advanced NMR's technology was not to sell it, but to *prevent* it from reaching the marketplace while GEMS developed its own competing echo planar technology. Second, the company's management discovered that, outside of a few medical institutions that used the device for clinical research, there was not a market for its product.

Rather than abandon their partnership, the company chose to continue its contract with GEMS because, at that time, its entire future was dependent on the relationship. By acknowledging the problems with the relationship, however, and the bad strategic position in which this placed the company, management was forced to rethink its business strategy. It asked several fundamental questions: Was the company's technology operative independent of a host system? Was it entirely dependent on GEMS? Did it have any other products that could create revenue?

The answers to these questions were not ideal. The technology required a host system to operate, and that host system was provided by GEMS. Furthermore, the company had no other product that was independent of GEMS that was capable of creating revenues. This left Advanced NMR in an extremely vulnerable position when GEMS blocked its technology from the market.

It took Advanced NMR management about a year to realize what was happening. Part of the reason it took so long was the emotional investment the company had tied up in its technology. According to Jack Nelson, "Subjective and objective passion seized the moment. Part of the greatest problem in any technology device company is you become so overly involved, you become so drunk on your own wine you believe with the deepest passion you can't be wrong. Having come in late to this game, I was drawn into the idea that we were really going to change the face of medical diagnostics. It is the most painful thing to sit back and have to dispassionately analyze the precepts on which a company's entire financial plan is based."

In August of 1996 Nelson announced a new strategic direction for Advanced NMR. This new strategy resulted from two decisions that management believed would turn the company around. The first decision was to spin off a product that would not be tethered to GEMS, a product that would not require a host system, but would function independently. The technology provided to GE was used by Advanced NMR's affiliate, Advanced Mammography, to develop a dedicated breast imaging system that was exclusively their own.

The second decision, made simultaneously, was to identify a company that fit with Advanced NMR's product and that could expand the reach of the company's revenues. The company identified and bought an MRI services company, which at the time added $25 to $30 million in revenues to the income statement. The company eliminated research, development, and production of its InstaScan technology and reduced its workforce in order to refocus on research and development. After spinning off a subsidiary to the public, the transition was complete: Advanced NMR was no longer a technology company. It was a service-oriented company.

Reflecting on his experience, Nelson recognizes that timing and not being reluctant to take action were the keys to restructuring the company and moving away beyond its dependence on a corporate alliance with GEMS. "When you recognize that something will not work, you have a responsibility, if the opportunity presents itself early on, to seize the moment. There were moments when InstaScan [the technology developed for GEMS] had the passions of the investor community. People were buying it. It was logical. It made sense. The investor community bought that. That was a moment in time when we had to act, and we did."

Advanced NMR struggled through a difficult period, acknowledges Nelson. Writing in 1996/1997, he says, "Over the course of the past year, management has taken drastic action to save the company. We have curtailed dramatically out technology development and production. We have sold our Medical Diagnostics imaging [services] business. The company now has the wherewithal to pursue a strategic direction which we believe will convert our strugglers of the past into successes of the future."

The completion of Advanced NMR's acquisition of Advanced Mammography marked the first step in that new strategic direction. According to the company's press release, the marriage of the two companies provides each with its missing ingredient for success.[3] Advanced NMR gained the market power and opportunities related to the commercialization of Advanced Mammography's Aurora system. In return, Advanced Mammography has the financial support to complete its product development and testing and commercialize its product.

The GEMS saga also has a successful ending. In August 1997 GEMS invested $5.1 million in the acquisition of $2.7 million of Advanced NMR stock, and for the acquisition of Advanced NMR's InstaScan whole-body MRI business (the two companies previously had collaborated in the development of these systems).[4] GEMS continues to develop, manufacture, sell, and service these systems. GEMS' investment in Advanced NMR was an indicator of its confidence in the future of the company and its desire to build on its strategic relationship by becoming an Advanced NMR shareholder.

Today, as Caprius, Inc., the company owns Strax Institute in Florida (acquired in July 1998), which provides comprehensive breast care services, performing some 24,000 procedures each year. It also performs bone densitometry to monitor osteoporosis. But the company's primary activities are now in the therapeutic drug monitoring industry, and are centered around subsidiary Opus Diagnostics' Innofluor line of diagnostic assays. Caprius acquired Opus in June 1999. Its diagnostic tests—which ensure safe and effective use of drugs in human bodily fluids—monitor the intake levels of more than a dozen different therapeutic drugs, including Johnson & Johnson's Toprimate and Aventis' Teicoplanin. Caprius sells its testing products in more than 30 countries.

Caprius completed a private placement in April 2000, raising almost $2 million, which was used to reduce outstanding debt and provide funds for working capital. The company continues to acquire complementary companies, for example, its 2002 acquisition of MCM Environmental Technologies, a company that developed a compact medical waste treatment and disposal system approved by the Environmental Protection Agency.

COMPANY PROFILE: SYNAPTIC PHARMACEUTICAL CORPORATION (NASDAQ: SNAP)

Since scientists have mapped the human genome, biotechnology and pharmaceutical companies find that their most significant growth opportunities lie in developing drugs that exclusively target receptors that are most closely associated with the symptoms and causes of a disease. Synaptic Pharmaceutical is a biotech company that is developing a process by which to discover and clone human receptor genes associated with specific disorders. By developing drugs designed to work with certain receptors (which receive cell-to-cell signals within the human body), the company hopes to create treatments that are

Date of incorporation:	1987
Corporate headquarters:	Paramus, NJ
Collaborative partners:	Procter & Gamble
	Grunenthal GmbH
	Kissei Pharmaceutical Co. Ltd.
	Eli Lilly
	Glaxo Group Ltd.
	Novartis Pharma AG
	Johnson & Johnson Research & Development

more effective and have fewer side effects than traditional drugs. Receptor-specific drugs are a new paradigm in drug discovery that may improve the state of the art in the treatment of many serious and common diseases.[5]

The company focuses on several disorders, including depression and other central nervous system (CNS) conditions, obesity, diabetes, and incontinence. The investment company, Warburg Pincus, owns approximately 35 percent of the company, and in November 2002 the Danish drug maker H. Lundbeck announced it was buying Synaptic Pharmaceutical. In March 2003 this acquisition was completed and Synaptic became a wholly-owned subsidiary of Lundbeck.

Since its founding in 1987, Synaptic has pioneered this paradigm with seminal discoveries in genomics (the cloning of genes) and functional genomics (the identification of a given receptor's physiological function). In February 2002 the company launched its first Phase I clinical trial of a receptor-specific compound, SNCE-2.

Synaptic uses a set of proprietary methods and technologies—called the SNAP Discovery Platform, which isolates and characterizes specific receptors and allows for synthesis of an effectively tailored compound. Today the company is positioned to be the leader in the development of pharmaceuticals that target G-Protein-Coupled Receptors (GPCRs), the largest and most promising class of target receptors with proven therapeutic relevance.

NOTES

[1] Company Web site, www.hgsi.com.

[2] Press release, January 27, 1997, "28 Patent Applications for Human Genome Sciences," distributed by Human Genome Sciences, Inc., and 1996 annual report, Human Genome Sciences, published April 1997.

[3] Press release, May 27, 1997, "Advanced NMR Systems and Advanced Mammography Systems Announce Plans to Merge," distributed by Advanced NMR, Inc.

[4] Press release, August 19, 1997, "GE Medical Systems Invests $5.1 Million for Acquisition of Securities of Advanced NMR Systems, Inc.," distributed by Advanced NMR Systems, Inc. and GE Medical Systems.

[5] Company Web site, www.synapticcorp.com.

CHAPTER 9

Tax Planning Strategies

How an organization is structured is oftentimes governed by the goals of the parties making up the organization. It's important to ask questions up front: How do I want to be taxed? What kind of flexibility do I want? What kind of protection from liability is important to me?

—Laurence Kraemer, Director, Deloitte & Touche LLP

Tax planning is important for all business entities, but perhaps even more so for the emerging high-tech or biotech company whose very survival may depend on its ability to manage cash flow. For these entities, tax planning is an effective way to help:

- Manage the burn rate during the company's start-up phase, before it begins to generate revenues
- Maximize the amount of after-tax cash flow the company receives once it commences operations

CHOICE OF ENTITY

In the excitement of creating a new corporation, many entrepreneurs overlook a very basic, but very significant, facet of corporate organization: choice of entity. Which corporate structure should we choose? How do we minimize tax? For almost all start-up companies, the considerations that should be in the forefront are:

- Tax and tort liability issues
- Cost of maintenance of the entity
- Size and complexity of the entity

- Regulatory requirements that the local, state, or federal government has placed on the proposed business activity

Historically, most start-up companies choose to organize as corporations taxable under Subchapter C of the Internal Revenue Code, despite their profits being taxed twice—once at the corporate level and once again when distributed to equity holders. In the early 1990s a new form of legal entity known as a limited liability company (LLC) was devised, which has now been implemented in all 50 states. This corporate structure eliminated many of the restrictions usually associated with organizing as a C corporation. S corporation, limited liability partnership, and joint ventures are other structures used frequently today. The next sections summarize the general characteristics of these entity choices.

C Corporations

A C corporation is a business entity, created under state law, that continues indefinitely (unless the articles of incorporation state otherwise). The C corporation can have few shareholders (closely held) or a large number of owners with shares sold on the public market (publicly held). The C corporation is managed by its directors and officers, who need not own shares in the corporation.

A C corporation is deemed to have these characteristics:

- Associates
- An objective to carry on business and divide the gains
- Continuity of life
- Centralization of management
- Liability for corporate debts limited to corporate property
- Free transferability of interests

When organizing a C corporation, the original shareholders may contribute cash or property in exchange for their share interests. This contribution will result in no gain or loss (for federal income tax purposes) if the taxpayer receives stock in exchange. Likewise, the corporation will not be taxed on this initial receipt of property. The basis of the taxpayer's stock is the same as the basis of the property transferred to the corporation. Stock issued in exchange for services or indebtedness, however, does result in a taxable event.

Taxation of a C Corporation   The C corporation is deemed to be a separate entity legally and for taxation purposes, distinct from its owners and shareholders. The C corporation is subject to corporate-level taxation at graduated rates of up to 35 percent. If and when a corporation distributes its earnings and profits to its shareholders, the shareholders recognize ordinary income. This, essentially, creates a double layer of tax—first, at the corporate level, and second, at the individual level (after earnings are distributed).

This is an obvious unfavorable characteristic of the C corporation. Such double taxation may effectively be eliminated in many closely held corporations, however, by a "zeroing-out" of the corporate taxable income by distributing *all* of the net income as deductible compensation to the employee-shareholders of the entity. This effectively eliminates an entire tier of taxation.

The primary advantage to the C corporation form is the insulation from liability that its owner enjoys. Because the corporation is deemed to be an entity separate and distinct from its owners, its debts and obligations belong to the corporation, not the owners. Additionally, because the corporate form enjoys free transferability of interest, its owners are granted a flexibility that is not found in partnerships.

Other Tax Considerations C corporations enjoy additional tax benefits over other corporate forms. For example, a full tax deduction is available for health insurance benefits in a C corporation, whereas only a fractional deduction is available in an S corporation or LLC.

S Corporations

The S corporation is an alternative corporate form that requires an election, generally done at inception, to select S corporation status. The effect of this election is that the corporation bears no federal income tax consequences at the entity level. Instead, all corporate income (and loss) is deemed to *pass through* the corporate level to its shareholders.

To be eligible for S corporation status, the corporation must:

- Be a domestic (United States) corporation
- Have no more than 75 shareholders
- Have no nonresident alien shareholders
- Have only permissible shareholders generally individuals and certain trusts
- Not have more than one class of stock

The S corporation retains all the characteristics of the corporate form—except for its pass-through tax status—and all the same disadvantages as the ordinary corporate form. A further disadvantage to the S corporation shareholder is that he or she is taxed on the pro rata share of the corporation's income, even if the income has not yet been distributed. The result is that a shareholder may be required to make a tax payment without the very cash distribution he or she may need to make such a payment.

Other Tax Considerations The S corporation shareholder receives a pro rata share of the corporation's losses, which may serve as an effective tax shelter against other income that the shareholder may earn. These losses are *only* available to the extent of the shareholder's basis (e.g., the amount the shareholder paid for the shares plus any amounts of taxable income attributed to the shareholder, but not distributed). Additionally, the use of this loss as a tax shelter is significantly diluted because the shareholder can not include a share of the entity debt in his or her basis in the shares of the S corporation (unlike a partnership), and the opportunity to increase basis and avail oneself of these losses is limited.

Of additional note, S corporations do not receive the same advantages as C corporations with respect to the tax treatment of healthcare insurance and pension plans. Deductions for health insurance are limited to 40 percent of the premium cost. Pension plans in an S corporation are treated as they are in partnerships, in that separate plans are required for employee-owners and employees.

General Partnerships

A general partnership is nothing more than an association of two or more persons (or entities) organized as co-owners to carry on a trade, pursuit, profession, or business for profit. A general partnership envisions that the partners share prorate to their partnership interests in the profit and loss of the business. All partners can act on behalf of the partnership and may perform any activity that is permitted by their partnership agreement. (Obviously, unlike a corporation, a general partnership does not have centralized management.) The acts of any partner will bind the other partners, notwithstanding any agreement to the contrary. For state law purposes, the partnership "form" is deemed to be a separate entity from that of its members. The assets of the partnership therefore are treated as belonging to a separate business entity, separate and distinct from the individual assets of the partners.

Similar to the corporation context, no gain or loss is recognized on a partner's contribution of property to the partnership in exchange for a partnership interest. The tax basis of the partner's interest is the tax basis of the transferred property. Similarly, the partnership recognizes no income on the contribution event.

The greatest advantage of the general partnership corporate form is its tax treatment: the partnership is a pass-through entity that avoids the double taxation at the corporate level and then again at the partner level. In the partnership, the income passes directly to the partners.

The greatest disadvantage of the general partnership is that personal liability exists with respect to each general partner vis-à-vis the debts and obligations of the partnership. This liability exists regardless of whether the partner was at fault. Additionally, a general partnership does not enjoy a free transferability of interest. A general partner may transfer his or her right to profits, but may not transfer other partnership attributes, such as the right to participate in management. If a partner sells or assigns his or her partnership interest, the purchaser does not become a partner or succeed to the partner's right to participate in management.

Limited Partnership

A limited partnership is a partnership of two or more persons formed under the limited partnership law of a state. The limited partnership must comprise at least one general partner and one limited partner. In this arrangement, the limited partner's liability for the partnership's debts or obligations is limited to the extent of the capital that that partner contributes to the partnership. Alternatively, the general partners remain personally liable for the debts of the partnership.

The limited partnership enjoys the same advantages as the general partnership with this additional advantage: The limited partners are not personally liable for the partnership's debts. This general rule of thumb is discarded if the limited partner status is merely a subterfuge and the limited partner is actually the one making all the important business decisions.

Limited Liability Partnership

A limited liability partnership (LLP) possesses all of the characteristics of a general partnership but has the added advantage of giving partners partial limited liability. A partner remains personally liable for his or her own wrongful acts (and the wrongful acts of those he or she supervises), but the partner's personal assets are protected from claims against the copartners (for their wrongful acts). This form does not, however, protect the partnership's assets (including a partner's individual investments) from any claim against either partner.

Limited Liability Company

This corporate form has emerged in the past few years as a popular alternative to the partnership arrangements just outlined. The limited liability company (LLC) is a hybrid entity that borrows the advantages of both the corporate and partnership form to create a more flexible business arrangement. The members of an LLC enjoy insulation from liability to the same extent as a corporation, but may be treated as a partnership for tax purposes. Additionally, all members of the LLC are given the option of participating directly in the management of the business, if they so choose.

The LLC is a comfortable alternative to the S corporation. Prior to the Internal Revenue Service's recognition of the LLC as a viable corporate form, taxpayers seeking to achieve corporate limited liability with pass-through tax treatment were limited to the use of the S corporation.

The advantages of the LLC over a partnership include:

- Lack of personal liability for the members—even though the limited partnership insulates all limited partners, nevertheless one partner still must be personally liable.
- More flexibility of management (all members can participate, or there can be centralized management)—in a limited partnership, if the limited partner increases his or her role in management, this will affect his or her insulation from liability
- The LLC can designate managers to manage the business, thereby severing management from ownership, if the members so opt.
- The LLC can freely transfer interest, although a transfer to a nonmember does not confer the right to participate in operations of the LLC to the nonmember unless all members consent.

The advantages of the LLC over the S corporation include:

- The LLC can have an unlimited number of members (an S corporation can have no more than 75 shareholders).
- No restrictions exist on who can hold stock.
- There is no one class of stock requirement, as in the S corporation corporate form.
- There is no limitation on the amount of contributions by a member to the LLC.
- There is no recognition of gain on distribution to the LLC members.

SUMMARY: HOW TO CHOOSE THE RIGHT CORPORATE STRUCTURE

There are a number of corporate structures available, and those just listed represent today's more popular choices. How an organization is structured is

TAX VERSUS FINANCIAL ACCOUNTING

Companies will treat certain expenses differently for tax and financial accounting purposes. For example, for tax accounting purposes, a start-up company may choose to capitalize its research and development expenses, which minimizes the company's net operating losses and instead creates deductions in future years.

For financial reporting purposes, just the opposite is true. Under generally accepted accounting principles, R&D costs must be expensed in the period in which they are incurred. Doing this creates large losses for the start-up company, but results in a lean balance sheet without a significant amount of intangible assets.

often governed by the goals of the parties making up the organization. It is important to ask questions up front: How do I want to be taxed? What kind of flexibility do I want? What kind of protection from liability is important to me? Many organizations are turning to the LLC option because of its flexibility and the insulation it offers its members from personal liability. Because it retains the best characteristics of both the C corporation and the S corporation, it is becoming the entity of choice in many situations. However, it may not be an appropriate choice if the company is expecting to do a public offering in the near future.

RESEARCH AND DEVELOPMENT AND OTHER START-UP EXPENSES

During the start-up phase of a business, a company typically has several types of expenses, and decisions must be made as to whether these should be capitalized or expensed for tax purposes. In some instances, the company may have to file a formal election with the Internal Revenue Service (IRS) to declare the tax treatment of certain items. The following table describes the typical expenses incurred by a start-up enterprise and the related tax treatment:

Expense	Tax Treatment
Taxes	Expense in the period incurred
Interest	Expense in the period incurred
General & administrative costs	Capitalize and subsequently amortize once the company begins business
Research & development	Can either expense or capitalize

Research and Development: Capitalize versus Expense

As the table indicates, the one area where companies most need to make decisions—and, therefore, the one area where they most need to conduct tax planning—is in the tax treatment of R&D expenditures. The overall objective of the company's tax planning strategy is to minimize tax expense and thus maximize cash flow, both in the short term and in the foreseeable future. When planning for the tax treatment of R&D expenditures, two important considerations must be kept in mind:

1. *Lack of taxable income in start-up years.* During a company's start-up years, it will be incurring net operating losses (NOLs; as opposed to earning taxable income). These net operating losses will be carried forward to offset future taxable income.

2. *Restrictions on NOL carryforwards.* There are certain restrictions on a company's ability to utilize NOL carryforwards in future periods. Some of the most important restrictions are triggered when a company has greater than a 50 percent change in ownership, which is not unusual for an emerging company that goes through several rounds of financing.

Typically, most companies expense R&D costs as they are incurred. Doing so will increase the company's net operating loss for the period, which will hopefully be used at a later date as a deduction against future taxable income.

However, taking a current deduction for R&D costs is not always the best choice for the long term. In some cases, the company may be far better off electing to capitalize R&D costs and amortize them in the future when business commences. At that future time, the company may want to seek permission from the IRS to currently expense then current costs while amortizing the old capitalized R&D expenses.

Why would a company elect to capitalize R&D? Earlier chapters have focused on the variety of ways a company can raise money, with the clear implication that—particularly in high-tech and biotech industries—companies will go through several rounds of financing before they can stand on their own, generating revenues from their products. Raising money frequently involves giving up equity, and if a company goes through several financings in a short period of time, it may encounter restrictions on the use of its net operating loss carryforwards.

The tax laws impose certain restrictions on the use of NOL carryforwards if the company has a 50 percent change in ownership during any three-year period. This test is applied cumulatively. If a company elected to *expense* its R&D costs during its start-up phase (i.e., in the years before it

---

CAPITALIZING RESEARCH AND DEVELOPMENT COSTS: A CAVEAT

A company that capitalizes its R&D costs is *not* guaranteed to get the full tax deduction for these costs once the company begins business. Technically, the tax code contains certain limitations on "net unrealized built-in losses" that are similar to the limitations on loss carryovers.

However, as a practical matter, if a company is successful at raising equity capital, that essentially indicates that the market believes the company is worth a significant amount of money. In that case, the company probably will not have any unrealized built-in losses because the ability to raise equity capital demonstrates the value of the intangibles created by the capitalized R&D costs. This should allow for the full amortization of these costs once business commences.

generates taxable income), the danger is that the company (through successive financing rounds) will have a 50 percent change in ownership that triggers limitations on the use of NOL carryovers. If the company *capitalizes* its R&D costs instead of adding them to its early-year net operating losses, it may be in a position to capture the future amortization of those costs without any limitations associated with change of ownership.

In addition to avoiding the limitations on NOL carryovers when there has been a change in ownership, other reasons for capitalizing R&D costs include:

- *Alternative minimum tax (AMT) considerations.* When a company begins to use its loss carryovers, even if it does not otherwise have any net taxable income, it may have an AMT to pay, generally a 2 percent tax on the prenet operating loss taxable income. Future amortization of capitalized R&D expenses can avoid this problem.

- *State tax considerations.* Certain states can impose limits on the use of NOL carryforwards that are even more restrictive than federal laws. In Massachusetts, for example, the NOL carryover period is only five years (as contrasted with the federal limit of 15 years for losses incurred before 1998 and 20 years thereafter). This is a significant limitation, and a Massachusetts company that is considering expensing R&D costs should consider whether the resulting net operating losses could be used within the limited carryover period. In one real life example of a Massachusetts technology start-up, the differing carryover periods resulted in a federal tax payment for a particular year of $15,000 and a Massachusetts state tax payment of $150,000 for the same year.

Of course, capitalizing R&D expenses is not the best choice for every situation. Some companies may have interest income and, absent interest expense, may need to expense at least some of their R&D costs to shelter this income.

If a company elects to expense R&D costs and include these amounts in the NOL carryforwards, management must remain aware of where the company stands in relation to the 50 percent change in ownership test and whether the company is in danger of severely restricting or losing a portion of its carryforwards.

For example, suppose a company has $1 million of NOL carryovers and has had a 48 percent change in ownership. Management is considering another equity offering, perhaps in the next year or two. Assume that during that time, the company will incur additional losses of $10 million.

If the company does nothing, it most surely will pass the 50 percent change in ownership threshold at its next equity offering. In that case, the $1 million of existing carryforward *plus* the $10 million in losses during the next two years will all be subject to the NOL carryforward limitations, and future deductibility will be limited or even lost.

In this situation, the company should *accelerate the change in ownership* before incurring the additional $10 million in losses. If the company issues another 3 percent of stock immediately, it crosses the 50 percent threshold and restricts the NOL limitations to the previously incurred $1 million loss carryforward.

At that point, the 50 percent test starts all over again. When the company undergoes its next round of financing, it gets a fresh start on the change of ownership test and has a much better chance of being able to use the $10 million of net operating losses as taxable deductions in future periods.

Making the Election

The election to capitalize or expense R&D costs must be made in the *first year's* tax return for which the company incurs any R&D costs. The amortization period for capitalized research and development also must be elected at that time, even though it may not commence for several years. The way in which a company treats R&D costs in that first year establishes an accounting method for tax purposes. Therefore, a company should carefully consider how expenses are classified in its initial tax return. In some situations, a company will take a deduction for an item such as salary expense that was, in fact, an R&D cost. By taking its deduction, the company inadvertently established an accounting treatment for future R&D costs.

Entities have the ability to change their tax accounting method with the permission of the Internal Revenue Service. Typically, these requests for change are granted; however, the IRS would undoubtedly be reluctant to grant a series of successive changes in a period of only a few years.

GET PROFESSIONAL SERVICES ADVISORS INVOLVED EARLY

A company engaged in R&D activities should seek the advice of its tax advisors *before* it files its first tax return to ensure that the right election for R&D costs is reflected. The company's first return establishes the tax treatment for all future R&D costs, and changes can be made only with the permission of the Internal Revenue Service.

Many start-up companies understandably try to put every single dollar into research and development and do not want to spend precious cash on professional fees. That strategy can backfire if the company chooses the wrong election for R&D costs in its first tax return and creates net operating losses that later cannot be utilized fully. Consulting with knowledgeable professionals to develop a tax strategy up front is not that expensive and can significantly reduce a company's tax liability in the future.

The election to capitalize or expense R&D costs can be made on a project-by-project basis. Thus, if a company has more than one R&D project, it can elect to expense one and capitalize the other. In its election filed with the IRS, the company should clearly identify the project it is capitalizing. If it starts in year 1 and capitalizes Project A while expensing Project B, the company's general method is the expense method and Project A is merely the exception. All future R&D costs on new projects would be expensed.

MILESTONE PAYMENTS

As described in earlier chapters, a company's corporate partnering arrangements may call for milestone payments. Depending on their nature, these payments may or may not be considered taxable income.

Milestone payments can take many forms. Some are essentially investments in stock. Others are considered shared research because the agreement calls for sharing of ownership of any resulting patents and technology. Payments for investments in stock or under shared research are not treated as income. Other milestone payments are so closely tied to the ultimate business of the company that they are considered business receipts and, therefore, taxable income.

In certain cases, the milestone payments may be deemed to be loans with contingent repayments. In this case, there would be no income from the transaction, because it involves the receipt of loan proceeds. Even though the payback may take the form of "royalties" for a specified period or amount, these are considered contingent repayment obligations.

Typically, most milestone payments are considered to be taxable income, but that determination requires a great deal of judgment. In making the determination, a key consideration is the economic substance of the transaction and whether it constitutes the receipt of business income and the commencement of business activities.

Business Commences

In a broad sense, business typically was thought to commence for tax purposes in the year in which a company begins to generate revenue from its business activities. In some instances, that might have been when the company began to receive milestone payments.

For example, suppose the partnering agreement stipulates that the corporate partner is to pay $10 million when the company reaches milestone A, and if the company ultimately generates a commercial product, the corporate partner has rights to manufacture and sell that product, paying the company a royalty. Under those conditions, the milestone payments are so connected with the ultimate business and the ultimate royalty that business was thought to have commenced when the company earned the milestone payments.

However, the attitude of the IRS toward R&D companies seems to be notably different from its attitude toward other companies when it comes to defining when business commences. Rather than looking to the time when business revenue is first generated, for tax purposes business appears to have commenced when the R&D activities begin. (See the section entitled "R&D Companies May Have No Capitalizable Start-up Costs.")

Once business commences, the company should begin to amortize any capitalized start-up costs. From that point forward, new start-up costs will be deducted currently. Capitalized R&D costs, however, would be amortized beginning when the taxpayer first realizes benefits from the R&D. Typically, this would be when the results of the R&D costs are put to an income-producing use.

If the company has been capitalizing its R&D costs and/or start-up costs, and if it is uncertain as to whether the milestone payments really do constitute the commencement of business (or the realization of benefits from the R&D), it should file a request with the IRS to begin deducting R&D costs/ and or general and adminstrative costs currently. That way there is no question it can take current deductions to offset any taxable income from the milestone payments.

CROSS-BORDER PAYMENTS

Some companies enter into agreements with overseas corporate partners and then receive cross-border milestone payments. Depending on how these agreements are structured, they may be subject to withholding by the foreign government.

In one example, a company entered into a partnering agreement with a French corporation that called for milestone payments and later royalties for the right to manufacture and sell future products. When the company reached its milestone and received its first payment, 15 percent of the amount had been withheld by the French government, which took the position that the payment constituted royalties subject to withholding.

The U.S. company and its tax advisors argued that the milestone payment was essentially a reimbursement for shared research expenses and therefore was not subject to the withholding. This argument failed. The U.S. company was allowed a tax credit for the amount withheld by the foreign government, but the company would much rather have received the cash. Such a situation is particularly true if the entity is not generating any taxable income, because tax credits are subject to certain limitations, and without current taxable income, it is uncertain whether they can ever be utilized.

A company can avoid having withholdings taken on cross-border payments in two ways:

1. *Tax review.* Any agreement that calls for cross-border milestone payments should be reviewed by a tax expert. If it appears that the payment might be subject to foreign withholding, the agreement should be restructured, if possible, to recharacterize the nature of the payment.
2. *Renegotiate.* If the agreement cannot be restructured and the payment will be subject to withholding, the U.S. company may be able to renegotiate the amount of the payment so that the net amount received is what the company needs. This type of arrangement may be difficult to negotiate, but the company's position should be that (a) it is selling its technology for a negotiated amount and that taxation at the source should be the responsibility of the buyer; and (b) it needs a certain amount of cash flow to continue its research after its milestones are achieved and it would be unwilling to enter into the agreement unless that cash flow would, in fact, be available.

TAX PLANNING FOR THE START-UP COMPANY

Start-up companies may generate little, if any, taxable income. Still, these companies cannot ignore tax planning and other tax-related decisions. With solid advice and an eye toward the future, a start-up company can take advantage of elections and provisions in the tax code to minimize its burn rate and maximize the after-tax cash flow once it begins operations.

R&D COMPANIES MAY HAVE
NO CAPITALIZABLE START-UP COSTS

Taxpayers have been wrestling with the troublesome subject of start-up costs since the U.S. Court of Appeals for the Fourth Circuit decided in 1965 that Richmond Television Corporation had not commenced its business until it obtained its Federal Communications Commication (FCC) license and began broadcasting. Subsequently, Congress codified the conceptual result in *Richmond Television* by enacting Section 195 of the Internal Revenue Code, which states that no current deduction is allowable for start-up expenditures.

That section also made available for the first time an election by taxpayers to amortize such expenditures over 60 months or longer, commencing with the month in which the active trade or business begins, provided that such election is contained in the tax return for the period that includes that month. However, Congress did not see fit to add any significant guidance on the factual questions of just when a taxpayer's business is to be treated as having begun.

For R&D companies—most notably in the biotech field—this question involves many millions of dollars and typically, many years. Indeed, most would prefer to capitalize early years' costs for income tax purposes rather than create or increase the operating losses, which, when used, might not completely eliminate the alternative minimum tax. Furthermore, some states have relatively short loss–carryforward periods before such losses expire— remember that Massachusetts, where a large number of biotech companies reside, only allows a five-year carryforward period.

Recently the National Office of the IRS was presented with this question. In the case of one biotech research company, it ruled, surprisingly, that R&D activities constituted the active trade or business for which the taxpayer was created (even though the taxpayer had not yet commenced manufacturing or selling any product or licensing any technology). Thus, once research commenced, the taxpayer had no capitalizable start-up costs.

The IRS ruling letter stated that "the taxpayer was organized to develop drugs for certain diseases. Therefore, its active trade or business began when the taxpayer began to function as a going concern (acquired the necessary assets, personnel, and resources) and performed those research and development activities for which it was organized." It is most significant that the IRS viewed the taxpayer's mission as one to "develop" drugs rather than to "make and sell" such drugs once they are developed.

This ruling was made in response to a request for a change in accounting method, and thus will not be published. While it applies only to the taxpayer to whom it was issued, it does indicate the current attitude and policy of the IRS National Office on this question. Taxpayers who desire certainty on this point should consider submitting their own request for ruling, rather than run the risk of the IRS audit division reaching a different conclusion in the course of an audit and then risking the possibility that the National Office personnel are not the same ones as those who issued the current ruling and may not agree with it.

Those requesting this private letter ruling have suggested to the IRS that a Revenue Ruling be published on this question, and it is hoped that one will appear in the near future Taxpayers would then be able to rely on that ruling and obtain certainty in their planning and tax returns without the need to obtain their own rulings.

Because the conclusion in this ruling would render all general and administrative expenses of a research company currently deductible, such companies may find it desirable to elect to capitalize all of their R&D expenses and amortize them over five years or longer, beginning with the month in which the taxpayer first realizes benefits from the R&D expenses (i.e., first puts the process, formula, invention, etc., to which the expenses relate to an income-producing use). This rule is different than the start-up rule, which focuses on the commencement of an active trade or business rather than the realization of benefits. Caution should be exercised, however, as the amortization period must be elected in the tax return when the R&D capitalization election is made, rather than in the return for the later year when income is first generated.

The IRS views the treatment of start-up costs as a method of accounting. Even erroneous methods cannot be corrected unilaterally by the taxpayer. A request for change in accounting method must be filed with the IRS in almost all cases to initiate a voluntary change. Failure to do so could leave taxpayers at the mercy of examining IRS agents, who would be free either to accept the taxpayer's method or to force a change to a correct method, which could result in the permanent loss of amounts not deducted in the correct periods as determined by the IRS.

INDEPENDENT CONTRACTORS VERSUS EMPLOYEES

Employment status is often one of the most misunderstood concepts in tax law. Many employers (and employees, for that matter) do not fully understand the distinction between independent contractors and employees. Unfortunately, there are also those who do understand the distinction, but exploit the relationship because it is to their advantage to do so. Many employers sidestep the distinction, thinking it irrelevant, not realizing that it is very significant and implicates two separate tax treatments and reporting requirements.

When a company hires an employee, that company then has the obligation to withhold federal, state, and social security (FICA) taxes. It also must pay unemployment and worker's compensation insurance and provide other benefits, such as paid sick leave, vacation and health insurance, and stock options and other such incentives to retain these employees. *When a company hires an independent contractor*, it does so with an understanding that the contractor will work pursuant to the terms of the contract that he or she bargained for. No taxes are withheld, no employee benefits are provided, and the scope and degree of the business relationship is determined by the conditions negotiated for in the contract. Clearly, the differences are quite extensive.

The IRS is very interested in ensuring that "workers" are correctly classified. Because companies do not withhold taxes for independent contractors, these contractors are required to pay their own taxes quarterly. Many independent contractors do not and therefore cheat the system of millions of dollars. Conversely, companies that deliberately misclassify employees as independent contractors forgo the payment of FICA, disability, and unemployment insurance and thereby deprive useful government programs of funding—which is, effectively, a depletion of rightful benefits for all workers in the entire system. Muddying the line between independent contractors and employees also enables companies to try to control the worker as an employee but deprive him or her the wages of an independent contractor.

EXHIBIT 9.1 Independent Contractor or Employee? The Word According to the IRS

Primary Factors	Yes	No
1. **Instructions:** Does the employer have right to require compliance with significant instructions?		
2. **Hours of Work:** Does the employer have the right to set the hours of work?		
3. **Order or Sequence:** Does the employer have the right to set the order or sequence of services to be performed?		
4. **Right to Discharge:** Does the employer have the right to discharge the worker?		
5. **Hiring Assistants:** Does the employer have the right to hire, pay, and supervise assistants, as the nature of work requires?		
6. **Realization of Profit:** Does the worker have no ability to realize a profit or loss?		
7. **Equipment:** Does the worker have no investment in significant tools, materials, and other equipment when such items are necessary to accomplish the task and are customarily provided by the employer?		
8. **Investment:** Does the worker have no significant investment in facilities when they are necessary to accomplish the task and they are customarily provided?		

Secondary Factors	Yes	No
9. **Training:** Does the employer train the worker?		
10. **Oral/Written Reports:** Does the employer have the right to require oral or written reports?		
11. **Rate of Payment:** Does the employer pay by the hour, week, or month?		
12. **Business/Travel Expenses:** Does the employer pay for business and/or travel expenses?		
13. **Services Rendered Personally:** Does the employer have the right to require personal service?		
14. **Multiple Employment:** Does the worker usually not work for more than one firm at a time?		
15. **Type of Relationship:** Does the worker maintain a continuing relationship with the employer?		
16. **Employer's Premises:** Does the worker work on the recipient's premises? Is he or she required to work on the premises?		

EXHIBIT 9.1 *(Continued)*

Secondary Factors	Yes	No
17. **Full Time Required:** Does the worker devote substantially full time to the employer?		
18. **Right to Terminate:** Does the worker have the right to terminate the relationship at any time without incurring liability?		
19. **Integration:** Is the worker integrated into the employer's business?		
20. **Availability:** Does the worker not make his or her services available to the public on a regular and consistent basis?		

If companies misclassify workers, they risk getting audited by the IRS or the Department of Labor. The stance taken is fairly aggressive, with the IRS sometimes requiring the company to pay all back withholding taxes plus interest—in addition to any fines it might impose. In some cases, misclassified workers have successfully sued for back benefits, such as retirement, disability, worker's compensation, and even stock options.

A worker cannot be classified as both an employee and an independent contractor—he or she must be classified as one or the other. The IRS has attempted to remove the indecision and confusion surrounding the employee-independent contractor status issue by developing 20 common law factors that provide guidance on those facts that are indicative of either one status or the other. Each of these two factors embraces the principles of control and independence. Are the services of the worker subject to the employer's will and control over what must be done and how it must be done? Exhibit 9.1 outlines the 20 factors.

Obviously, the determination is one that is strictly fact sensitive. A "yes" answer to a majority of the factors enumerated in the exhibit indicates that the worker is an employee; however, if the worker can offer sufficient facts (from those factors to which he or she replied "no") that indicate an independence from control by the employer, he or she may be classified an independent contractor. In making this determination, it is not necessary that the employer *actually* direct or control the manner in which services are performed; as long as the employer has the *right* to do so, the worker will be deemed an employee.

EBUSINESS: INTERNET TAX ISSUES

Despite the veritable implosion of the Internet and tech sectors on the stock market over the past few years—and the resulting economic malaise caused by the wreckage of that implosion—there is probably no marketplace more viable and dynamic than the Internet. Free from the restrictions and overhead costs of traditional bricks-and-mortar companies, Internet businesses have flourished, and will continue to flourish, as more and more people around the world log on to the Net. But perhaps the greatest restriction from which Internet entrepreneurs are free is that of having to pay taxes. The Internet is essentially a sales tax–free zone. Why? Simply put, the government does not know what to do with it.

The Internet is a relatively new entrant into the economic marketplace. Long the haven of pleasure-seekers chatting in cyberspace or battling cyberdemons across servers, it has developed into an opportunistic arena for barter and exchange that could not have existed 20 years ago. Products are finding their way to consumers who, but for the evolution of the Internet, may never have known of their existence. Because of the facility of this business model and the reduction of significant overhead costs (e.g., rent), the Internet has expanded rapidly and, as a consequence, has brought attention to the nontaxation aspect of its use.

A New York consumer can purchase articles from a New York company over the Internet and not pay a penny in sales tax. Yet if that same consumer walks across town to the same company and buys the same product, he or she may pay as much as 8.5 percent in sales tax. Equitable? Probably not.

The argument in favor of this model has always been that the only way to encourage and foster a thriving Internet economy is to create some incentive for consumers to use it. That incentive has long been the absence of any tax on a transaction consummated over the Internet. The alternative argument against this model is that nontaxation creates an unfair advantage to Internet retailers and deprives the government (both state and local) of necessary tax dollars.

Congress began reviewing the issue in early 1998, but because it could not arrive at a consensus, it passed the Internet Tax Freedom Act (Public Law 105-377, October 21, 1998), which placed a three-year moratorium on taxation of the Internet. So, for the term of the moratorium, Congress would not impose any new federal taxes on Internet access or e-commerce. This act expired in November 2001, thereby giving Congress an opportunity to revisit the issue and deliver a final determination of how Internet commerce is to be taxed. Congress opted to pass on the issue a second time—possibly as a result of sensitivity to the events of September 11 and a faltering economy—and extended the act until November 1, 2003.

Proponents of the act asked to make it permanent, leaving the Internet a tax-free zone. Opponents of the act asked Congress to grant states the power to enforce sales tax collection if the states can make sales tax compliance simpler. As it is unlikely that the states could introduce any meaningful simplified system of sales tax collection within the next few years, the two competing sides in Congress compromised and extended the Internet Tax Freedom Act.

Multistate Income Tax

While the act does not specifically address multistate income taxation, it has evolved into an increasingly hot issue as Internet companies start to realize profits from increased sales. No state may impose income tax on a company until that company has established a minimal jurisdictional presence in the state or nexus. But what qualifies as nexus? What activity supports that minimal jurisdictional presence?

Nexus is generally found when a remote seller has a certain quantity and quality of sales and marketing in the taxing jurisdiction. A company can be taxed only if it had sufficient "minimum contacts" within the taxing jurisdiction and a "substantial physical presence" in the state. With Internet businesses, a remote seller will utilize either an in-state or an out-of-state server to make his or her sales over the Internet. The act specifically states that an out-of-state server is not enough to claim nexus; however, the Act does not preclude a finding of nexus where the seller's Web site is hosted on a server that is located in state. Other factors that tend to support nexus include the employment of individuals in the state and active participation in marketing efforts in the taxing jurisdiction.

Because some states take the position that even a single sale in their jurisdiction creates nexus, a company would be well served to consult an attorney or accountant to discuss any potential tax liability.

Sales and Use Tax

Sales and use tax is one of the crucial issues of debate in the tax laws affecting the new Internet economy. The act, as promulgated, limits a state's right to impose sales and use tax on products sold over the Internet because it explicitly prohibits any discriminatory taxation. Local sales and use taxes are believed to be discriminatory because different jurisdictions charge varying rates of sales for various products, leading to disparate tax treatment of sales in different jurisdictions. With over 5,000 individual taxing jurisdictions in the United States, a small retailer would face an administrative nightmare trying to comply with them all. As stated earlier, each state would be required to simplify sales and use tax compliance before any effective method of taxation could be implemented.

What Next?

For now, the issue of Internet taxation has been placed on a hold. With so many Internet companies struggling just to stay in business, the government is not likely to launch a tax scheme that will further exacerbate their economic tribulations. If the economy improves by the time the Internet Tax Freedom Act expires in November 2003, the government may, indeed, opt to tax Internet transactions. With that in mind, many businesses should be prepared to adapt to the changing business climate. As of this writing it appears that the issue of taxation of Internet transactions is going to be bifurcated. The latest information indicates that Internet services, such as the provision of an internet connection, may be granted a five year moratorium from taxation. As to product sales, there is currently no legislation on the docket for the current congressional session. The practical result of this non-action is the de facto extension of tax exemption for Internet transactions beyond November 2003. With national elections looming in 2004, it looks more and more likely that this hot button issue will not be dealt with until 2005 at the earliest.

CHAPTER 10

How to Attract and Retain Quality Employees and Management Teams

Ultimately, the success of a business depends more and more on people. We can't just make a huge investment in a machine or in land—it's the people who are going to make a business successful, especially in the technology area.

—Martin Somelofske, Principal, Deloitte & Touche LLP

One of the most important issues for an emerging company of any kind—technology or otherwise—is knowing how to assemble the highest quality management and employee teams possible and, once assembled, how to retain them. Experienced investors always say that they would rather invest in a company with an "A" management team and a "B" product than in one with an "A" product and a "B" management team. But it is not unusual to see a highly creative, highly entrepreneurial person trying to launch a company without a clue about how to attract and retain other employees.

The art of compensation—and the tax and accounting issues that accompany it—is rife with pitfalls and missed opportunities. One of the most commonly mishandled elements of compensation is stock ownership, or equity-based compensation. While the whole practice may be getting a bad rap during this time of corporate scandal, there really are some very good reasons for using stock ownership as a way to reward employees. However, there are also many entrepreneurs who have gotten into trouble down the road when they issue stock to employees and investors without good long-range planning.

There are a few critical things to understand when tackling the complicated world of equity-based compensation. From the requirements of the

Financial Accounting Standards Board (FASB) requirements regarding the recognition of the accountingfor equity-based compensation to issues of dilution and overhang—which will be discussed later in this chapter—to the ultimate issue of board governance, the arena of equity-based compensation is not for the fainthearted.

OVERVIEW OF EQUITY-BASED COMPENSATION

Equity-based compensation involves the use of a company's own stock, options for its own stock, or both, to reward employees. Start-up companies use equity-based compensation for two main reasons:

1. *To improve cash flow.* Offering employees stock or options reduces the amount of cash a company must spend on compensation, leaving more to be used for the company's research and development (R&D) efforts.
2. *To attract, retain, and motivate key employees.* No start-up company can or should try to compete with larger, more established companies in setting the amount of cash compensation for its employees. However, that does not mean that the start-up can afford anything less than the best people. Employees who receive equity-based compensation will be better off than if they received more cash if the company does well. By receiving equity "kickers" instead of cash, the employees are tied more closely to the company's results and have greater incentive to perform.

From the time of the first Silicon Valley start-up, cash-strapped high-tech companies have used the promise of future wealth embodied in stock option plans to attract key executives. Thanks to the overall increase in the stock market over the years for both high-tech and biotech companies, this technique has been extremely successful, at relatively little cash cost to the companies (see Exhibit 10.1).

Maximizing Cash Flow

Equity-based compensation arrangements allow a company to conserve its cash by reducing, though not eliminating, the cash paid out for salaries.

When a company pays salaries, its total cash outflow is equal to the amount of the salary *plus* the employer's share of social security and Medicare taxes (currently at 7.65 percent). Thus, if a company were to pay an employee a cash salary of $100, the company's total cash outflow would be $107.65.

In addition to the employer's portion of social security and Medicare taxes, the company also must withhold the employee's federal and state income taxes and the employee's portions of the social security and Medicare taxes. This withholding does not increase the amount of the company's cash outflow; instead, it decreases the amount of cash received by the employee. If

EXHIBIT 10.1   Equity Utilization

High-tech companies grant twice as much as other industries as a percentage of shares outstanding.

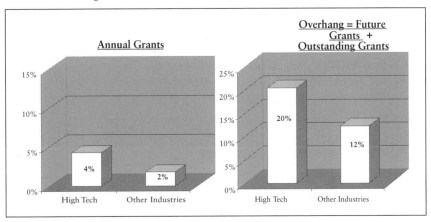

Source: NASPP 2000 Stock Plan Design & Administrative Survey.

a company paid a cash salary of $100, and assuming a 28 percent federal tax rate and no state taxes, the total cash flow paid out by the company would be:

Net paid to employee ($100 – 28 – 7.65)	$ 64.35
Paid to federal government	
Employee federal tax withholding	28.00
Employee social security & Medicare withholding	7.65
Employer social security & Medicare tax	7.65
Total cash outflow	$ 107.65

The granting of stock or stock options eliminates the cash paid for salary expenses, but it does not relieve the company of its obligation to pay the federal government the employee withholdings plus its own share of social security and Medicare taxes.

Assuming that a company paid an employee's salary of $100 in stock rather than cash, the total cash outflow to the company would be:

Cash paid to employee	$ 0
Paid to federal government	
Employee federal tax withholding	28.00
Employee social security & Medicare withholding	7.65
Employer social security & Medicare tax	7.65
Total cash outflow	$ 43.30

In this example, the fair market value of the stock granted to the employee was $64.35, which is equal to the total salary minus the employee's withholdings.

The amount taxable to the employee is based on the difference between the fair market value of the stock and the price paid by the employee. The last example assumes the stock had a fair market value of $64.35 and the employee paid nothing for it. If the company granted the employee a stock option that required the employee to pay $10, the social security and Medicare taxes would be based on a salary expense of $54.35—the difference between the fair market value of the stock and what the employee paid for it.

Tax Treatment of Equity-Based Compensation

The use of certain forms of equity-based compensation can generate a tax deduction to the employer in an amount equal to the income reported by the employee. The deductions generally are recognized during the same period in which the employee recognizes taxable income. To take such a deduction, the company must file a W-2 or a 1099 form with the Internal Revenue Service (IRS) and the recipients of the income.

In practice, the tax deductions for equity-based compensation are of limited current value, since start-up companies typically generate net operating losses that will not be utilized for many years.

A more important consideration is the timing and amount of taxable income recognized by the employee and whether that income is taxed at ordinary or capital gains rate. The receipt of stock is a taxable event to the employee, as is the exercise of stock options if they are nonqualified options (NQOs). If that employee does not have sufficient cash to pay the taxes, equity-based compensation arrangements actually can be a *disincentive* for the employee. For that reason, companies entering into equity-based compensation agreements should consider the effect these agreements will have on the tax liabilities of its employees.

In general, when an employer transfers property to an employee as compensation for services rendered, the employee recognizes taxable income equal to the fair market value of the property transferred. When stock of a nonpublic company is transferred, valuation can be difficult. Nevertheless, some objective determination of fair market value should be made when the stock is transferred to the employee so as to provide support for the deduction in case the IRS later questions the value during an audit.

It is also advisable to transfer the stock to employee as early in the company's life as possible. The earlier the transfer is made, the easier it would likely be to justify a low value to the stock and therefore less income to its employees. For example, if a biotech company had a new drug that was already undergoing Phase III clinical trials, the stock of the company would clearly be worth more than if the company was just beginning to assemble its research team. An earlier grant also may help to avoid other potential problems, such as net operating loss limitations due to changes in ownership, as discussed in the last chapter.

Equity-based compensation arrangements can be broken down into two types: grants of stock and grants of stock options.

GRANTS OF STOCK

Outright Grant of Stock

An outright grant of stock is one in which the company grants the stock to an employee without any temporary restrictions, which would require the employee to return the stock if he or she leaves the company before a certain period of time has passed. When stock is granted outright, the employee is taxed on the excess of the value of the stock less any amount he or she is required to pay for the stock. (If the amount is greater than the value of the stock, there are no further income tax consequences to the employee.)

Any fair value of the stock above the amount per share that the employee is required to pay, if any, is included as wages in the employee's W-2. The employee is then responsible for paying any income taxes on this amount, either with the filing of the tax return or periodically by making estimated tax payments.

The employee must come up with the cash necessary to make these tax payments. While this amount is less than if the employee had to pay full value for the stock, it is still a burden on the employee, and the timing required for the payments is often not ideal.

A number of techniques are available to reduce the cash flow burden on the employee. Two of these techniques are:

1. A permanent buyback provision *places a permanent restriction on the stock, such that the employee is obligated to give the company a right of first refusal on any subsequent sale of stock. For example, assume that stock worth $10 is granted to the employee for $1. At a 40 percent ordinary income tax rate, the employee would owe $3.60 in federal income taxes (40 percent multiplied by the $9 difference between the fair value of the stock and the employee's purchase price).* If the terms of the stock grant included a permanent buyback provision, then whenever the employee decided to sell the stock, he or she would be obligated to first offer it back to the company at the then fair market value less $9. In effect, the permanent buyback provision means that the employee has paid full value for the stock at the date it is granted ($1 in cash plus $9 at the time it is sold back to the company). Since the employee has paid

full value, there is no income and therefore no tax. The downside is that the employee forever gives up the built-in gain that exists at the date of the award.

2. The *grossed-up bonus technique* requires the company to pay a bonus to the employee so that, after taxes on the bonus are paid, enough cash remains in the hands of the employee to pay the tax on the stock award. In the above example, a bonus of $6, taxed at a 40 percent rate, would generate net cash proceeds to the employee of $3.60—just enough to pay the tax on the stock award.

While a cash bonus is good for the employee, the employer's objective of preserving cash would defeated at least in part. Employees prefer grants of stock for another reason. If they hold unrestricted stock for longer than a year, any appreciation in the fair market value of the stock is taxed at the capital gains rate and not as ordinary income. Additionally, certain small businesses have been targeted for even lower capital gains tax rates, which make stock grants even more attractive.

Restricted Stock and Restricted Stock Units

Part of the advantage to offering equity-based compensation is that it helps a start-up company retain its key employees. The company wants the employee to use his or her best efforts for at least a few years, improving the performance of the company (and its stock price) for the mutual benefit of both employee and employer. Under an outright stock grant, the employer is vulnerable to having the employee take the stock and leave the company.

To protect itself, the company might choose to lock in the employee for a period of time before granting full, unrestricted ownership of the stock. For example, the company might require that the employee return the stock if he or she leaves the company within five years. Companies considering this type of arrangement should consider its implications carefully. While this type of arrangement satisfies the employer's desire, it could have a disastrous tax effect on the employee.

In this situation, any income tax consequences are deferred until the time that the restriction lapses—that is, at the end of five years. However, the income is not measurable by reference to today's stock value, but by reference to the value at the time the restriction lapses—namely, five years from now, even if the employee paid full value at the date the shares actually were transferred. While the company clearly expects the stock value in five years to be significantly higher then than it is now, this good news can put the employee in an untenable tax position.

For example, assume the same facts as in the previous example: The company grants stock to an employee, requiring a payment of $1 for stock with a fair market value of $10. Assume the agreement obligated the employee to return the stock if he or she left the company within five years.

If the value of the stock at the end of five years increased to $30, the employee in the example has a federal tax liability of $11.60, as calculated:

Fair market value of stock when fully vested	$30.00
Employer's basis in stock	1.00
Gain	29.00
Ordinary income tax rate	40%
Tax liability	$11.60
Cash netted by employee	$18.40

Note that the gain is calculated at the ordinary tax rate rather than the more favorable capital gains rate. It is also significant that the taxable event is *not* the sale of the stock (which would generate cash to pay the taxes) but the expiration of the restriction period. If the company is not yet public (or even, in some cases, if it is), the employee may not even be able to sell shares of stock to raise the cash needed to satisfy the liability at the time that the restriction expires. In this situation, the employee would have to find some other source of cash to pay the tax—not good for employee morale, which was one of the reasons for granting stock in the first place.

To reduce this onerous tax bite, the employee can file a Section 83(b) election within 30 days of the original restricted stock grant. The effect of this election is to treat the stock—for tax purposes only—as if the five-year vesting provision did not exist. The employee voluntarily elects to be taxed, at ordinary rates, on the value of the stock at time of grant (less any amount paid for the stock). Making this election puts the employee in the same tax position as if he or she had been granted the stock outright. A portion of the tax, calculated at the *ordinary income tax rates*, would be assessed at the date of the *stock award*, based on the difference between the then-fair market value and the amount the employee pays for the stock. A second tax, calculated at the *capital gains tax rate*, would be assessed at the date the stock is *sold*.

In this example (assuming the employee sold the stock at the expiration of five years), if the employee had filed a Section 83(b) election, the total tax would have been:

Tax assessed at date of award (assuming 83(b) election)	
Fair market value of stock at grant date	$ 10.00
Employee's basis in stock	1.00
Gain	9.00
Ordinary income tax rate	40%
Tax liability	$3.60

Tax assessed at date of sale

Fair market value of stock at date of sale	$30.00
Employee's basis in stock	10.00
Gain	20.00
Capital gains tax rate*	15%
Tax liability at date of sale	3.00
Total tax liability	$6.60
Cash netted by employee	$23.40

*Assuming a holding period of more than 18 months.

The employee enjoys two significant advantages by making a Section 83(b) election: (1) the overall tax liability is reduced by $4, and (2) the bulk of the tax is paid on the sale of the stock, when cash proceeds are available to pay the tax.

As a trade-off, the employee must pay a portion of the tax immediately, at the stock award date. However, the employer and the employee can deal with this liability in the same way as they would have in the case of the out-right grant—namely, using the permanent restriction or the cash bonus. However, in most instances employers are unwilling to grant cash bonuses. If the stock price goes down and stays down, the employee will have paid tax on income, which he or she will never realize in cash. An employee's decision to make an 83(b) election is impacted by his or her degree of confidence that the value of the company's stock will increase. If it does not increase, there is no refund on the taxes that the employee elected to pay in an earlier period. Thus, careful consideration should be given before this technique is employed.

Employees wishing to make a Section 83(b) election have only 30 days from the date the stock is received to file the election. No extensions are available. In some situations, if the company is generating taxable income, it is quite common for the company to insist that employees make the Section 83(b) election so the company gets a tax deduction in the year in which it gives the stock to its employees.

Restricted Stock Units

Another twist on the use of restricted stock, and one which is gaining in popularity at the time of this writing, is the granting of restricted stock units (RSUs). With restricted stock grants, shares are issued to the employee and vest over specified future timeframes. With RSUs, the right to stock is granted, but the stock itself is given to the employee in the future, generally at the time of vesting, although it could be later, for example, at retirement. The tax treatment difference arises because no property is transferred at the date of grant. Therefore no tax event occurs.

However, a special rule applies to FICA related to the value of such grants. Check with a tax advisor for the specific implications. The advantage of RSUs is that the taxation on the value of the stock is deferred until the stock is delivered to the grantee. No 83(b) election is available, since no property changes hands at grant. The value of the stock is considered to be compensation upon delivery and taxed just like cash compensation. Properly implemented, an RSU plan can defer taxation beyond vesting, a feature not available using restricted stock.

> *On the bright side, equity-based compensation has driven many young entrepreneurs and employees to real wealth. Examples like Bill Gates and Michael Dell are well known, but there are a lot of other millionaires out there who you never hear about, and it's all because of these stock options.*
>
> —Martin Somelofske, Principal, Deloitte & Touche LLP

STOCK OPTIONS

Stock options provide several advantages over stock grants, both outright grants and vesting stock. These advantages include:

- *No initial cash is required.* The employee does not have to pay the company for the option, so no cash is required at the grant date. Just as important, the granting of an option is not considered a taxable event, so there is no income tax liability to satisfy.
- *Cashless exercise is possible.* Some plans permit employees to exercise their options without paying cash. This can be done either by turning over already owned stock to the company or by forfeiting some of the options. This technique, however, does not eliminate the need to provide the cash required to satisfy the company's withholding liability of the individual's tax liability, and there may also be negative financial accounting consequences.
- *It provides incentives to employees.* A stock option allows the company to meet one of its primary objectives: to attract and provide incentives to employees by giving them an opportunity to get a piece of the action if the company does well.

However, stock options have their own tax and financial accounting pitfalls that must be addressed before an informed decision can be made as to the proper form of equity-based compensation to be used.

Stock options can be divided into two types: incentive stock options (ISOs) or nonqualified options (NQOs).

Incentive Stock Options

Incentive stock options are creatures of the tax law and, as such, come with their own statutory baggage. In order to qualify as an ISO, all of these conditions must be met:

- Shares acquired from the exercise of the option cannot be sold within (a) two years from the granting of the option, or (b) one year from the exercise of the option.
- Only *employees* can be granted ISOs (i.e., not directors or independent contractors)
- The option price must at least equal the fair market value of the stock at the time the option is granted (if the employee already owns more than 10 percent of the outstanding stock, the price must be at 110 percent of the fair market value)
- The value of the underlying stock exercisable for the first time cannot exceed $100,000 in any calendar year

If these requirements are met, the transfer of the stock to the employee on the exercise of the option is not taxable for regular income tax purposes. However, the difference between the fair market value of the stock at the date of exercise and the exercise price of the option is an item of tax preference for alternative minimum tax (AMT) purposes.

Postexercise the employee has a tax basis in the stock equal to the exercise price, and the holding period begins on the date of the exercise. Assuming that the employee holds the stock for at least one year (both for ISO purposes and to satisfy the long-term capital gains holding period), the sale of the stock will generate a long-term capital gain equal to the difference between the sale proceeds and the exercise price. For AMT purposes, the gain would equal the difference between the sales price and the fair market value at the date the ISO was exercised.

For example, let us assume:

- In year 1, an employee was granted an option to purchase 100 shares of company stock for $5 per share, which is the fair market value of the stock at this time.
- In year 4, the stock is trading at $15 per share, and the employee exercises the option, paying $500 (100 shares multiplied by the exercise price of $5 per share) for stock now worth $1,500.
- In year 7, the employee sells all 100 shares for $3,000.

Assuming that all the conditions for an ISO have been met, the tax treatment for the employee at certain key dates is:

Year 1: Granting of the option	Not a taxable event
Year 4: Exercise of the option	Tax-free for regular income tax purposes Preference item for AMT purposes is $1,000 (difference between fair market value of $1,500 and exercise price of $500) Tax basis in stock is $500

Year 7: Sale of the stock	Capital gains tax calculated on $2,500 (difference between $3,000 price and tax basis of $500) AMT preference item is $1,500 (difference between $3,000 sale price and $1,500 fair market value of stock when option was exercised)

Generally, a company is required to pay social security and Medicare taxes and the employee withholdings only when the employee recognizes ordinary income. In the example just described, the employee never recognizes ordinary income, only capital gains. Thus, under most ISO plans, the company does not have a cash outflow. Indeed, it has a cash inflow when the employee exercises his or her option.

However, the mirror image result of this is that the company is not allowed a tax deduction. A tax deduction is allowed only if the employee recognizes ordinary income. If the company is a start-up generating net operating losses, the loss of this deduction will not be a great sacrifice.

Nonqualified Stock Options

Any option that does not qualify as an incentive stock option is considered to be a nonqualified option (NQO). Although the granting of a NQO option is not a taxable event, the exercise of one results in significant tax consequences both to the employee and to the employer. Also, if the employee makes a disqualifying disposition of an ISO (i.e., within two years from the grant or one year from exercise), the ISO retroactively becomes an NQO, with all the attendant tax consequences.

On the exercise of an NQO, the individual recognizes compensation income, measured by the excess of the fair market value of the stock over the exercise price. This income is taxed at ordinary income rates. The individual must be able to satisfy this tax liability, and generally will not be able to dispose of enough shares to do it. Therefore, the source of cash to meet this liability becomes a concern. This is true whether the individual is an employee or an independent contractor (including a director).

If the recipient of the NQO is an employee, the company has a responsibility to withhold income and social security taxes on the exercise of the option. Generally, the tax consequences (to both the company and the individual) and possible mitigating strategies on the exercise of an NQO are similar to those resulting from the granting of stock.

FINANCIAL ACCOUNTING CONSIDERATIONS

In addition to the income tax implications, start-up companies also should consider the accounting treatment of equity-based compensation and how

THE EMPLOYEE PERSPECTIVE:

Five Things to Remember about Equity-Based Compensation

#1 *Early Exercise and Sec. 83(b)*

Before joining a company, be sure that you can make an election to exercise your options early and then consider electing to be taxed on the spread under Internal Revenue Code Sec. 83(b) if you are confident that the stock price is likely to rise. This combination will reduce your taxes to the minimum and will maximize your long-term capital gains. (Also, there is no AMT issue when ISOs are exercised.)

#2 *You Always Begin in the Hole*

With stock options, you always begin in the hole. Think of stock options as playing poker: You need to ante up before you can play; so you are in a loss position right off the bat. The challenge is to minimize your loss position—i.e., pay the smallest ante possible.

#3 *Long-term Capital Gains*

With nonqualified options, exercise and hold for 12 months and you'll receive long-term capital gains. With ISOs, you must first exercise and hold the stock for 12 months—and for at least two years from the date of grant. Meet these two ISO requirements and when you sell the stock, you'll be entitled to long-term capital gains.

#4 *Generally, with Start-ups, the Longer You Hold the Options, the Larger the Spread*

As a general rule with start-ups, the longer you wait to exercise your options, the greater the spread will be, since the stock value should be climbing. And the larger the spread, the greater the adverse tax consequences will be when you exercise. For ISO stock, the spread is subject to the AMT. With nonqualified options, the spread is taxed as compensation.

#5 *Maximize Your Annual AMT Credit*

On an annual basis, exercise ISOs to the extent that there is no AMT. Although ISOs are a tax preference item under the AMT, there is a small exemption, $33,750 for single filers and $45,000 for joint filers, against the imposition of the AMT. Unfortunately, the AMT calculation is so complex, your actual exemption amount could be much smaller. Nevertheless, each year you need to determine the maximum number of ISOs that can be exercised without incurring AMT—and you need to exercise that amount on or before December 31st.

Source: Robert L. Sommers, "The Five Major Points to Remember About Compensation Stock Options," January 2001, *www.taxprophet.com.*

these arrangements will impact their financial statements. There are two basic methods of accounting for equity-based compensation:

1. *The intrinsic value method.* The intrinsic value method measures compensation expense as the excess—if any—of the quoted price of the stock at the measurement date (usually, the date the option is granted) over the amount the employee must pay to acquire the stock. Thus, for an ISO, where the exercise price of the stock must be equal to or greater than the market price of the stock at grant date, there is no intrinsic value, and no compensation expense would be reported on the income statement.

2. *The fair value method.* Under the fair value method, compensation cost is measured at the grant date of the option based on the estimated fair value of the option as determined using an option pricing method. The most common model in current use is the Black-Scholes model. Incentive stock options typically do have a determinable fair value at grant date (even though the exercise price is equal to or greater than the then-fair value of the stock), because of time, usually several years, during which the option is exercisable and this amount must be reported as an expense on the company's income statement.

Under current accounting rules,[1] companies are encouraged, but not required, to adopt the fair value method of accounting for stock-based compensation. Companies may continue to use the intrinsic method; however, if they do, they must make pro forma disclosures of net income and, if presented, earnings per share, in the footnotes to their financial statements as if the fair value-based method had been applied.

In practice, the fair value method invariably results in lower reported earnings because stock options do have a measurable economic value even if the exercise price is greater than or equal to the fair value of the stock at the grant date of the option. For that reason, until recently most companies have elected to calculate earnings using the intrinsic value method and then make the required fair value disclosures in the notes to the financial statements.

As this volume goes to press, the discussion of whether to continue to allow the intrinsic method of accounting is again being renewed. There is tremendous activity among accounting standard setters both in the United States and around the globe to mandate a fair-value-based method as the required method of accounting for equity based compensation. In all likelihood a change to a fair-value only methodology will be implemented, possibly as early as 2004.

Intrinsic Value Method

Compensation expense under the intrinsic value method is measured as the quoted market price of the stock at the "measurement date" less the amount, if any, that the employee is required to pay to acquire the underlying stock. In the example used previously, if an employee receives an option to purchase 100 shares of company stock at $5 per share at a time when the fair value of the stock is also $5 per share, then no compensation expense would be recognized for financial accounting purposes under this method.

When applying the intrinsic value method, the determination of the measurement date can have an impact on the amount of compensation expense to be recognized. The measurement date is defined as the first date on which both of the following are known:

- The number of shares that an individual employee is entitled to receive
- The option or purchase price

For many plans, those two conditions are met on the date an option is granted or stock is awarded to an individual employee. However, the measurement date may be later than the date of grant or award in plans with variable terms that depend on events after the date of grant or award other than the passage of time. Plans that have a measurement date subsequent to grant date include:

- *Performance-based vesting.* Some stock options arrangements call for performance-based vesting that allows the employee to exercise the option only if the employee achieves certain performance goals. Under these types of plans, compensation expense is not accrued until it becomes probable that the performance goals will be achieved.
- *Stock appreciation rights.* Stock appreciation rights entitle employees to receive cash, stock, or both as the market value of the company's stock increases over a specified price. Under these types of plans, compensation expense and accrued compensation should be adjusted at the end of each reporting period to reflect the changes in the price of the company's stock.

The danger with variable equity-based compensation plans is that the impact on earnings is beyond the company's direct control. Changes in the company's stock price or the performance of its employees can significantly impact the income statement—particularly if the plan applies to a large block of employees. Large fluctuations in earnings can alter plans to go public, especially if the public offering is based primarily on earnings.

Fair Value Method

Under the fair value method, compensation cost is measured at grant date based on the fair value of the stock or options awarded to the employee. This amount is then recognized as an expense over the employee's expected service period, which is usually the same as the vesting period.

The fair value of a company's stock and stock options is determined as follows:

- *Nonvested stock.* The fair value of nonvested stock is its market price or estimated fair value, if the stock is not publicly traded. To determine fair value, assume the stock was fully vested and issued on the grant date.
- *Restricted stock.* As used in the accounting literature, restricted stock means shares that are contractually or governmentally restricted after they are vested and issued to the employees. For example, if the employee is obligated to offer the company a right of first refusal on any subsequent sales of the subject stock, those shares would be considered restricted. The fair value of those restricted shares is established by the fair value of similarly restricted stock issued to nonemployees.
- *Stock options.* The fair value of a stock option should be estimated using an option pricing model.

Numerous computerized models exist to help companies estimate the fair value of their stock options. The accounting literature describes two (Black-Scholes and binomial) that may be used for this purpose, but it does not require the use of a specific model. In practice, the Black-Scholes model has gained widespread acceptance. The only requirement is that whichever model the company uses, it must take into account:

- Exercise price of the option
- Expected life of the option
- Current market price or fair value of the underlying stock
- Expected dividends on the stock
- Risk-free interest rate for the expected term of the option

Additionally, if the company's stock is publicly traded, the option pricing model also must consider the expected volatility of the underlying stock. This is generally determined by reference to its historical volatility, if available, or to the historical volatility of comparable companies in the same industry.

With a computerized pricing model, calculating an estimate of an option's fair value is not difficult. However, the validity of the resulting amount depends totally on the accuracy of the underlying assumptions. Estimates of the expected life of the option or dividends on the stock (or, for public companies, the volatility of the stock) may be highly judgmental and have a significant impact on the estimate of fair value and, ultimately, the income statement.

For years technology companies fought to convince accounting standard setters to continue to allow the intrinsic method of accounting for stock options. One round of that fight ended in 1995 when the Financial Accounting Standards Board issued FASB Statement No. 123, which encouraged, but did not mandate, a fair-value approach to option accounting. Events of the past three years including the bear market, Enron, and other scandals and movement on the international front to adopt fair-value accounting have brought the issue into the headlines again. As mentioned

STOCK OPTION EXPENSING—A "QUICK HIT" SURVEY

The list of major companies that are moving toward expensing employee stock options is growing. WorldatWork, the leading not-for-profit professional organization for compensation and benefits, surveyed over 500 members in July 2002 to gauge the opinions of professionals who administer stock option plans to see how they feel about this accounting switch.

While the vast majority (74 percent) of companies said they had not yet made up their minds about what they would do if legislation or regulation mandated the expensing of stock options, here is what the others said*:

10% would offer smaller stock option grants.

9% would shift to more performance-based stock options.

8% would discontinue providing stock options to employees below the highest/executive level.

7% would make stock option grants more infrequently.

6% would not change current practices.

1% would no longer provide stock options to any employees.

*Respondents checked all that applied; therefore, total percentage is greater than 100%.

previously, a fair-value method looks likely to be mandated as early as next year. However, earlier in 2003 a decision by a single company has reframed the debate.

In early July, Microsoft announced that it would voluntarily start expensing all existing options starting with the company's 2004 fiscal year. Moreover, it also will completely stop granting stock options and instead issue restricted stock units (RSUs), vesting over five years, to all employees on a go-forward basis. Microsoft's announcement was a highlight amid growing interest in restricted stock and RSUs with a corresponding shift away from options. Accounting issues alone were not the only motivating factors in this shift. Many companies discovered a dark side to options, which coincided with their stock prices going down—often substantially—in the recent, extended bear market. In many cases employees were left with "underwater" options (options with a strike price substantially higher than the market price of the underlying stock). Underwater options are perceived as worthless by employees and therefore the utility of options as a retention device is negated.

Restricted stock and RSUs, in contrast, retain some value even if the stock retreats, and thereby continue to have retention value during their vesting period. In addition there is an assertion that restricted stock better aligns with the interests of non-employee shareholders. Because fewer shares are granted versus options granted on a value-to-value basis, there is less dilution to shareholders. Additionally the accounting charge is based on the actual value of the shares rather than on a multi-variable option pricing model. The next twelve months will likely demonstrate whether Microsoft's approach is part of a trend away from options.

STRATEGIES FOR ADOPTING EQUITY-BASED COMPENSATION PLANS

Determining appropriate equity-based compensation plans can depend on the company's stage of development. At or near the beginning of the company's history, the fair market value of the company's common stock is likely to be at its lowest point, possibly not much in excess of par value. In this situation, direct grants of stock subject to vesting formulas with timely Section 83(b) tax elections, or grants of RSUs, may be the most appropriate vehicle from both the company's and the employee's point of view.

As the company matures (and, it is hoped, its technology development is achieving success), it becomes more difficult to sustain a low fair value calculation for its stock. Therefore, to minimize the potential cash burdens to the company and the individual, options—both ISOs and NQOs—have traditionally been the equity vehicles of choice, although RSUs are making inroads as described previously. Even though the company permanently forgoes a tax deduction on ISOs and defers such deduction until the income recognition event of the employee under NQOs and RSUs, these tax considerations are most often outweighed by the reduced cash requirements inherent in options as compared with payment of cash compensation for emerging technology companies.

Compensation Committees

When a company reaches a certain size, the issue of equity-based compensation is just one of a myriad of decisions that have to be made in the area of compensation. The company's board of directors should begin by electing a Compensation Committee, whose members will be responsible for overseeing the executive compensation programs for the company's CEO, other top executives, and even outside directors. All compensation packages—including salary, stock options, health and other benefits, and bonuses—should be subject to strict standards, and the packages for senior management team members should conform to those standards and also withstand board scrutiny. The Compensation Committee plays an integral and visible role in the overall corporate governance of the company, including:

- Helping the full board balance the interests of shareholders and management
- Bearing responsibility for ensuring a strong link between executive pay and corporate performance
- Ensuring that compensation programs support the overall business strategies of the company

Role of the Compensation Committee

Compensation committees have a variety of roles within a corporate structure that, if performed responsibly, will provide the checks and balances needed to avoid the kind of corporate scandals that have rocked the business world in the early 2000s. Some of these duties include:

- Helping to design and implement compensation programs that will attract, retain, and motivate management and provide a strong link between pay and performance
- Serving an oversight role vis-à-vis management, including the development of compensation programs, performance appraisals, and often CEO succession plans
- Providing constant and ongoing communications with the full board of directors
- Ensuring a clarity of communications with shareholders and investors
- Conducting ongoing reviews of management relative to the performance of the company, reviewing stock plans, performance goals, annual incentive awards, and management succession
- Creating and/or updating a Compensation Committee charter that outlines roles and duties of the committee; discusses membership criteria; sets up guidelines to choose the chairperson; and defines the role that outside consultants will play
- Ensuring that the company's compensation philosophy is being implemented in an appropriate way

The Compensation Committee should be chosen through a full board process or though a preselected Nominating or Corporate Governance Committee. The most effective Compensation Committees are relatively small, having no more than five or six members maximum, with a recommended minimum of three, and—to avoid conflicts or the appearance of impropriety—the chairperson should be elected either by the full board or an appropriate subcommittee, never appointed by the CEO.

In fact, as proposed by the New York Stock Exchange in a recent Governance Proposal, the CEO should not even be a member of the Compensation Committee; it should, in fact, be composed of only "independent members." It is recommended that committee members rotate service for a number of years (typically three or four) and then rotate off. Likewise, it is recommended

KEY COMPENSATION COMMITTEE ACTIVITIES

Periodic	Annual	Ongoing
Establish and/or update committee charter	Assess corporate and executive performance and compare to pay levels	Respond to shareholder concerns
Develop appropriate compensation philosophy with pay-for-performance provisions	Approve compensation plans and pay levels for the CEO and other top executives	Ensure proper communications between the committee and the rest of the board, as well as appropriate members of the management team
Ensure proper succession and evaluation plans for the CEO	Determine appropriate levels of participation in various compensation plans	Ensuring the effectiveness of the executive compensation philosophy
Review the impact of the change in control provisions	Produce the annual Compensation Committee report	
Hire and/or approve outside consultants	Review and evaluate board of director compensation	

that the committee chairperson should rotate after one or two years of service as chair.

A typical Compensation Committee is responsible for a variety of activities, performed on a periodic, annual, or ongoing basis.

Pay for Performance

The Compensation Committee is responsible for ensuring that a strong link exists between executive pay and company performance. It is the committee's job to conduct regular assessments of company and executive performance and, in an ideal world, to see that there is a balance between the two. Doing this involves looking to the outside, as well, examining the financial performance and compensation philosophies of well-selected peer companies.

In examining the relationship between corporate and individual executive pay and the company's level of performance, the committee also must confirm that:

- The right performance measures are determined and used consistently
- The appropriate goals and/or performance targets are established
- The programs in place are aligned with the overall company goals (i.e., the achievement of the business plan)

COMPONENTS OF TOTAL COMPENSATION

The Compensation Committee is responsible for thoroughly assessing all the elements of the total executive compensation package. These elements could include:

- Base salary
- Short-term incentive: annual bonus
- Medium-term incentives: stock options, stock appreciation rights (SARs), restricted stock, RSUs, phantom stock (1)
- Qualified or broad-based benefits plans: pension plans, medical and dental plans, savings plans, life insurance plans, disability plans
- Other perquisites, as defined by the company

(1) Stock appreciation rights give the recipient the right to the monetary value of the increase in value of a specified number of shares of stock over a specified period of time. SARs are usually paid in cash, but could be paid in shares. Phantom stock is similar to SARs, but is more generally a bonus payable in cash at a point in the future and calculated as either the value of a certain number of shares or the value of the increase in value of those shares at the future point in time.

It's one thing for entrepreneurs to take huge risks in secret with their own money, for instance, but as a professional manager you are basically deceiving your clients—your shareholders—if you take a serious gamble with their money and don't tell them about it.

—Richard Schmalensee, John C. Head III Dean,
MIT Sloan School of Management[2]

CASE STUDY CORPORATE GOVERNANCE
BEST PRACTICES EXAMPLE: PFIZER, INC.

Certainly, the whole issue of equity-based compensation—and top management compensation in general—has come under scrutiny in the United States in recent years. Since the Enron and WorldCom and other scandals—and the taking down of a major accounting firm—serious attention is being given to corporate governance issues and the shoring up of principled management.

The pharmaceutical giant Pfizer, Inc., places a high priority on corporate governance and communicates that priority to its investors. This open communication results in minimum opposition from the company's shareholders.

Here is how it works at Pfizer:

- The company has a six-person Corporate Governance Committee and has a vice president of corporate governance on staff.
- Fifteen of Pfizer's 18 directors are outside directors.
- Pfizer is recognized for its tight linkage of executive compensation to performance.
- At least twice a year, the board meets—without presence of management—to discuss its outside auditors and to assess the pay and performance of its top executives.
- The CEO and chairman of the board are required to give an annual report of the senior management's potential to be his or her successor.

OPTION REPRICING

A caveat counterbalances the benefits of providing stock options as compensation to employees. In putting such a plan in place, a company's management hopes that stock options will encourage employees to care about the future of the company and contribute toward its long-term growth and earnings performance. Senior executives who sign on with the company understand the ups and downs of the stock market and the calculated risk inherent in holding options for stock that promises, but may not achieve, spectacular growth. If the worst happens and the stock plummets, the plan may become a disincentive for less savvy employees who do not understand why the money they expected does not materialize.

Opportunities to "reset" or "reprice" option stock prices—a modification resulting in a direct or indirect reduction to the exercise price of a fixed stock option—used to exist in situations where a company's stock price had declined considerably. But all that changed on December 15, 1998, when the FASB ruled that options could not be repriced without accounting ramifications and formalized it with FIN 44, which made it very difficult to reprice options without accounting ramifications. Companies today—with the stock market as a whole is not performing very well—can play within the rules and still use good accounting standards by canceling existing fixed stock options and subsequently granting replacement options with an at-the-money exercise price but only after waiting six months plus one day. But they must be mindful of securities regulations, accounting regulations, and tax consequences, both to the company and to the individual.

By way of example: If a company had an unlimited number of shares available, it would not even have to think about repricing the options in a bear market because it could just let the "bad" shares—those "underwater" options—sit out there until they *expired*. But because of concerns about overhang and dilution, which affect nearly all public companies a repricing may become necessary. If the board has already authorized 20 percent of the shares for employee option plans, they may not want another 10 percent allocated to such plans which further dilute the current shareholders. Wall Street analysts also do not like potential shares overhanging the market—even underwater shares—so practical limits are placed on how often companies can go back to their shareholders to authorize that additional shares be allocated to employee compensation plans.

NOTES

[1] The financial accounting treatment for equity-based compensation is principally described in Financial Accounting Standards Board Statement No. 123.

[2] Richard Schmalensee, "Ethics," *ROI: Periodic Statements from the MIT Sloan School of Management*, December 2002.

CHAPTER 11

Corporate Governance in a Post-Enron World

What makes it difficult for young biotechs is the fact that companies are growing and evolving. It's easy to make a decision when things are black and white and you can clearly distinguish right from wrong. But a lot of our operations are in that gray area. We may want to go down a certain path where there's a lot of uncertainty and "what-ifs," and you're not going to know if it's right or wrong—and I don't mean in a legal sense, I mean a business sense—until much later.

—Dr. Thomas E. D'Ambra, Chairman and CEO,
Albany Molecular Research, Inc.

The recent revelations about high-profile business scandals—Enron, WorldCom, and Tyco, to name a few—have placed us in a unique period in the history of American business. The call for corporate responsibility has never been greater, and the need to link sound corporate governance to effective controls has never been clearer. Consequently, in terms of restoring public confidence in the financial markets—and in American corporations in general—there has never been more at stake.

And while publicly traded companies are facing a large number of new federal regulations and stock exchange rules, private companies are facing equally strong and, at the moment, less formal pressures for corporate governance reform from investors anxious to avoid unpleasant surprises and to safeguard their investments. Most of it makes good common sense, while some of it may change the way boards are created and decisions made.

The Sarbanes-Oxley Act, signed by President George W. Bush in July

2002, is doing nothing less than rewriting the rules for corporate governance, disclosure, and financial reporting. And while reading through the pages and pages of legalese and accounting-speak is a daunting task, the underlying premise is simple: Good corporate governance and ethical business practices are no longer optional—they are the law.

But what exactly is "corporate governance"? In brief, it covers all those areas that affect how corporations direct and control their operations to ensure the honesty, transparency, and accuracy of their business results. It touches on the many diverse facets of a business that require specialized expertise, including the role of corporate boards, financial reporting, internal metrics and controls, and corporate values.[1]

Containing broad-based accounting, disclosure, and corporate governance reforms, Sarbanes-Oxley's intent is to restore confidence in the American business system and stress the importance of ethical standards in the preparation of financial information that is reported to investors. No more

INTERNAL CONTROL

Sarbanes-Oxley focuses on "internal control," which is a process effected by a company's board of directors, management, and other personnel that drives business success in three categories:

1. Effectiveness and efficiency of operations
2. Reliability of financial reporting
3. Compliance with applicable laws and regulations

Sarbanes-Oxley makes CEOs and CFOs *explicitly* responsible for establishing, evaluating, and monitoring the effectiveness of internal control over financial reporting and disclosure.

The SEC has proposed defining *internal controls and procedures* for financial reporting to mean "controls that pertain to the preparation of financial statements for external purposes that are fairly presented in conformity with generally accepted accounting principles." It defines *disclosure controls and procedures* (for both financial and non-financial disclosures*) as entities "designed to ensure that information required to be disclosed by a company in the reports filed by it under the Exchange Act is recorded, processed, summarized, and reported within the time periods specified by the SEC."

*Nonfinancial disclosure includes such items as the signing of a significant contract; developments regarding intellectual property; changes in union relationships; termination of a strategic relationship; legal proceedings; or required disclosures in the management's Discussion and Analysis contained on Forms 10-K, 10-Q, and 20-F.

can chief executive officers (CEOs) and chief financial officers (CFOs) of public companies claim they were unaware of such things as off-the-book partnerships and improper revenue recognition. Now measures instituted by Sarbanes-Oxley will strengthen internal checks and balances and enhance accountability.

To much media hype and publicity, CEOs and CFOs were in the spotlight in August 2002 as the first of the Sarbanes-Oxley provisions was carried out. *Section 906* of the Sarbanes-Oxley Act required CEOs and CFOs to sign and certify their periodic report containing financial statements. This executive certification states that the report complies with Securities and Exchange Commission (SEC) reporting requirements and fairly represents the company's financial condition and the results of its operations. Failure to comply with this requirement carries a high price: Fines of up to $5 million and imprisonment for up to 20 years can be imposed for knowing or willful failure to comply.

GOOD NEWS ABOUT SARBANES-OXLEY

Many of the new and proposed SEC rules affecting Sarbanes-Oxley are complicated, and their implementation will no doubt be costly and time consuming for public companies. But it is not all bad news. In addition to bringing pockets of corporate America back onto the ethical business practices track, it is important to understand that:

- Virtually all public companies already have some kind of internal control structure in place, although in some instances it may be somewhat informal and not completely documented.
- Many companies will be able to tailor existing processes to comply with the internal control provisions of Sarbanes-Oxley.
- Setting up a strong internal control structure to meet the mandates of Sarbanes-Oxley can provide benefits well beyond compliance. With these activities, the potential for revising and realizing new corporate visions and achieve new levels of corporate excellence abounds.

This is a significant piece of business legislation—some argue that it is the most significant financial legislation since the 1930s. Others liken it to the Federal Deposit Insurance Corporation Improvement Act (FDICIA) of 1991, which imposed significant reporting requirements on the banking industry in an effort to prevent large depository institution failures. With Sarbanes-Oxley, the American regulatory and business landscapes have been fundamentally changed, and public companies should not underestimate the task that lies before them. What is more, strict timetables are in place now, so immediate action is required. A description of two of the critical sections of Sarbanes-Oxley—Sections 302 and 404—follows.

COST OF COMPLIANCE

While not as costly as noncompliance, the cost of compliance can be high for companies. Smaller companies, especially, that have neither extensive staff nor a robust infrastructure may find compliance extremely taxing on their system.

Direct costs could include:

- Employee and consultant time for assessment, implementation, and monitoring
- Educating employees about internal control
- Cash outlays for new technology to support the internal control program
- Fees for independent auditors to perform control testing to support the company's assertion about the effectiveness of the new internal controls

Indirect costs could include:

- Reassignment of staff
- Realignment of other resources in the organization to create and maintain a better internal control structure

Section 302—Quarterly and Annual Certification of Disclosure Controls and Procedures

Under Section 302, CEOs and CFOs must personally certify that they are responsible for disclosure controls and procedures. Each quarterly filing must contain a certification that they have performed an evaluation of the design and effectiveness of these controls. These executives also must state that they have disclosed to their Audit Committee and independent auditor any significant control deficiencies, material weaknesses, and acts of fraud. The SEC also has proposed an expanded certification requirement that includes internal controls and procedures for financial reporting, in addition to the requirement related to the disclosure of controls and procedures. And it is now the CEO's responsibility—not the CFO's—to acknowledge responsibility for internal control.

Specifically, since August 2002, CEOs and CFOs must certify, in both quarterly and annual filings, that they:

- Are responsible for disclosure controls and procedures
- Have designed (or supervised the design of) these controls to ensure that material information is made known to them

- Have evaluated the effectiveness of these controls
- Have presented their conclusions regarding the effectiveness of these controls
- Have disclosed to their Audit Committee and the independent auditors any significant control deficiencies, material weaknesses, and acts of fraud that involve management or other employees who have a significant role in the company's internal control
- Have indicated in the filing any significant changes to controls

VIEW FROM THE TOP

Of course, different CEOs are having different reactions to Sarbanes-Oxley with regard to board composition in particular and corporate governance in general. The New York Biotechnology Association meeting in February 2003 generated a lively discussion at its CEO Roundtable on this issue. Moderator Peter Micca, a partner in Deloitte & Touche's Healthcare & Life Sciences practice, observed that there were three typical reactions:

On one side, there were CEOs whose boards were historically composed of high-techn or scientific experts who took an active interest in running the business. With the advent of Sarbanes-Oxley, these board members now feel the need to scale back their level of involvement because of increased liability issues and the fear that they will be perceived as an extension of the company rather than as part of corporate governance. At the same time, the CEOs are reluctant to give up what they perceived to be critical board seats in favor of a "financial expert."

On the extreme other side are the CEOs who do not really view Sarbanes-Oxley as an issue because they feel their businesses are relatively uncomplicated and that because they do not do any off–balance sheet transactions, they really should not be bothered. But they will go ahead and put another person on the board if that is what it takes, and maybe all the fuss will go away.

Somewhere in the middle, however, are the CEOs who are a little nervous. And because they are nervous, they do not really understand how Sarbanes-Oxley impacts their business because they have never had to deal with issues of corporate governance before. And maybe they do not have the best internal controls infrastructure, but it has worked all right so far. They are afraid for their own personal liability (with good reason or not), and they are looking for help.

Section 404—Annual Assessment of Internal Controls and Procedures for Financial Reporting

Section 404 is essentially a mandate for an annual evaluation of internal controls and procedures for financial reporting. In addition, it requires that the company's independent auditor issue a separate report that attests to management's (CEO, CFO) assertion on the effectiveness these internal controls and procedures.

As a result of Section 404, a company's annual report will need to include an internal control report from management that:

- Affirms their responsibility for establishing and maintaining internal controls and procedures for financial reporting
- Evaluates and reaches conclusions about the effectiveness of internal controls and procedures for financial reporting
- States that the company's independent auditor has attested to, and reported on, management's evaluation of the company's internal controls and procedures for financial reporting

Most public companies must comply with the Section 404 rules for fiscal years ending after June 15, 2004. In other words, a company with a December 31 year-end would have to comply in their financial statements for calendar 2004. Certain small public companies effectively have an extra year to comply.

GETTING STARTED WITH COMPLIANCE

Public companies need to take several steps to address the internal control program mandated by Sarbanes-Oxley. The challenges faced by larger companies will be somewhat different from the challenges faced by smaller companies, and the extent to which companies already have a strong internal control framework in place also will bear significantly on how they meet those challenges. But in every case, three groups will play a prominent role:

1. *The board of directors,* which oversees the company's commitment to the task
2. *The CEO and CFO,* who acknowledge responsibility for ensuring compliance and communicate this information to key management and employees
3. *The Steering Committee,* which oversees and coordinates Sarbanes-Oxley activities across the organization

Companies may need to expand their technological capabilities, as well, as they take on the challenge of Sarbanes-Oxley compliance. Database programs and other proprietary tools can be a real boon in documenting control objectives, processes, and activities; identifying gaps and tracking actions to remediate deficiencies; and supporting self-assessment and monitoring activities.

While several suitable frameworks for internal control exist, the dominant model is likely to be structured around the Committee of Sponsoring Organizations of the Treadway Commission (COSO). The COSO framework breaks effective internal control into five interrelated components:

1. *Control Environment:* The foundation for all other elements of internal control, which includes the ethical values and competence of the company's employees
2. *Risk Assessment:* The identification and analysis of relevant risks that can hinder the achievement of business objectives
3. *Control Activities:* Specific tasks to mitigate each of the risks identified above
4. *Information and Communication:* Creating pathways from management to employees, and vice versa
5. *Monitoring:* The evaluation and assessment of internal control

First, companies will need to create—and empower—a *Disclosure Committee* as part of its internal control process. This committee performs numerous functions, among them: reviewing SEC filings, recommending parameters for disclosure, overseeing disclosure processed, and reviewing control deficiencies and material weaknesses with the CEO and CFO.

Once the committee has been established, the labor-intensive work of creating the internal control program begins. Companies can begin by building a project team to manage the internal control program. Smaller companies might be able to redeploy existing staff to the task on a part-time basis. Larger companies will likely need full-time personnel to manage the myriad details. In assessing the existing control environment, the project team should take into consideration elements such as:

- Integrity, ethical values, and competence
- Management's philosophy and operating style
- Delegation of authority and responsibility
- The directions provided by the board of directors

This kind of cultural assessment can aid in understanding and documenting a company's existing control environment.

Companies also will need to identify their financial reporting and disclosure risks, so they will know how to prioritize the tasks before them. Building a "controls repository" will be an immeasurable help to companies in their efforts toward compliance. This repository will serve as a clearinghouse for all the information and activities related to internal control, containing documentation on control objectives, design, and implementation, as well as methods for testing the operating effectiveness of such activities.

BEYOND INTERNAL CONTROL

While Sarbanes-Oxley focuses heavily on internal control, that is just one of the components of good corporate governance. Other considerations that need to be taken into account include:

- Integrity and ethical values
- Management philosophy and operating style
- Organizational structure
- Well-delineated roles and responsibilities for boards, management, and employees
- Commitment to excellence
- Effective and proactive boards and committees

Testing of the operating effectiveness of control activities should be ongoing and should be evaluated by all the individuals responsible for the controls, as well as by the designated project team. Likewise, the internal audit function should monitor the effectiveness of the entire internal control program and infrastructure.

A strong internal control structure can provide benefits well beyond mere compliance with Sarbanes-Oxley. It can help companies:

- Make better business decisions with higher-quality, more timely information
- Gain (or regain) investor trust
- Prevent loss of resources
- Comply with applicable laws and regulations
- Gain competitive advantage through streamlined operations

On the flip side, failure to comply can lead to disastrous results, including:

- Increased exposure to fraud
- Sanctions from the SEC
- Unfavorable publicity
- Negative impact on shareholder value
- Shareholder lawsuits or other legal actions

From a shareholder point of view, these new rules of compliance are meant to ensure that corporate boards will no longer tolerate unrestricted power or unethical behavior; will require the presence of financially literate directors; and will put into place strict internal controls that will aggressively protect their investment.

WHAT ABOUT PRIVATE COMPANIES?

The cost of corporate governance doesn't have to be strenuous for private companies. They can set up overlapping committees— audit, finance, and a board—with simultaneous agendas that can be discussed at the same time. And they can focus on the areas that significantly impact their financial operations: intellectual property, valuations, contractual arrangements, and compensation. The overriding theme is to go back to the basics, back to the cash management function. It's as simple as that.

—Peter Micca, Partner, Deloitte & Touche LLP

While private companies are not legally obligated to comply with Sarbanes-Oxley, they may choose to adopt certain components of the act as part of an overall plan to improve their business operations. However, as the Sarbanes-Oxley rules are woven into the fabric of public company governance, the market itself may dictate that private companies must de facto adopt at least the broad strokes of the Sarbanes-Oxley Act. It became painfully clear, as investors watched wave after wave of companies in the hot seat, that many corporate boards had not been paying attention to what was going on and, further, that many boards were not made up of the kind of financially astute members who were likely to understand what was happening—even if they had been paying attention.

Sarbanes-Oxley makes very clear distinctions about who should sit on corporate boards. The act defines an *independent director* as someone who does not receive any consulting, advisory, or other compensatory fee from the company, beyond service to the board. Further, board members may not be affiliated with the company or any of its subsidiaries. *Financial experts* are defined as those board members who have equivalent education and experience to a public accountant, auditor, CFO, comptroller, or principal accounting officer, or someone who has performed similar functions in a previous position.

These distinctions can get complicated for private companies, as they often build their boards by adding or subtracting directors with each new round of financing. So it is important for private companies to build boards with independent, high-quality members right from the start. And private companies need to be prepared for the inevitable: In today's post-Enron environment, many candidates will be wary of the increased liabilities that come with serving on a board, so recruiting good candidates is becoming more and more difficult. With that in mind, sometimes more aggressive board compensation packages are required, and adequate directors' and officers' liability insurance coverage is key, to protect board members in the event of an investor lawsuit.

10 THINGS PRIVATE COMPANIES SHOULD DO TO IMPROVE CORPORATE GOVERNANCE

1. *Make sure executives and board members are up to speed on the new corporate governance regulations and fully understand the ramifications of the new Sarbanes-Oxley Act, SEC regulations, and stock exchange rules.* Even though they technically apply to public companies, many investors expect private companies to conduct themselves like their public counterparts.

2. *Take a close look at the composition of the board.* Ideally, private company boards should consist of a majority of nonmanagement members. Also, does the board include honest-to-goodness independent directors and "financial experts," and do formal audit and compensation committees meet at least quarterly?

3. *Review the directors' and officers' liability insurance policies.* Understand legal exposures, and ensure that insurance coverage will adequately cover an investor lawsuit.

4. *Sign up executives and board members for an executive education course on accounting and finance.* Given the increased liabilities associated with overseeing a company's financial results, it is imperative that they have a firm grasp on how to interpret and challenge the accounting details behind a company's income statement and balance sheet.

5. *Develop stringent internal controls to push responsibility for the accuracy of financial statements farther down the company.* All employees who contribute key information to the company's financial picture or who actually help prepare a company's financial must have clear guidelines for how to produce accurate, complete, and timely financial statements.

6. *Take care to avoid overly aggressive accounting practices that technically comply with GAAP,* but ignore the underlying financial principles and paint a deceptively rosy picture of a company's financial condition.

7. *Create a performance benchmark plan that details the strategic and operational risk factors as well as the underlying metrics that are critical for measuring the company's growth.* At a minimum, these metrics should be reviewed formally each quarter, with clear explanations detailing the reasons for both positive and negative variances.

8. *Develop a formal ethics policy so that employees understand how the company's guiding principles apply to what they do.* This is now a SEC requirement for publicly traded companies, but private companies would be well advised to follow suit.

9. *Make sure to create a plan that consistently and regularly communicates corporate ethics policy and values.* Do not bury the values in an employee handbook.

10. *As part of a system of corporate checks and balances, create a mechanism for employees to report confidentially to the audit committee any dubious business practices they may encounter.*

Source: Antiphony White Paper, "What Private Companies Need to Know About Corporate Governance," p. 7.

As with public companies, it is important for board members to be educated about generally accepted accounting practices (GAAP), as well as the details that are behind the company's income statement and balance sheet. In short, companies need to make financial knowledge a requirement and reporting a top priority for prospective board members, moving forward. But equally important is the task of creating a formal ethics policy for the company—and communicating it frequently to the employees. Values and ethics come from the top, so senior management should lead by example and must ensure that the policies and procedures that are put in place are consistently communicated and reinforced.

Sarbanes-Oxley is about reestablishing trust among investors and customers. For business owners, it is important to remember that before a business can create any value, it must create trust—in its products and services, in its management team, and in the statements that it makes about its business operations and financial results.

NOTES

[1] Antiphony White Paper, "What Private Companies Need to Know About Corporate Governance," p. 2.

CHAPTER 12

Biotechnology Beyond
the U.S. Borders

Europe's entrepreneurial health sciences community is coming of age . . . [with] nearly 1800 businesses across Europe and in Israel and the pace of growth shows no sign of slowing. New companies are constantly being created looking to unblock bottlenecks in the drug discovery and development pipeline. There is no dominant location in Europe but rather about ten hotspots—in the UK, Germany, France, Switzerland and the so-called Medicon Valley, which takes in Northern Denmark and Southern Sweden.

—Stuart Henderson, U.K. Head of Life and Health Sciences,
Deloitte & Touche[1]

Just as individual biotechnology companies continually evolve and grow, so does the industry. While biotech has been centered in key U.S. cluster areas up until this point—Boston, Massachusetts; New Jersey; greater Philadelphia, Pennsylvania; the New York metropolitan area; San Diego, California; and the Bay Area of California—major technological advances have created centers of excellence in Canada, Australia, the United Kingdom, the Netherlands, Israel, and Japan, to name just a few. With the accelerated pace of discovery and the promise of the sequencing of the human genome, there are essentially no more boundaries, and the centers of incubation, discovery, and development are to be found in virtually every corner of the globe.

Deloitte & Touche LLP, the international professional services firm, has partners throughout the world who are committed to facilitating the growth of the life sciences field in every sector. Early in 2002 and again in 2003 they collaborated on a report called "Borderless Biotechnology," which describes how biotech is taking the global stage in a "clustering" strategy in key countries. The following information has been summarized from that document, as well as from interviews with some of the collaborators.

OUTLOOK: CANADA

Canada has one of the largest biotechnology industries in the world, with more than 400 companies and a bright outlook. Reinvigorated investment from venture capitalists and government and strong research-based universities are laying the foundation for continued growth.

Because many Canadian biotechs are younger and more dependent on venture capital than their U.S. counterparts, the decline in life science funding that spilled over from the United States affected the industry greatly. However, the Canadian government has stepped in to help fill the investment gap. Recognizing the strong economic potential of biotech clusters, many provincial and regional governments are joining forces with the federal government to launch venture funds, incubators, and research centers.

According to Nathalie Duchesnay, a manager in Strategic Planning, Life Sciences, for Deloitte & Touche's Montreal office, financing opportunities continue to be one of the biggest challenges faced by Canadian life science companies. Predictably, small, research-stage companies that have yet to produce a product (or a profit) are most likely to be affected. But on the optimistic side, Duchesnay reports that "in the most recent [2002] Canadian Venture Capital Confidence Survey, life sciences was named as the preferential area of investment, with more than half of the venture capitalists in Canada planning to increase funding in genomics and biotech companies."

Here and around the world, strong research universities are magnets for research and development (R&D)-intensive biotech ventures. Canadian life sciences companies are putting hefty dollars behind R&D spending and growing major biotech clusters in areas where there is significant university and hospital network support, such as Montreal, Toronto, Vancouver, and Edmonton.

Canada has seen its share of major merger and acquisition (M&A) activity, including the 2001 sale of BioChem Pharma to Shire Pharmaceuticals Group for US$4 billion to form the Quebec-based subsidiary, Shire BioChem Pharma. And while M&A activity is expected to continue to grow, a recent Canadian trend is the increasing independence of biotech firms. "Instead of automatically joining forces with big pharmaceutical companies," says Duchesnay, "many biotechs are venturing into commercialization on their own," She cites as an example Aetenna's spin-off company, Atrium, which sells fine chemical ingredients for the nutraceutical, cosmeceutical, and pharmaceutical industries. And the emergence of contract marketing organizations in Canada will allow more biotech companies to outsource the marketing of new drugs or products.

R&D TAX CREDITS IN QUÉBEC

The Québec R&D tax credits have been a key success factor in the clustering of biopharmaceuticals. Québec recognizes the key role played by business investment in ensuring sustained economic growth and durable prosperity.

Québec and Canadian tax incentives take the form of deductions, with respect to eligible R&D expenditures when taxable income is calculated, and of tax credits, several of which are refundable when they exceed the tax payable. R&D incentives are claimed in the taxpayer's annual income tax returns. Such incentives have the same monetary advantages as grants, without the attendant inconvenience.

These measures, which substantially reduce the net cost of R&D expenditures, make it possible to reduce the risks inherent in such activities and accelerate or enhance these activities, since more than twice as much R&D can be carried out for a given investment.

"As this trend becomes increasingly popular," says Duchesnay, "many biotech companies will need additional support to strategically manage their R&D investments to maintain a steady pipeline and ensure long-term growth."

With more Canadian venture funds specializing in life sciences and more U.S. funds making investments in Canada, the industry is looking forward to solid growth.

OUTLOOK: AUSTRALIA

Compared with the United States and Canada, Australia—which has historically excelled at basic research—is dominated by smaller biotech companies. These companies are largely still in the research phase, with relatively few generating income from the sale of products at this point. And therein lies the challenge.

Australian biotech companies are clustered predominately on the eastern seaboard, with New South Wales (Sydney), Victoria (Melbourne), and Queensland (Brisbane) home to 71 percent of companies by market capitalization.

Despite the relatively early stage of the science in many Australian biotech companies, there is a high percentage of listed biotech companies in the country—with more than a third having a market cap of less than $10 million Australian (AU).

The majority of Australian biotech companies derive their income from interest and government grants. And while the local biotech venture capital market has been somewhat immature in the past—which may account for the high percentage of small-cap companies—that is beginning to change. But according to David Black, a client director in Life Sciences and Growth Companies in Deloitte & Touche's Sydney office, Australian venture capital firms need to understand that biotech is a long-term investment that is not going to bring products to market in a year or two.

"Despite the small size of most Australian companies, three biomedical firms are truly global players," says Black. ResMed and Cochlear are in the device end of the market, the former making a machine to alleviate sleep disordered breathing and the latter a competitor in the bionic ear business. A company called CSL is in more of a core biotech business, working in the area of blood plasma and vaccines. And ResMed, while still developing its products in Australia, has a corporate head office in San Diego, California, and is listed on the New York Stock Exchange.

Two other Australian companies, SIRteX Medical Limited and Biotechnology Frontiers (BTF), release products on to the U.S. and European markets. Still other companies are already trading on the Nasdaq exchange.

"The biggest barrier that Australian companies face is distribution," continues Black. "The key markets are Europe and the U.S. That's where the money is, and that's where the distribution channels are. You'll never make your fortune selling exclusively to the Australian market in this business—there are only 20 million of us here." He sees the real challenge in Australian biotech not in the technologies or the research—which are strong—but in getting the funding and the distribution, which means getting the global pharmaceutical companies interested in what is happening 17 hours and half a world away.

The state and federal governments recognize that biotech is a huge growth area and have put several funding schemes into place; the problem with several of them, however, is that they rely on matching grants. And while good science is being developed in university settings, it takes a long time for products to see the light of day and, therefore, for venture capitalists to get interested. The government-sponsored Biotech Innovations Fund provides some "proof of concept" money, but that, too, requires matching funds.

However, there are several biotech funds in Australia. One Australian exchange–listed fund, Biotech Capital, raised $40 million AU in 2000 to invest in early-stage biotech companies using a portfolio approach. Two years later, it is still only 50 percent invested.

Says Black, "On the one hand, you've got all these small companies saying we need more venture capital, we need people with a longer-term view who understand the sector. And on the other hand, we've got a specialist fund that's sitting 50 percent invested. So there's a bit of a gap at the moment." He sees it as an education hurdle on both sides: educating scientists to the business imperatives of financing and educating investment managers that biotech is a longer-term play than they are used to.

ALIGNING REGIONAL INITIATIVES

Biotechnology has been recognized by all state and federal governments as crucial to the future of the Australian economy. In January 2001 the federal government announced a series of measures to promote research, development, and innovation in Australia. A further announcement, "Backing Australia's Ability," provides more funding, including proof of concept grants (Biotech Innovation Fund) and funding for a national Biotechnology Center of Excellence.

This support is backed up by more general business incentives including the federal R&D tax concession scheme that allows for a premium rate of 175 percent for certain eligible R&D undertaken in Australia and a cash rebate available to small-loss companies that undertake eligible R&D. The amount of the rebate is equivalent to the R&D tax concession. Combined with the federal initiatives are a number of state initiatives focusing on clustering.

Most Australian biotechs realize that they are not in business to become a manufacturing or distribution company. They are in it to get to Phase II and then license off to a big pharmaceutical partner who can provide funding for trials and, ultimately, global distribution.

OUTLOOK: JAPAN

If biotechnology is regarded as "a technology to produce valuable materials for human beings using biological functions," then Japan can be considered an early leader in the field, given its traditional brewing and fermentation businesses, which produce such traditional Japanese foods as sake, miso, or soy sauce. Today life science in Japan comprises two industries: biotechnology and pharmaceuticals. Many market analysts expect that the market size of the biotech industry in Japan will expand rapidly over the next 10 years, from $10 billion US to $250 billion.

The Japanese biotechnology market—including traditional food production, medical applications (i.e., tailor-made medical treatments), and information technology (i.e., bioinformatics)—surpassed $10.5 billion in 2001. The medical, agricultural, and food sectors comprised 30 percent of the market share in the biotechnology industry, and both chemicals and R&D fields comprised approximately 20 percent. Agriculture and food, R&D, and electronics are the growth fields and jumped by 15 percent in 2001. The growth of the agriculture and food fields is due largely to the increasing importance of genetic recombination foods. Bioinformatics and proteomic-related businesses in the R&D field also have shown significant growth.

Since 2000 the government has increased its budget and support for the biotechnology industry, and, as a result, the demand for data analysis in genomics and proteomics has expanded. The market size of bioinformatics-related businesses grew by 81 percent in 2001, from $128 million to $232 million. With increasing budgets in the biotech sector, further growth in the R&D field is expected.

Encouraged by the past success of support programs, the Japanese government has continued to promote emerging biotech ventures with technical seeds in research institutions and universities. In 1998 the Japanese version of the Bayh-Dole Act was enacted, with the result that more technologies have been transferred successfully from universities to venture companies through 30 technology licensing organizations. In addition, government ministries such as the minister of economy, trade, and industry, in cooperation with local governments, have encouraged the formation of industry clusters that undertake revitalization projects.

"The biotechnology industry is considered one of the most important in Japan," says Akihiro Sano, a manager in Life Sciences in Deloitte & Touche's Tokyo practice. "Along with government support, financial institutions and venture capitalists have been increasing investments into bio ventures, positioning Japanese biotechnology well for continued growth."

OUTLOOK: THE UNITED KINGDOM

Historically, the United Kingdom has been home to many key scientific milestones within the biotechnology industry. From the discovery of the structure of DNA, through the early efforts of protein and DNA sequencing, to the development of monoclonal antibodies and the cloning of Dolly the sheep—the United Kingdom boasts a rich pool of academic achievements in the fields of molecular biology that spawned a vibrant, robust, and entrepreneurial biotech sector.

At the end of 2002 there were approximately 430 biotech companies operating in the United Kingdom, employing nearly 28,000 people and investing more than $1.37 billion in R&D, resulting in revenues of more than $2.9 billion. The United Kingdom accounts for half the publicly quoted biotech companies in Europe and nearly two-thirds of the market capitalization.

Many of Britain's emerging pharmaceutical and biotech companies are now major, world-class players, including Shire Pharmaceuticals, Celltech, Cambridge Antibody Technology, Oxford Glycosciences, and Acambis—which won the U.S. government contract to supply and maintain stocks of the smallpox vaccine. U.K. companies lead the European field in having biotech products not only developed, but also actually achieving profitability.

Most of the U.K. biotech activity is focused in a handful of clusters in Cambridge, London, Oxford, northern England, and Scotland. These regions have developed a critical mass, not only of biotech companies, but also of support industries such venture capitalists, accountants, and law firms, which are essential for continued growth.

Within Europe, British investors have an advanced level of experience with the biotech market. The London Stock Exchange has allowed biotech companies to list since 1992, compared with other European exchanges, which opened up to biotech only in 1996. In November 2001 the London Stock Exchange launched techMARK mediscience, the world's first international market for healthcare companies.

According to Nigel Mercer, head of the Life Sciences group for Deloitte & Touche's U.K. practice, many executives who gained valuable experience in earlier biotech companies have sought to establish new initiatives in the United Kingdom, making it one of the fastest-growing regions for new company formations. "During 2001, venture capitalists invested £30 million, of a total of £830 million in European biotech funding, to companies in the U.K.," says Mercer. "More significantly, the top four European biotech venture capitalists financings were in British companies."

The United Kingdom is a leading market for European biotech, and it continues to benefit from support from the highest levels of the British government.

OUTLOOK: THE NETHERLANDS

The Netherlands is home to advanced research centers, a supportive governmental attitude, and one of the most accessible economies in the world. This may help explain the explosion in bioscience start-ups. Since 1999, according to Hans Verloop, senior manager in Life Sciences in Deloitte & Touche's Leiden office, the Netherlands has experienced a 30 percent increase in start-ups, outperforming the European average growth rate of 15 percent.

"The bioscience sector in the Netherlands has grown substantially in the last decade, and shows no signs of slowing down," says Verloop. "In the last two years alone, 45 bioscience companies were founded here—that's about 16 percent of total Dutch bioscience companies."

Almost 90 percent of bioscience companies operating in the Netherlands today are of Dutch origin, yet have a significantly global perspective and base. The other 10 percent of bioscience companies operating in the Netherlands originate primarily from the United States, such as Amgen, Biogen, Centocor, and Genencor.

New Dutch bioscience companies number around 75 and employ some 1,000 people. The majority of these companies focus on general biotechnology (45 percent) or human health (44 percent). The remaining 11 percent, the agrifood sector, is less developed, reflecting the more cautious European approach to biotech in the agricultural arena.

Bioscience in the Netherlands is clustered primarily in three science parks: Amsterdam Science Park, Bioscience Park Leiden, and BioMed City in Groningen. While all three have unique characteristics, each benefits from collaborations with nearby universities, medical centers, and research institutions. To encourage further R&D activities, the Dutch government is in the process of developing six incubator centers, including three in these science parks.

The Dutch government has a positive attitude toward the bioscience sector and its potential applications in human health and agrifood. Economic and innovative developments are considered carefully. The government regulates and monitors the biotech industry closely through R&D programs, clinical trials regulations, and a food and drug safety charter. Recently the Dutch Ministry of Economics initiated the BioPartner Program to encourage new life science start-ups, which will direct $40 million US into venture capital and the development of the six incubators.

Centrally located, and with excellent access to major European markets, the Netherlands boasts attractive tax laws, a strong R&D sector, and a relatively swift drug approval process (compared to the United States), all of which make it a viable environment for bioscience activities going forward.

A counter factor for biotech in the Netherlands is the lack of a strong tradition of entrepreneurialism among Dutch universities and the scientists resident there. In addition, under Dutch law, inventions made by university-based scientists typically belong to the university. This decreases the likelihood of scientists forming the fledgling entities that have proved such a boon to commercialization of science in other locales, especially the United States.

OUTLOOK: ISRAEL

It is no surprise that Patricia Hewitt, the U.K. secretary of state for trade and industry, recently remarked that Israel, second only to the United States in its commitment to biotechnology, "probably has the highest density of scientific and technical expertise in the world."[2] with significant governmental support and a considerable research focus—35 percent of research conducted in Israel is in life sciences—the current opportunities for biotech success in Israel are good and growing.

An influx of scientific and technical know-how from the former Soviet Union during the 1990s does not hurt. Add to that the support of seven major universities and five major research institutes plus a growing number of international partnerships, and you have got a recipe for success.

Some of the more notable Israeli biotech companies in operation today are Teva Pharmaceutical Industries, Ltd., in Jerusalem; Pharmos Corporation in Rehovot and Iselin, New Jersey; D-Pharm in Rehovot; and NeuroSurvival Technologies in Tel Aviv. Medical devices companies tend to be clustered in northern Israel and in Haifa, where knowledge sharing is common, and a viable low-cost manufacturing base has been found in many kibbutz groups.

KEY PLAYERS IN ISRAELI BIOTECH RESEARCH TODAY[3]

The Hebrew University of Jerusalem
Yissum Research & Development Company Ltd. signed 130 contracts in 1997

Tel-Aviv University in Ramot
A high-tech incubator in Tel Hashomer Hospital focuses on diagnostics

The Technion—Israel Institute of Technology
This progenitor of Medical Device development now has annual sales in excess of $1 billion

Hadasit Medical Research, Service & Development in Jerusalem
A center for cancer therapeutics, osteoporosis, diabetes, cardiovascular, orthopedics, etc.

Bar-Ilan University
Bar-Ilan R&D Company, Ltd. focuses on electro-optical blood cell diagnosis for cancer

Ben Gurion University of the Negev
This will become the national research center for biotechnology; currently houses the Institute of Applied Life Sciences and is active in technology transfer and applications

According to Brian Lovatt, CEO of Vision Healthcare Consultancy and of Lovatt-Mills & Co. Ltd. of Caterham, England, the key issues that face biotechnology's continuing growth in Israel are the vast number of start-ups that need financing and attention (in excess of 3,000 in 2002); limited local manufacturing capacity; and the limitations of venture capital growth funds.[4]

The Israeli biotech industry has realized, as have others, that overseas market listing is a major benefit and that collaborations and partnerships are the key to survival for many enabling technologies. To that end, Israel has entered into several partnerships with U.S. entities, including:

- U.S. Israel Binational Industrial Research & Development Fund (BIRD), which provides off–balance sheet financing for basic R&D and start-up companies and matches Israeli high-tech companies with strategic partners in the United States
- U.S. Advent Venture Fund and the Walden Israeli Venture Capital Group, an independent affiliate of the Walden Group of International Venture

Capital Funds, providing early-stage and start-up financing and working with entrepreneurs to build successful and long-lived companies
- Relationships with chambers of commerce
- U.S. Israel Science & Technology Commission (USISTC), established by President Clinton and Prime Minister Yitzak Rabin in 1993, which includes a working group in biotechnology; USISTC works to identify and promote areas of common interest where both countries can profit from strategic partnerships
- U.S. Israel's National Committee for Biotech
- U.S. Israel Biotechnology Council

OUTLOOK: EXTENDING THE BIOTECH VISION

According to French public health specialist Dr. Pierre Anhoury, "If you have no public funding of academic research, you will have no biotech companies in the future. The United States understands this very well." His research indicates that, on a per capita basis, the United States is investing 57 times more on public academic research than France. From his perspective of working with biotech companies in France, the United Kingdom, and the Netherlands, the major players in the world today in the area of biotechnology are still the United States, the United Kingdom, and Germany (home to more mediscience companies than any other European country), with Japan not far behind.

The Sixth Framework Programme for Research & Technological Development, recently launched by the European Commission (EC), is designed to support biotech research and the formation of biotech companies. It is considered by many to be a decisive step toward the involvement of Europe's research and scientific networks in the transformation of the European Union into the most dynamic and competitive knowledge-based economy in the world.[5] It is open to all public and private entities, large or small. The overall budget covering the four-year period 2003 to 2006 is $17.5 billion. The key areas for the advancement of knowledge and technological progress are:

- Genomics and biotechnology for health
- Information society technologies
- Nanotechnologies and nanosciences
- Aeronautics and space
- Food safety
- Sustainable development
- Economic and social sciences

But while there is this big push at the EC level, issues still abound. One is that many believe that it is simply too little too late and that the European markets might never achieve the critical mass they need to compete on a global basis.

Another is the definition of biotechnology itself. Terms like "biotech," "life science," and "mediscience" are often used interchangeably. But, says Anhoury, "When you say 'medi' you omit agri and food biotech. 'Medi' means human health. But human health concerns are much more prevalent in our industrialized countries. Go to any biotech meeting in China and it's about rice. Go to Africa, and it's about cotton." A broader definition is to say that "life sciences" mainly encompass healthcare, agriculture, nutrition, and the environment.

An important new vision in Europe involves a kind of competition between the *national* initiatives and the *transnational* initiatives. The term is Euro bioclusters. One example is the Munich-Bonn-Strasbourg cluster. "In the middle of that triangle you have one of the highest densities of science in the world—all the big pharmas are there, plus a research biocluster called Bio Valley," says Anhoury. "There's another one formed by Brussels-Paris-Lille, another one in Denmark and Norway, and another under way in Spain." But it gets interesting when you consider that within this cluster structure lies the national financing of academic research, spanning the gamut from raw discovery all the way to commercialization.

Of course, every city or region wants its own incubator and its own bioplatform, and that can dilute the overall biotech effort. For example, in France there are probably 20 incubators right now, when 5 would be enough. So while space and researchers are a good start to doing good science, there are a dozen or so other factors that go into building a successful discovery process, and not every incubator will be able to realize all those factors. According to Anhoury, public money is being given for political reasons—out of good intentions, to create a biotech platform that the individual country can be proud of—but the current way of distributing funds for research is actually spreading already limited resources too thin among too many groups.

It is also true that each country has its own set of challenges in this area.

BIOTECHNOLOGY: AN IMPORTANT PART IN LIFE SCIENCES[6]

Biotech firms are companies that are developing products or services derived from the study of living systems or that use living systems in their research and development. Such companies usually are working in the fields of human or animal healthcare, including diagnostics, therapeutics, vaccines, nutrition and environmental protection.

In Europe, the biotech sector has come back after being ignored by disillusioned investors flocking into Internet stocks. Today biotechnology is a major area of economic activity with the potential to create future wealth and improve quality of life.

One of the ways that information can be shared is through the World Life Sciences Forum BioVision Conference, which is held every other year in Lyon, France. Created in May 1998 at the request of former French prime minister Raymond Barre, and in partnership with the Académie des Sciences de l'Institut de France, the first BioVision Conference was held in 1999.

BioVision 2001 brought together more than 1,000 leading representatives from around the world from the fields of politics, science, consumer organizations, the media, and nonprofit organizations. Designed as a constructive dialogue among science, society, and industry, BioVision 2001 focused on four broad areas:

1. Healthcare: better efficiency through biotechnology?
2. Agriculture and environment
3. Food: safety and public acceptance
4. Industrial Revolution through life sciences: the dawn of the biological agency

BioVision creates an environment where some of the most important and timely issues of the day can be discussed and evaluated in terms of opportunities versus risk: genomics, stem cell research, cloning, genetically modified organisms (GMOs), neurosciences, and bioinformatics, which combines high-speed data processing to biological systems. The previous conferences have been so well received that another has been put into place: BioVision in odd years, and the Alexandria Conference, a kind of North/South BioVision, to be held in Egypt in even years. At the first Alexandria Conference in 2002, 40 countries were represented and about 80 percent of the discussions were about GMOs and the impact of biotechnology on food and agriculture.

Beyond the U.S. borders, the good news is that the politicians have recognized the potential of the biotechnology sector and are working to create funding and programs to facilitate growth and discovery. Cooperation and information sharing between scientists and governments will add to the understanding and development of new products that will serve us all well.

NOTES

[1] Stuart Henderson, "Dealing with Growing Pains," *The Pan European Mediscience Review*, 2002, Deloitte & Touche.
[2] Brian Lovatt, "Israel Biotech: An Opportunity?" presentation to New York Business Forums, September 25, 2002.
[3] Ibid.
[4] Ibid.
[5] The European Union On-Line Web site, http://europa.eu/int/comm/research/fp6/index.
[6] World Life Sciences Forum Web site, BioVision Information Kit, www.biovision.org.

CHAPTER 13

Technology's Future—
The View from the Frontier

There is no doubt . . . that medicine will advance more in the next 100 years than it has in the past 100,000.

—WebMD[1]

Predicting [the impact of advancing technology] is even harder. Recall ADL's famous prediction that the entire world market for the computer was likely to be less than ten units—or the skepticism with which the telegraph was initially greeted. Truly important, world-changing technologies have a history of being used in ways that no one—least of all their inventors—really expected. Who would have predicted that the teenage market would be vital to the development of wireless communications?

—"The Next Technological Revolution: Predicting the Technical Future and Its Impact on Firms, Organizations and Ourselves"[2]

"What's going on here," asks the marketplace? "What happened to technology and tech stocks? Is anyone investing? Will they ever invest again? How do you reconcile so many stocks with 90 percent fall-offs from their highs with the future progress of technology?"

So the business cycle has not been repeated after all. Boom does lead to bust. And the current bear market (recently ended?) has been long and severe. It was led by the dot-com bubble bursting, exacerbated by deflation, and extended by worries of terrorism and ongoing war.

Those of us with long memories have seen a series of cycles in tech investing. Even when investing in technology is out of favor, as at this writing, advances in technology itself are not halted. When I sit with entrepreneurs, their zeal is undiminished, even if their lives are more difficult and capital is scarce.

While timing the market is nearly always an unproductive effort, there is strong precedent to believe that—despite the slowdown in technology uptake brought on by the current economic climate—the next 20 years will bring even more rapid technological advances than the previous 20.

THE WEB

A number of areas of technology that are likely to lead the way, not the least of which is the web. The collapse of many dot-coms does not change the fact that the web has revolutionized the way we communicate and do business. The demise of numerous dot-coms with flawed business plans has not reversed this process. Consider how ubiquitous e-mail has become, how we send electronic versions of documents and slide presentations to each other without requiring or even considering fax or hard copy first. Another way to look at this revolution is to consider how lost we are if our connectivity fails or even slows down. Realize, too, that the power of the web is a function of the fatness of the pipe connecting people to it.

Although an estimated 80 percent of households in the United States are currently connected to the web, only 20 percent have broadband links such as DSL, satellite, Wi-Fi, or cable modem. The web gives users the power to move any information, anywhere, any time, nearly instantaneously with a fat enough pipe. True-recorded video on demand and real-time video are but two examples of what the web can deliver with a fast enough delivery mechanism. The web's business applications are, and will continue to be, a huge source of ongoing productivity gains.

Fundamental changes in the ways that businesses order from each other and take orders from their customers have been driven by the availability of web-based applications. Despite the dot-com blow-up, the level of activity on the web continues to increase. The volume of retail purchases on the web keeps rising. Pricing information available online is an extremely powerful inducement to buy there, and this situation will only continue to accelerate.

BIOTECHNOLOGY

But the web is not the only area that will continue to be revolutionary in the next 20 years. Biotechnology is another. Biotechnology was in its true infancy 20 years ago. Today major headway has been made in the biology and chemistry required to speed the development of biotechnology and the drugs it promises. Many have commented that what is behind us in biotech is 10 percent and what still lies ahead is 90 percent of the ultimate benefits we will see.

We are in the midst of one of the most remarkable revolutions in the history of mankind. The revolution was sparked by scientific curiosity about life, but its consequences will be so far-reaching as to touch every aspect of society. It is an information revolution, unlocking databases of human heredity and evolutionary history. It is a medical revolution, holding the prospect that our children's children will never die of cancer. And it is an intellectual revolution that may reshape—for better or for worse—our notions of human potential. I refer, of course, to the revolution in Genetics and Genomics.

—Dr. Eric S. Lander,
Director of the Whitehead Center of Genome Research,
Professor of Biology at MIT[3]

In 1976 venture capitalist Robert Swanson and biochemist Dr. Herbert Boyer came together to discuss the commercial potential of recombinant DNA technology. That discussion led to the creation of Genentech, Inc., which launched the biotech industry.

Advances in the biotech industry have been based on three significant events:

1. *Monoclonal antibodies.* In the past, the search for an antibody against a disease target involved injecting an antigen into a rabbit to produce a serum containing a collection of antibodies (polyclonals). Within that collection, one of the antibodies acted on the target, but which antibody was effective was unknown. The development of monoclonal antibodies allowed scientists to isolate the specific antibody from the collection and to deliver these antibodies to specific targets for both imaging and therapeutic purposes. This process of creating only the antibody necessary for the target was faster, cheaper, and far less labor intensive than the previous polyclonal process.

2. *Genetic engineering.* Advances in genetic engineering have allowed scientists to isolate a gene or gene fragment out of nature and reconstruct it in a known medium such as *E. coli.* This has made possible the development of medical treatments that focus on the genetic source of diseases (see "The Human Genome Project," below).

3. *Methods of conducting research and development.* Concurrent with the advances in technology, methodologies to convert them to practical, cost-effective applications were being developed. Most critically, improvements were made in the ability to separate, purify, and measure proteins. For example, the *ultra-centrifuge* permitted high-speed separation of cellular components, such as the nucleus. The *amino acid analyzer* allowed one to quantify the amino acid content of a protein, and *sequencers* provided knowledge of the amino acid sequence in a protein. Each new

method ended up being faster and cheaper than its previous method, paving the way for commercial production.

Advances in the science of biotech have led to expanding business opportunities. One of the more significant trends during the past 25 years has been increasing diversity in biotech applications.

In the early years of the industry, biotech companies focused almost exclusively on human health applications. The reasons were economic—only healthcare offered the possibility of high returns to offset the high costs of research and development (R&D). As the economics of the industry improved through more efficient methods, the door opened to more commodity-oriented applications, such as those in chemical and agricultural production. Crops such as tomatoes, carrots, and corn have been improved through biotechnology to last longer, taste better, and resist disease and pests. By 1997 biotech crops were being grown commercially on nearly 5 million acres around the world, in Argentina, Australia, Canada, China, Mexico, and the United States.[4] Other applications, such as environmental remediation, DNA fingerprinting, and new enzymes for food processing and textile manufacturing, will provide additional business opportunities in the future.

Healthcare applications also will play a significant role in the future of the industry. According to Jim Vincent, chairman and chief executive officer of Biogen, "Most scientists today would tell you that most of the remaining serious health problems, cancers, cardiovascular conditions, etc., have a significant genetic component to their solution." Biotechnology will be looked to not only as a means to solve these problems, but to do so in a cost-effective manner, slowing the increase in healthcare costs.

HUMAN GENOME PROJECT

Arguably the most comprehensive project in the field of biotechnology to date, the Human Genome Project (HGP) is an international effort that began in 1990 with two major objectives:

1. To sequence all of the approximately 3 billion base pairs (DNA letters) that comprise human DNA
2. To identify all 30,000 to 40,000 genes in human DNA that collectively make up "the human genome"

Since genes may have hundreds or even thousands of DNA letters, this is an exceedingly complex undertaking—even for a computer. In a sense, the HGP is as much a computer project as it is a biology project.

Participants in the HGP come primarily from government—including the U.S. National Institutes of Health and the U.S. Department of Energy—industry, academia, and the nonprofit world (e.g., the Wellcome Trust). Other participants include the men and women who have donated their

The breakthroughs in biotechnology have led to a series of essential ethical issues and ensuing debates, including the following:

GENOMICS

Pluses: This study of the relationship between gene structure and biological functions will lead to the prevention of genetic, infectious, and nutritional diseases. It also will lead to better medicines (pharmacogenomics), as drugs will be customized to patients according to their individual genetic profiles.

Minuses: Through prenatal diagnosis, it will be easier to prevent the birth of children suffering from serious handicaps—potentially resulting in a new form of eugenics.

STEM CELLS

Pluses: Pluripotent cells that can be grown into normal cells to replace dead ones, stem cells can be used to find new genes responsible for serious diseases and also enable the pharmaceutical industry to more rapidly test the efficacy and safety of new drugs. They could be very useful one day in treating chronic diseases such as Alzheimer's, Parkinson's, and Diabetes.

Minuses: Conflicts revolve around authorizing publicly funded stem cell research in light of the current political, ethical, and moral issues about the human embryo and when "life" begins.

CLONING

Pluses: Biotech companies around the world are working on unraveling the mystery of genetics, which could lead to the development of new treatments and drugs.

Minuses: Concerns have arisen about therapeutic cloning, and countries have taken different stances on the issues. In the United Kingdom, research on embryo stem cells has been authorized, while France is opposed to therapeutic cloning based on the belief that it could lead to reproductive cloning and a possible trafficking in human eggs.

GENETICALLY MODIFIED ORGANISMS (GMOS)

Pluses: Technology for genetically modifying foods offers a great opportunity to dramatically improve the lives of millions of people by helping to feed the hungry in developing countries, as well as offering an alternative to today's agricultural methods. Common transgenic crops include herbicide- and insecticide-resistant soybeans, corn, cotton, and canola.

Minuses: GMOs are the subject of continuing controversy around a number of issues, including human and environmental safety, labeling and consumer choice, intellectual property rights, ethics, food security, poverty reduction, and environmental conservation.

NEUROSCIENCE

Pluses: The central nervous system has been a prime target of the revolution in neuroscience, neurophysiology, and neurochemistry. With the advent of a new generation of antidepressants and modern neuroleptics, for example, beta interferon, patients with multiple sclerosis have been given new hope.

Minuses: Along with new hope, come questions of philosophical and ethical import. Where will full understanding of brain activity lead us? Can we/should we try to eradicate the darkest aspects of human behavior—drug abuse, mental illness, sociopathic behavior? What is our responsibility?

Source: Adapted from material on the World Life Sciences Forum Web site, "Key Issues: Opportunities versus Risk."

DNA to the project. Originally scheduled to take 15 years, the project will be completed during 2003—two years ahead of the original schedule. A "rough draft" of the human genome was completed in June 2000, making the project already 90 percent complete. Projections call for a cost in excess of $3 billion when the HGP is complete, including funds allocated to study ethical and moral issues and the protection of individual privacy.

Once the identification and sequencing of human genes is complete, there is still a lot of work left to do before we can say we truly understand human genetics. Scientists will have to tackle the functionality and variations in genes, to better understand the basis for differences in disease susceptibility between humans. To the field of molecular medicine, this also will mean early detection and improved diagnoses of disease; early detection of genetic susceptibility to disease; personalized prescribing of existing drugs; development of new drugs to treat the root cause of disease; and gene therapies.[5]

But the implications of work of the HGP go far beyond that. Its benefits will be felt in the areas of microbial genomics; risk assessment; bioarcheology, anthropology, evolution, and human migration; law enforcement and identification; and agriculture, livestock breeding, and bioprocessing.

Steve Jurvetson, a managing director of Draper Fisher Jurvetson, one of the world's leading venture capital firms, recently commented, "We will learn more about molecular biology and the origin of disease in the next 20 years than we have in the past 2000."[6]

As discussed previously, the *human genome* has been sequenced successfully—a great achievement. However, in terms of relative complexity, look at it this way: Think of the DNA in the genome as an alphabet, which in turn acts as the building blocks for the creation of a myriad of complex and highly interactive proteins. Think of the proteins as an unabridged dictionary for all the words that are just now being created. The full creation and definition of all those words is what lies ahead in the field of *proteomics*.

How will we be able to harness all this detail and complexity? Through confluence. The fields of biotechnology, molecular engineering (i.e., *nanotechnology*; more on that later) and computing are cross-fertilizing each other. These formerly discrete disciplines are becoming intertwined. And it is exactly this cross-fertilization that accelerates our abilities to engineer products across the entire spectrum of biology, chemistry, physics, and mathematics. Jurvetson goes on to say, "*Lab Science*, from biotech to nanotech, is becoming *Information Science*—designed on a computer, not a lab bench. With replicating molecular machines, physical production itself migrates to the rapid innovation cycle of information technology. Matter becomes code."[7]

The drug development process itself is changing in fundamental ways as *rational drug design* emerges and becomes the dominant paradigm. Nearly all drugs on the market today interact with one or more of the 500 or so basic enzymes and chemical reactions that scientists have known about for decades and that they knew played roles in the onset and progression of diseases. That limited focus is rapidly morphing into a completely different starting point—the underlying molecular workings that actually are the triggers of disease and that are set off sometimes years before the afflicted person feels a thing.

This new paradigm moves along a continuum from the species level of blockbuster drugs for the mass of humanity to the individual DNA level and specific cures focused on the uniqueness of my DNA as compared to yours. The fundamental enabling technologies needed to bring about this paradigm shift combine biology and computing; some have called it biodigital medicine.

"Ten years ago, five years ago, two years ago, the biotech revolution was still more science fiction than fact," says Dr. Scott Gottlieb. "It is Moore's Law, the doubling of computer power from an already impressive base, that is transforming the once far-fetched promise of the human genome into a medical, entrepreneurial and commercial reality."[8]

The tremendous advances in computing speed—exponential in power—put biotech at a rare inflection point. The paradigm switchover to come relates to process and a focus on digital technology. It moves discovery focus away from wet lab work to the electronic medium where Metcalfe's law (which states that the usefulness or utility of a network equals the square of the number of users of the network) and Moore's laws drive the speed of discovery. Instead of working with compounds mixed in a test tube, the new starting point is to instruct a computer about what the underlying molecular structure of an effective drug against a particular condition is likely to look like and also what it probably should not look like. And if a particular drug is known to be harmful to the liver or is poorly metabolized, then the computer can be instructed to design away from those problem properties.

All historical movement in medical development is away from treating symptoms to discovering underlying processes and causes. The first diseases that we could prevent, such as typhus or malaria, were those caused by specific outside agents: germs delivered via mosquito. Those based mainly on processes internal to the human body, such as heart disease and many cancers, are a lot more complex in terms of causation and are taking a lot longer to understand and conquer. Now, for the first time, the keys to that understanding are within our comprehension. The next 20 years should be the golden age of biotechnology.

RISE OF NANOTECHNOLOGY

We are on the verge of a new industrial revolution—the convergence of Information Technology, Life Sciences and Nanotechnology. . . . Nanotechnology, the study of matter at the atomic scale, promises to revolutionize our view of materials and offers unprecedented options for new machines and intermediate products. . . . As the newest of the three, nanotechnology has achieved the fastest start from a funding perspective and is poised to surpass biotechnology and semiconductors in both size and scope.

—"The Next Technological Revolution: Predicting the Technical Future and Its Impact on Firms, Organizations and Ourselves"[9]

Another tremendous enabling technology is just beginning to emerge into the consciousness of the financing community. Nanotechnology—the technology that allows measuring, seeing, predicting, and making things at the scale of atoms and molecules—can readily be called the Industrial Revolution of the 21st century. Nanotech affects everything—biology, chemistry, physics—and its importance is hard to overstate. It will affect almost all aspects of our lives, including the drugs that are being developed, the speed of our computers, how we harness energy to power our world, even our food.

Much of this impact is yet to come, and one might compare the nanotech industry now to the computer industry of the 1960s, before the integrated chip, or to the biotech industry of 20 years ago, before the recent breakthroughs in genomics. One of the fundamental fascinations and opportunities of nanotech is that at the scale of atoms and molecules, the ordinary physics that we are used to observing in everyday life, are superceded by quantum physics. At the nanoscale we can observe, and it is hoped harness, changes in mechanical properties.

Although many aspects of nanotechnology are still in their nascent stages, others already are approaching the product stage. A number of nanomaterials are already on the market. Nanoparticulate zinc oxide is already in use in sunscreens. Nanoparticles are also in use as abrasives, in paints, as coatings for eyeglasses (making them more scratch-proof and less breakable). It is possible that soon Teflon will be surpassed in slipperiness by nanocomposites. The first textile applications are already on the market. Nanoparticles protect fabrics from stains without changing the texture of the cloth. Not far off are more advanced applications in the arena of textiles—"smart" fabrics that change properties depending on ambient conditions or can even monitor vital signs.

The medical applications of nanotech are far reaching, as well. In one example, certain nanoparticles can be tuned to emit light at particular, controllable frequencies. Ultimately this can lead to tagging of DNA and the identification of diseases at their earliest moment of development, long before any symptoms arise or even before blood-based diagnostics could detect the disease's presence.

Nanotech holds great promise in the arena of drug delivery, as well. One of the great difficulties in using drugs at the site of diseases such as cancer is the lack of differentiation of healthy versus cancerous cells as they come under attack blindly by the therapeutic agent. Loads of healthy cells get targeted along with the diseased cells, hence the incidence of sometimes severe side effects. Nanotech can overcome this problem by delivering less of the active agent but delivering a higher payload more precisely to the desired disease site.

The ability to manipulate materials at the molecular level can lead to approaches to cellular manipulation. It may be a long time before we see nanobots doing complex construction inside our vital organs. However, the hope is that nanotech can help find ways to regrow tissue, for example, nerve cells, which could lead to treatments to reverse paralysis and offer help in other central nervous system (CNS) diseases.

TECHNOLOGY: POISED FOR GROWTH

So biotechnology may provide the answers to long-studied disease conditions. And computers and computer chips—already in our homes, cars, appliances, and the workplace—will proliferate, and these areas will become more and more automated. Nanotechnology is emerging and will touch everything.

But of course, investing in technology, biotech, and nanotech is not without risk, as anyone who lived through the bubble of the late 1990s understands. There are certain to be periods of tremendous volatility brought on by growth and setbacks in these two industries. Not all companies will fare equally well, and the prudent investor will have to choose carefully when deciding which ones to fund.

One of the important trends during the late 1990s was that the size of the individual investments in the high-tech and biotech sector increased dramatically. Institutional investors, venture capital firms, and corporate partners discovered that it takes just as much effort to evaluate a $10 million deal as it does a $100 million deal. In the future, as the total dollar value of investments in these sectors increases, the number of firms receiving that financing may not increase at the same rate. Fewer companies will receive financing, but in greater amounts. Additionally, more companies have entered the high-tech and biotech industry, and all of them are looking for financing. Thus, although capital will continue to flow into high-tech and biotech companies, the competition for that capital will only increase.

VIEW FROM THE ACADEMIC MEDICAL ORGANIZATIONS

From a futuristic perspective, it's all throttles open.

—Dina Elliott, Elliot Consulting

Among the hotbeds of discovery in the medical field are the regional academic medical organizations (AMOs). The statistics speak for themselves. At this writing, there are 164 AMOs—combined research and teaching institutions—in the country, all competing for R&D dollars. With government funding drying up, most of these AMOs are beginning to look to commercialization of products to fund future research. More and more, that means hooking up with a giant pharmaceutical company that can fund the doctors' teaching and research activities. According to Dina Elliott of Elliott Consulting Group, money also comes from organizations around the world that are willing to provide grants and funding, such as the National Institutes of Health in the United States, World Relief, or the Christian Children's Fund.

"If you're a doctor, the money isn't in patient care anymore," says

Elliott. "Many doctors are leaving medical school and going right into research, never seeing a patient. Providing care today is a maintenance activity, and most doctors want to cure disease. And they take a research track for that."

Elliott's company conducted a study during the summer of 2002 among AMOs in the New York metropolitan area to learn more about the issues they face and the major initiatives they have in place. Her findings are compelling. AMOs, which include some of the most prestigious teaching and research institutions in the country—among them Yale-New Haven Hospital, Mount Sinai Hospital, New York Presbyterian Hospital and Health System, and Columbia University's College of Physicians and Surgeons—consider themselves to be in crisis mode.

Elliott's feedback suggests that AMOs feel that their viability and position as world healthcare leaders is threatened by significant pressure from every possible angle: societal changes; the regulatory environment; and the demands to innovate and improve their services, given the constraints in resources, including funding, human capital, and technology. AMOs strive to strike a balance among their three core functions: research, patient care, and teaching. And as custodians of their respective community's healthcare—and "the engine driving all other healthcare around the world"—they are in agreement that emphasis on research is likely to increase, while emphasis on patient care will decrease over the next three to five years.

In spite of this somewhat bleak situation, AMOs continue to be hopeful about the future. They are clear about what needs to happen in order to relieve the current systemic burdens before they can move forward with the research that will make a difference in the quality of patient care around the world. Some of the most pressing issues include:

- Finding a way for AMOs to have access to capital markets
- Developing creative options for fund-raising, such as risk-sharing alternatives
- Modeling for and facilitating integration of mission-based budgeting
- Fixing reimbursement systems and processes to maximize returns
- Initiating programs to hire and retain the best people
- Rebuilding technological resources to be integrated and cutting edge
- Integrating financial performance and clinical performance data
- Helping to drive legislation that is supportive of AMOs and their overriding mission

FINANCING STRATEGIES IN A VOLATILE INDUSTRY

I will argue this business [raising money for technology-driven companies] is more regular and unchanging than changing. We may think because we're close up that it's changing all the time, and there are new trends and new ways, but if you think back a little bit, it's fundamentally the same old thing.

People get excited over great ideas—they're prepared to invest when they feel good. Then they get disappointed and run away. And always, always, it takes a lot more money than anyone believes.

—Stelios Papadopoulous, Former Managing Director, Healthcare Investment Banking, PaineWebber[10]

In order to take advantage of future business opportunities, high-tech and biotech companies will need to continue to raise large sums of money. Although some of the tactics for raising that money will change with the industry, many of the strategies described in this book will continue to apply. These strategies have been shaped by several broad themes and trends.

More Sophisticated Investors

As the high-tech and biotech industries have matured, investors have become more knowledgeable and sophisticated. As a result, they are more discriminating when choosing the companies and technologies to finance in these sectors.

In the early days of the industry, investors would take a chance on a promising technology and a reputable scientist. That is no longer true. Today companies must be product oriented, not research oriented. They need to demonstrate proof of principle in order to attract financing. For example, in the early years of biotech, many companies went public with only Phase I clinical data. Now Phase III data is more the norm.

Single products aimed at narrow markets will not attract large numbers of investors. Companies must develop multiple pathways to the market and enabling technologies that can be applied across numerous products. Corporate partners have also become more sophisticated, using venture capital techniques to evaluate possible funding arrangements with emerging companies.

Many investors also have become less patient. They are no longer willing to hold speculative investments for long periods of time. They look for corporate earnings sooner and for liquidity of their investment.

Need to Build and Nurture the Investor Base

Companies will go through several rounds of financing before they can begin to generate revenues and stand on their own. Many of these financing rounds may be necessary during bear markets. To increase the chances of raising money during these times—and to maintain investor support during the ups and downs of a company's early years— management must work to cultivate the relationship with its investors.

Some investors—for example, venture capital firms or corporate partners—may be involved more directly in the operation of the company. These kinds of investors provide more than just financing, offering expertise and access to a vast network of resources. It is especially important for chief executive officers (CEOs) to manage these relationships to make sure the company takes advantage of all they have to offer.

Credibility Matters

CEOs must work to establish credibility with their investors and potential investors. Projections and assumptions about the future can be optimistic, but they must have a realistic chance for success. "Hockey stick" projections (which chart flat or modest growth for a few years, followed by dramatic growth to reach annual sales of $100 million) will not impress investors because such projections simply are not believable.

When courting potential investors, CEOs must have a realistic view of their company and how much equity they should give up to get the financing they need. The goal is to "get across the desert" to develop and launch successful products. To establish credibility, CEOs must do their homework.

ON PREDICTING THE FUTURE[11]

No one can predict exactly what science and technology will produce over the next decade or two, because of the challenges that face the commercialization of any new technology. However, we can make some guesses. First, there are likely to be obviously "disruptive" effects on particular firms. Second, these technologies are likely to have a very significant impact on all individuals. The initial rumblings as to the importance of individual privacy that have surfaced around the Internet and around the increasing consolidation of commercial data banks are likely to become a shout. Third, there is the possibility that these technologies will change the very structure of firms and organizations, and open up qualitatively different development paths for some of the developing economies, enabling some regions to "leap frog" their way to leadership. Finally, our research suggests that the days when technology could be safely left in the hands of R&D are over, if they were ever here. The return to managing technology strategically—to being fully aware of what is likely to happen and to having thought through how the organization will respond to it—are likely to skyrocket.

They must know how much money they need (as opposed to asking investors how much they would be willing to spend) and how those funds will be used. Finally, they should know and understand the investment criteria on which their deal will be judged.

> *When I was an investment banker and I had scientists coming in to see me, I would say, young person, you're about to go on a journey across the desert. Here's one bottle of water and 100 pounds of gold on your back.*
>
> *And what always happens, as you reach the middle of the desert, you're out of the water, the sun is beating down on you, you're going to die, and all the gold is doing is weighing you into the sand.*
>
> *Along comes a caravan. What they want is all of your gold, but they have all the water you need. The dumb person dies in the desert with the gold on his back.*
>
> *But the smart person gives up as much gold as he needs to, gets as much water as he needs, and reaches the other side. Because at the other side you still have more personal wealth than you ever really deserved.*
>
> —Jay Moorin, Former President and CEO,
> Magainin Pharmaceuticals (now Genaera Corporation)

High-tech and biotech companies will be the source for the creation of great personal wealth in the near future. But in order to realize that wealth and to take advantage of those business opportunities, the people involved in these industries must overcome significant barriers. Of these, the most pressing is the need for large amounts of financing.

Financing is the fundamental prerequisite for the continued survival of a research, technology-oriented company. Without financing, there is no company. It dies because it has no way to "cross the desert" and develop products that reach the market. But with adequate financing, a start-up technology company can survive, grow, and, it is hoped, take advantage of the opportunities of tomorrow.

NOTES

[1] WebMD Web site, http://my.webmd.com.
[2] Ellen Brockley, Amber Cai, Rebecca Henderson, Emanuele Picciola, and Jimmy Zhang, "The Next Technological Revolution: Predicting the Technical Future and its Impact on Firms, Organizations and Ourselves," Paper prepared for MIT Sloan School 50th Anniversary Celebration, October 2002.

[3] Dr. Eric S. Lander, Millennium Evening at the White House, October 12, 1999.

[4] www.bio.org/er/timeline.asp.

[5] WebMD Web site, http://my.webmd.com.

[6] *Red Herring*, June 15, 2001, p. 42.

[7] Ibid., p. 43.

[8] Gilder Biotech Report, September 2001.

[9] Brockley et al., "The Next Technological Revolution."

[10] Stelios Papdopoulus, "What's New in Biotechnology Funding," Presentation at the annual meeting of the New York Biotechnology Association, New York, NY, October 1995

[11] Brockley et al., "The Next Technological Revolution."

afterword

Donnell P. O'Callaghan, Jr.[1]

There's a better way to do it. Find it!

—Thomas Edison

The next 10 years will be remarkable ones in the field of life sciences and healthcare. Whether your creativity takes you to healthcare delivery, pharmaceuticals, biotech, medical devices—or something quite undefined as of yet—the road to discovery is waiting for you. Are you ready? Informed? Armed with questions and theories? Feeling confident about financing? Ready to tackle the day-to-day business and technical aspects of your venture? We hope so. We need you.

This arena of healthcare and life sciences encompasses a lot more than was traditionally believed. In the past, professional services organizations defined the industry so narrowly that it was conceivable that a practice dealing with hospitals might never have medical schools and training or pharmaceuticals or medical devices or insurance on its radar screen. In retrospect, a huge mistake, since they are all so interdependent.

Today, Deloitte & Touche approaches the industry from a much more holistic point of view, bringing the payers, providers, and life sciences companies into the fold together, to participate in our own process of discovery. When you talk about the delivery of healthcare or the delivery of medicine or the practice of medicine—regardless of whether you are a hospital chief executive officer (CEO) or the head of a large insurance company or a consumer—

---

[1]*Managing Partner, TriState Healthcare & Life Sciences, Deloitte & Touche LLP, May 2003.*

you have to think in the broadest of terms, because all these segments overlap, converge, and influence each other. Being open to understanding how they overlap, converge, and influence one another is a futuristic way to think about healthcare, and it is going to be vital in the coming years. That is what we try to do in our practice at Deloitte and Touche, by bringing an approach and a set of services and capabilities that are responsive to what we think makes this industry unique. And that's what Richard Shanley has tried to do in *Financing Technology's Frontier.*

The future is all about discovery. In the healthcare field, this is nowhere better illustrated than in the metropolitan academic medical organizations (AMOs), which, on a daily basis, are balancing patient care with teaching with the research that could lead to discovery and commercialization. Increasing cost pressures on AMOs will continue to force these institutions to focus on their core competencies, with research being a top priority. It is in these environments—the incubators, the academic institutions, the AMOs, the bioparks—that research thrives. And it is out of these environments that the cures and state-of-the-art processes of the future will emerge. And we will all be the better for it.

Did you know that the tristate area, encompassing New York, New Jersey, and Connectictut, is a hotbed of biotech discovery? Projects that come out of the New York regional AMOs represent an enormous export to almost every corner of the globe—more biotech research activity than from any other metropolitan region.

Hospital CEOS across the country recognize that new discoveries, new drugs, new medical devices—once they are tested, brought to market, and embraced by the insurance industry—will have a huge impact on how healthcare is delivered and received. The multiple crises impacting healthcare, including regulatory pressures, budget cuts, economic slowdowns, increased cost of care, and bioterrorism, are threatening the delivery of America's healthcare daily. Experts agree that biotech discovery holds a threefold promise: reduced costs for the insured customer, improvements in hospital care, and important new products to pharmaceutical companies.

As voters, taxpayers, and consumers, we all make a huge commitment to the cost of healthcare each year, and it is always top of mind. But the scientists, physicians, entrepreneurs, and investors who are at work right now promoting discovery are helping to create remarkable, cost-effective solutions that we cannot even imagine today.

We are ready for the future. Are you?

Office Depot, 49
Online gaming, 23–25
OnLink Technologies, Inc., 48, 148–149
Option repricing, 203–204
Opus Diagnostics, 22, 161
Osteoporosis-related issues, 75
Ottoman Empire, healing arts in, 1
Outsourcing, and virtual companies, 12
Oxford Glycosciences (UK), 221

PaineWebber, 239
Papadopoulous, Stelios, 239
Park 'N View, 49–50
Partnering, corporate. *See* Corporate partnerships; Strategic alliances
Pasteur, Louis, 2
Pasteur Merieux Connaught/Ora Vax, 151, 154, 158
Pataki George, 94
Patents:
  as competitive advantage, 35
  and HGS, Inc., 152
Patricof, Alan J., 49
Patricof & Co. *See* Apax Partners
Pennsylvania Private Investors Group, 80
Performance, monitoring, 20–21
Performance-based pay, 201
Performance-based vesting, 196
Performance guarantees, explained, 66–68
Pfizer, Inc., 147, 202–204
Phantom stock, 202
Pharmaceutical industry
  collaborations in, 117
  innovation in, 4–5
  product failure rates, 86
  rational drug design, 234
Pharmacia & Upjohn Co., 151, 154, 155, 158
Pharmos Corp. (Israel), 223
Philanthropy, venture. *See* Venture philanthropy
Phosphorylcholine (PC), applications for, 12–13
Photonics Center, Boston University, 92

Pioneer Hi-Bred International, Inc., 151, 154
PIPE transactions, 67, 68
Pitching, venture capital, 38–41
Pogo.com, 30
Polf, William, 94–96
PPL Therapeutics, 51
Praecis Pharmaceuticals, 156
"Prayer Model," 9
Premarin (pharmaceutical), 35
Presbyterian Hospital, 94
Price, Frederic D., 21, 133
Private companies, governance issues, 213–215
Private investors:
  and PIPE transactions, 67, 68
  as venture capitalists, 43–44
Private placements:
  case study of, 75–76
  regulation of, 68–72
Procter & Gamble (P&G), 138, 139–140, 161
Products:
  versus companies, 39–40
  as part of business plan, 19
  as venture capital criterion, 34–35
Program-Related Investment (PRI), 85–86
Proprietary products. *See* Products
Protein engineering technologies, 137–142
Proteomics, defined, 137
Public markets:
  advantages of, 53–56
  bear market strategies, 65–68
  case study of, 72–75
  cyclical nature of, 58–65, 76
  investor base, 56–58
  IPO underwriters, 56

Quantum physics, and nanotechnology, 236
Quest, acquisition of Unilab, 147

Rabin, Yitzak, 225
Rate of return (ROI), 26–27
RBC Dain Rauscher, 57
Recombinant Biocatalysis, Inc., 51